**DO NOT REMOVE
CARDS FROM POCKET**

EUROPE'S STAGFLATION

EUROPE'S STAGFLATION

Edited by
MICHAEL EMERSON

CLARENDON PRESS · OXFORD
1984

Oxford University Press, Walton Street, Oxford OX2 6DP

London New York Toronto
Delhi Bombay Calcutta Madras Karachi
Kuala Lumpur Singapore Hong Kong Tokyo
Nairobi Dar es Salaam Cape Town
Melbourne Auckland
and associated companies in
Beirut Berlin Ibadan Mexico City Nicosia

Oxford is a trade mark of Oxford University Press

Published in the United States
by Oxford University Press, New York

British Library Cataloguing in Publication Data

Europe's stagflation.
1. European Economic Community countries
—Economic policy
I. Emerson, Michael
330'.94   HC241.2
ISBN 0-19-828487-X

Unless otherwise indicated the views expressed in this book are
attributable only to the authors in a personal capacity and not to any
institution.

Set by Joshua Associates, Oxford
and printed in Great Britain
at the Alden Press, Oxford

Preface

The present book has its origins in a conference entitled 'Western European Priorities', which the Centre for European Policy Studies organized in Brussels as its inaugural event in December 1982. Oxford University Press are also publishing two other books based on the conference: R. Masera and R. Triffin (eds.), *Europe's Money*, and A. Jacquemin (ed.), *European Industry: Public Policy and Corporate Strategy*. We hope that together these books will constitute a significant contribution to the discussion of central questions of public policy at a European level, complementing and reinforcing the contributions that the Centre has already begun to make through the *CEPS Papers*.

Although based on the conference, essays in the present book have been updated to take account of more recent events, and in one or two cases heavily revised. Michael Emerson has also written an introduction which explains the overall scope and purpose of the volume. The end product is, therefore, somewhat more than a haphazard collection of contributions to a conference, and I should like to take this opportunity to acknowledge the work that Mr Emerson has done in moulding the present volume.

Neither the contributions of the authors nor the efforts of the editors would however have materialized at all, had it not been for a grant from the Ford Foundation, which in this way as in others, provided support to a new centre when it was most needed. It is therefore, finally, a particular pleasure to thank the President of the Ford Foundation and his staff for their help.

Centre for European Policy Studies,   PETER LUDLOW
Brussels, 1984

Contents

Notes on Contributors

Andrea Boltho has been a fellow and tutor in Economics at Magdalen College, University of Oxford, since 1977. Before that he was at the Organisation of Economic Co-operation and Development, Department of Economics and Statistics, where his posts included editor of *Economic Outlook* and head of the Growth Studies Division. In 1973-4 he was Japan Foundation Fellow at the Economic Planning Agency in Tokyo.

Michael Bruno is professor of economics at the Hebrew University of Jerusalem and a research associate of the National Bureau of Economic Research in the US. His research has been on economic development and trade, focusing more recently on macroeconomics.

Lars Calmfors is a senior research fellow at the Institute for International Economic Studies at the University of Stockholm, where his research is in macroeconomics with emphasis on stabilization policy, inflation, and unemployment.

Jean-Michel Charpin is currently *Directeur de Cabinet* of the Minister of Economic Planning, in France. Previously he was head of division at INSEE (National Institute for Statistics and Economic Studies), where he was one of the authors of the D.M.S. (Dynamique Multi-Sectorielle) econometric model, and worked in the Directorate General of Economic and Financial Affairs at the Commission of the European Communities.

Michael Emerson is currently Director for Macroeconomic Analyses and Priorities at the Commission of the European Communities, Brussels. His earlier positions included economic adviser to Commission President Roy Jenkins and various posts at the Organisation for Economic Co-operation and Development in Paris.

Kees P. Goudswaard has been assistant professor of public finance at Leiden University (the Netherlands) since 1981. His research programme covers debt-management policies and economic effects of income-transfer programmes.

David Grubb is a research officer at the London School of Economics'

Centre for Labour Economics. His research interests include multi-country econometric studies, productivity growth, and the size distribution of earnings.

Victor Halberstadt has been professor of public finance at Leiden University since 1974 and a crown-member of the (Netherlands) Social Economic Council since 1972. His publications are in the field of national and international economic and social policy.

Richard Layard is professor of economics at the London School of Economics and head of the Centre for Labour Economics there. He has worked extensively on income distribution and on unemployment.

Bart le Blanc has been adviser in social economic policies and financial affairs to the Office of the Prime Minister of the Netherlands, Director-General for the Budget, and Deputy Director-General for Public Service. At present he is a member of the executive board of F. van Lanschot Bankiers N.V.

Harmen Lehment is director of Advanced Studies in International Economic Policy Research at the Kiel Institute of World Economics, which he joined in 1976. He has published numerous titles in the fields of international macroeconomics and international financial markets.

J. S. V. Symons has been working for the past few years on the effect on employment of changes in wages, the price of raw materials, and interest rates for Britain and a number of other countries. He is at present developing complete models of the labour markets of a number of OECD countries in order to trace the causes of the general rise in unemployment.

Introduction

MICHAEL EMERSON

As the conference met, in December 1982, the European economy was concluding its third successive year of recession. Far from there being a strong upturn in sight, latest data pointed to a renewed weakening in economic activity in late 1982—a double-dip in the European recession. The unemployment rate in the EC as a whole had, in the autumn of 1982, passed the 10 per cent level, thus approaching double the level reached at the last cyclical peak of activity in 1978-9. The reduction in the average rate of inflation in Europe was proving a very sticky process. By the end of 1982 the rate of consumer-price increase (over the previous twelve months) had decelerated to 10 per cent in the EC as a whole, compared with 14 per cent in 1980 at the height of the oil-price and dollar shocks. This was a much more limited stabilization achievement than that seen in the United States or Japan.

Against this sombre background the issues taken up in the eight conference papers reproduced in this volume were essentially the following:

Can we account for what has been happening to the European economy in the present recession, notably the behaviour of output, prices, real incomes, budget balances, employment, and unemployment?

Can we separate the contributions of the second oil-price rise and endogenous reactions of the economy to it, from the impact of governmental policy decisions made in the last few years?

Can we diagnose structural problems underlying the European economy's weak performance, for example in the domains of public finance and income distribution and formation?

How should policy now be addressed to the overwhelming need to generate a sustainable recovery? What would be the most advisable budgetary–monetary–incomes policy mix in present circumstances? What policy cocktail is needed in particular for the employment problem?

Are these problems basically tractable, or intractable, in terms that economists can reasonably present to politicians?

Andrea Boltho presents a policy-oriented assessment of Europe's economic performance since the second oil shock of 1979-80. He

considers the initial policy reactions to the second oil shock to have
been better co-ordinated than after 1973, and that the private sector
shows signs of lessons learned. Real wages were more flexible relative
to the first episode. In 1974–5 there was a very large real-wage increase
in Europe which led to a severe liquidity squeeze on enterprises and
thus a sharp destocking and investment-cutting process. Policy was
also initially more coherent after the second oil shock. The effects
of the Bonn Summit budgetary expansion in Germany in 1978–9
eased intra-European balance-of-payments problems, which otherwise
would have further complicated the process of adjustment to the
oil-price rise. However, as US monetary policy became increasingly
restrictive from 1979 onwards, the concerted tightness of budgetary
and monetary policy in Europe and the OECD area as a whole increased
the length of the recession, and the recovery process was repeatedly
delayed. Boltho gives four measures of the policy stance: a fiscal policy
impact, a high employment budget balance, real money supply, and
the real interest rate. For each of these measures the policy stance was
more restrictive in 1980, 1981, and 1982, than in the comparable
years after the first oil shock, 1974, 1975, and 1976.

Boltho analyses this stance in terms of a policy dilemma, contrasting
a contemporary 'expectations trap' with the Keynesian 'liquidity trap'
of the 1930s. The present policy dilemma arises from the different
processes of formation of expectations in the financial and industrial
parts of the corporate sector. In particular, policy can be immobilized
in a situation in which (a) expansionary policies could lead to exchange-
rate depreciation and/or higher interest rates as the financial sector
'imbibed with monetarist orthodoxy' expects inflation to accelerate,
whereas (b) restrictive policies would depress the much more Keynesian
expectations of the industrial sector. Thus, in the 'expectations trap',
policies are functions of expectations, but expectations are also a
function of policies; both remaining locked in a condition of
depression.

The behaviour of the European economy in the wake of the oil-price
shocks of the last ten years is analysed econometrically by *Michael
Bruno* within the framework of a small set of estimated equations. The
experiences of individual EC countries, the US and Japan, and of EC
countries combined (either as the EC aggregate economy, or in pooled
regression analyses of all individual countries together), are carefully
sifted in a variety of tests.

Bruno's main argument is that 'an increase in the real cost of material
and energy inputs pushes back the aggregate supply schedule of final
goods. This supply-side shock will be more aggravated the more rigid
the real cost of labour tends to be, since profits will be squeezed and
both short-run as well as long-term output supply will be reduced and

prices will be increased. The adjustment process is further compounded by the contraction in aggregate demand. The latter is partly caused by the real income effects of the worsening terms of trade and partly exacerbated by contractionary monetary and fiscal policy which was followed by most countries in response to the supply shocks, for fear of inflation and balance-of-payments deficits. It is thus difficult to disentangle that part of unemployment and the productivity slow-down caused by real factor price increases from that which follows more conventional Keynesian, cyclical arguments, although it is clear that both types of phenomena were at work.'

The commodity-price shocks of the past ten years are found to have had systematically depressive effects on GDP and employment and an accelerating impact on inflation. The effects wear out after about two years of lagged reactions. Thereafter contractionary monetary policy reactions take on a more important role, with the fall of real output subsequently attenuating the rate of inflation. For the period 1967 to 1981 as a whole, Bruno's equations for the EC aggregate economy predict 4.9 per cent out of the actual 5.2 per cent increase in the level of unemployment, and 8.1 per cent out of the actual 8.5 per cent increase in inflation.

As regards the issue of real-wage reactions to the price shocks, Bruno finds all EC countries to have been more rigid than the US or Japan after the first oil shock, but perhaps somewhat less so in the second episode. The policy conclusions point to the key role of in-comes policies in directly fostering higher employment, as well as in enabling co-ordinated expansion policies to be pursued among the industrial countries. Bruno also argues for commodity-price stabiliza-tion policies at the world level to avoid some of the extreme gyrations in activity and losses in productivity.

Issues of wage formation and behaviour, and conversely of enter-prise profitability are further examined in several contributions.

Richard Layard (*et al.*)[1] first sets out for European countries, the United States, Canada, and Japan the results of econometric re-search with equations explaining the evolution of nominal wages in terms of current inflation, the previous year's wage increases, and an unemployment term. Price inflation is explained in terms of current and lagged inport-price increases, and trends in productivity growth and unemployment. Overall Layard finds that these equations provide a rather robust explanation of current price and wage developments.

Layard then examines empirical evidence in support of neo-classical labour demand theory which suggests that real-wage changes should have an important and inverse impact on employment. For the countries studied the essential findings were that the elasticity of labour demand to the real wage tended to be in the range of -0.7 to -1.4. Thus a real-wage cut of 1 per cent would lead to an increase in labour demand of between 0.7 and 1.4 per cent. Empirical investigation of this question has for a long time proved inconclusive. Layard considers that his results overcame problems not resolved in other research by including real import prices in the explanation of labour demand.

For Layard the main policy question is how to achieve changes in wage behaviour that will either directly create extra employment, or reduce the level of unemployment at which inflation does not accelerate thus permitting faster demand expansion. He advocates supply-side labour market programmes and measures to discourage voluntary unemployment, especially better income support for poor working families and stricter enforcement of the work test for the unemployment benefit. His main proposal, however, is for a decentralized, market-oriented, tax-based incomes policy. The employer would be taxed in the event that he agreed to pay rises for his enterprise in excess of the national norm for the rate of growth of hourly earnings. The tax would overall be revenue-neutral; the receipts of the tax authority would be rebated to employers at a flat rate through adjustment of social security contribution rates. Thus employers who settled for the wage norm or less would be net gainers from the system, whereas employers who agreed to 'excess' wage increases would be net losers.

Layard's proposal for better decentralized incomes policies is envisaged for large or medium-size economies. Turning, on the other hand, to the setting of more centralized wage negotiation in the smaller European countries, *Lars Calmfors* examines a totally different approach —indeed he considers the Layard proposal to be inappropriate for such countries.

Calmfors bases his argument upon a comparative analysis of Sweden, Finland, Denmark, Belgium, the Netherlands, Austria, and Norway— seven advanced, open economies of comparable size. His concern is the interaction of financial policies of the government—especially the budget and the exchange rate—and the income negotiation process. In particular he contrasts the results that may be obtained, in an economic environment typical of the 1970s, from on the one hand explicitly co-ordinated financial and incomes policies and, on the other hand, game situations in which the government and social partners adapt to the expected behaviour of each other.

Calmfors sees the problems of real-wage adjustment to have become particularly serious in the smaller OECD countries in the 1970s. Not only did these countries fail to make real-wage adjustments after the first oil shock; in addition they allowed a relative cost deterioration to take place compared with the larger industrialized countries. This explains the prolonged stagnation in the sectors meeting international competition in many of these countries, and thence the large increases in balance-of-payments current account and budget deficits as resources became more concentrated in sectors producing non-tradable goods and services.

Three different approaches are identified for achieving real-wage adjustments that in turn should be adequate for inducing high employment levels: devaluation, non-accommodation policies, and incomes policies. Devaluation can lower the real wage and increase employment temporarily, but needs to be complemented by non-accommodating financial policies or incomes policies if the effects are not to prove ephemeral. The choice between these two back-up policies will depend essentially on whether the burden of adjustment is to fall on the unemployed minority or on the majority of employed wage-earners.

In relating these approaches to experiences of the 1970s, Calmfors cites Finnish economic policy since 1976–7 as a good example of how a policy of non-accommodation and devaluation can be successfully combined. The Swedish devaluation experience of 1977 is cited as a good example of a policy of devaluation alone proving inadequate to solve macroeconomic imbalances. He is agnostic whether the recent Swedish devaluations of 1981–2 will be matched by appropriate long-run demand policies.

Structural problems of public finance policy were the subject of the contribution by *Victor Halberstadt* (*et al*.)[2] with special reference to the cases of Belgium, Denmark, Ireland, Italy, and the Netherlands. Halberstadt qualifies the growth of the public sector in these five European countries concerned as 'truly amazing'. Public expenditure reached an average 57 per cent gross domestic product in 1981, representing a growth of 23 percentage points with respect to the average level of the 1960s. The single expenditure category to fall was gross capital formation. Only in this case were the techniques of budgetary expenditure control effective, but this fall merely served to aggravate the weakening of economic potential. The negative economic effects of this vast public-sector expansion are, according to Halberstadt, clear. They arise through increased labour costs for employers, the crowding-out of private investment because of high borrowing requirements, and the crowding-out of public investment through the growth of transfer and interest payments.

Halberstadt reviews the bulging list of new or renewed techniques of budgetary control such as global norms, cash limits, credit limits, staff ceilings, frames for real resource allocations, envelopes, etc. While noting the value of more sophisticated techniques, Halberstadt is sceptical of their overall effectiveness without the strongest political support. 'What really matters is the courage of politicians. The key question therefore is whether politicians agree on the necessity for fundamental changes in the size and composition of the public sector.

Are they able and willing to make difficult choices, also to resist adequately veto groups (for example the elderly), and to risk revenge from their party and the voters, especially when the decisions to be taken may take years to produce fruits?'

The macroeconomic implications of large public-sector deficits are further explored by *Harmen Lehment*, with special reference to Germany, and its central role in the concerted budgetary expansion announced at the Bonn Summit of 1978. The sharp increase of budget deficits in the 1970s in much of Western Europe is attributed to the attempt of governments to stimulate aggregate demand through expansionary fiscal policies. Lehment feels that this policy thrust was influenced by misleading macroeconomic model simulations, which overestimated what fiscal stimulation could do for real output and employment.

In particular Lehment criticizes the highly Keynesian models that were in vogue in the mid-seventies, which incorporated at best only part of the crowding-out mechanisms that are now more strongly represented in economic theory and some newer econometric models. In addition these model simulations typically assumed, either implicitly or explicitly, an accommodating monetary policy.

With respect to the 1978 concerted budgetary expansion, Lehment's argument is that policy-makers then underestimated how quickly this re-created inflationary pressures, and that in any case the policy mix at that time should have been more focused on monetary than just budgetary policy. In fact there was a strong monetary expansion in some key countries in 1977–8 including Germany, and this, if better recognized, would have warranted a more cautious budgetary policy.

Turning to the present situation Lehment puts several arguments in favour of reducing structural budget deficits. These relate to interest rates, confidence effects, and balance-of-payments deficits. He acknowledged the risk of negative demand effects, but considers that this could be adequately offset by a compensatory adjustment of monetary policy, in particular in the case of Germany. The balance of financial policy would in any case be aimed at keeping the expansion of nominal gross domestic product on a target path compatible with high capacity utilization and low inflation.

Jean-Michel Charpin explores the case for a major effort to adapt working time in order to reduce unemployment. His premise is that demand and supply policies are both now rather limited—economically or politically—in their capacity to do this in Europe.

He reviews the macroeconomic results of a number of historical episodes in which working time was sharply reduced: France in 1936, Germany in 1955–8, the Netherlands in 1961, the United Kingdom in the three-day working-week case in 1974, and France again with the experience of the Mitterrand government since 1981. His observations are, reduced to the barest summary, that the pre-war French case did see an increase in employment, that the German and Dutch cases did not because there was hardly spare capacity in the economy at the time, and that the British case illustrated the scope for productivity gains that may be obtained in the short run by reducing working time. Charpin feels it is too early to judge the current French experience, but early indicators suggest a much larger gain in productivity than in employment as a result of the shorter working week.

More generally Charpin discusses the issues that arise in trying to obtain higher employment from reduced and reorganized working time: the question of wage compensation, the potential flexibility of work organization, the extent of productivity gains, the extent of budgetary savings in unemployment allowances (and thus the potential for subsidizing the reduction of the standard working week), the need or not for internationally concerted action in this field, and finally the suitable degree of decentralization of negotiations within national economies.

On the whole Charpin advocates a cautious activism in the adaptation of working time. He recognizes the potentially harmful effects on the economy and perverse effects on employment if several exacting conditions are not respected—for example the avoidance of cost increases, or the differentiation between situations in which work organization can be more or less easily changed.

Many of the issues already mentioned are also taken up in *Michael Emerson*'s paper, for example the importance of the real-wage level and medium-term public finance trends in explaining the deepening stagflationary condition of the European economy. It is argued that Europe's unemployment problem has for these reasons become considerably deeper that in either the United States or Japan. Although the present recession has seen US unemployment levels rise to the same level as in Europe, the striking difference over the past decade has been the complete failure in Europe as a whole to achieve any substantial net employment creation at all—unlike in the US where the increase has been very large. Nominal demand has been kept up, but the split between real growth and inflation has drastically worsened.

As for the prescription, Emerson offers a menu of adjustment policies, which aims at unwinding the problems just mentioned. It is recognized that a policy strategy along these lines risks running into serious problems of transitional demand deflation unless these are explicitly countered. A promising framework for doing this lies in the setting of targets for the evolution of nominal gross domestic product (nominal GDP)—which combines both real growth and inflation together. Applying at the European level principles advocated by Professor Meade, it is argued that nominal constraints have to be imposed on the economy to prevent inflation running out of control. But nominal GDP targeting can be a safer guide to the management of financial policies than the rigid pursuit of money supply or budget deficit targets. The second feature of this approach is that real wage trends have to be recognized as a prime determinant of employment, whether or not an incomes policy is arranged in co-ordination with financial policies. With the setting of nominal GDP targets, a reasonable safeguard against demand deflation can be offered. Should a real-wage adjustment begin to cause a transitional problem of deflation this would show up in an undershooting of nominal GDP in relation to target, which would warrant an easing of financial policies to correct this.

It is also suggested that the approach has potential for improving the co-ordination of policies in Europe. Within the European Community and European Monetary System the co-ordinated setting of multi-year nominal GDP targets could offer an improved framework for the pursuit of economic convergence. Across the Atlantic, the Federal Reserve Board in the United States in the period ahead could make use of a nominal GDP targeting approach, given the downgrading now of M_1 targeting, and the need in these conditions to minimize uncertainty over future monetary policy management. This could be a practical contribution towards putting international monetary policy management on to a sounder footing.

In conclusion, while the group did not set itself the objective of working out a joint position on current issues of economic policy, the exceptional gravity of the economic situation in Europe provoked substantial discussion on this. A large majority of participants were of the opinion that endogenous developments were not about to set the European economy on a self-righting trajectory. Thus there was undoubtedly a problem for policy. It was also widely felt that an easing of financial policies in some key countries could not alone be expected to achieve the kind of correction now required. In addition an important real-wage/profit adjustment was necessary in much of the region, perhaps even in all European countries. Opinions differed on more precise issues of wage adjustment and financial policy.

Opinion was perhaps evenly divided as to whether the necessary shift of income distribution from wages into profits should be pursued through making real-wage cuts *ex ante*, or through holding back the growth of the real-wage level as an economic upswing increased profits. Here there are also important country differences and as regards Germany, for example, opinion was in the group more solidly behind the second alternative than the first, whereas for several other countries in Europe the first alternative was more strongly supported.

On financial policy, a minimal common denominator was that monetary policy should be eased in the period ahead so as to reduce real interest rates. Money supply growth should at least be sufficient to permit a reasonable trajectory for nominal gross domestic product in low-inflation countries. On budgetary policy the group evinced a wider spectrum of opinions, including from some the proposition that in present circumstances some fiscal stimulus was warranted in Europe on average, and from others the proposition that reductions in structural budget deficits should still be aimed at in 1983. On the structure of public expenditure there was widespread support for a reversal of recent trends which have seen growing transfer payments squeezing out public investment. However there was also a wide range of opinion on the advisable severity of action to curb the growth of current public expenditure.

At the conference there were no high expectations that the authorities in Europe would now devise a set of co-ordinated policies that could at one and the same time rekindle growth and curb a resurgence of inflation. It was therefore appropriate to ask what other forces might exist that could pull Europe out from semi-stagflation. Boltho concluded his paper on precisely this issue. Taking an eclectic view of historical adjustment periods of booms and slumps, and thus borrowing from both Marx and Schumpeter, he suggested that four conditions might have to be met for a new endogenous upswing of major proportions to occur: (i) the emergence of a reserve army of unemployed and falling wages; (ii) the accumulation of a backlog of unexploited innovations; (iii) the scrapping of a significant segment of the capital stock; and (iv) the emergence of a new generation of Schumpeterian entrepreneurs. In fact several of these conditions are beginning to be fulfilled in Western Europe at present, including the possibility that new technologies may be reviving growth possibilities for small-scale production. Such 'optimistic' reflections need, however, to be tempered by the dangerously long time-lags in such processes. Meanwhile the relatively passive response to increasing social difficulties and economic hardship could give way to more open forms of discontent. Boltho concludes: 'Policy-makers may have learnt some lessons from the first oil shock, but may, in the process, have forgotten some lessons from the 1930s.'

Notes and Sources

[1] R. Layard, D. Grubb, and J. Symons.
[2] Victor Halberstadt, Kees Goudswaard, and Bart Le Blanc.

Economic Policy and Performance in Europe since the Second Oil Shock

ANDREA BOLTHO

Introduction

This paper looks at macroeconomic trends and policies in Western Europe over the years 1979–82. To provide some historical perspective the discussion is often conducted with reference to the earlier 1973–6 cycle with which a number of parallels and contrasts can be drawn. In particular, a bird's-eye view of both periods suggests two major similarities and two major differences. Both cycles were strongly influenced by similar, OPEC-determined, oil-price rises[1] and in both cycles the course of activity and inflation followed broadly similar trends, at least in the years of expansion (1973 and 1979), slow-down (1974 and 1980), and recession (1975 and 1981). A major difference appears, however, when comparing 1976 with 1982—in the earlier year there was a sharp recovery, in the latter virtual stagnation. And economic policies have clearly been much more restrictive throughout the 1979–82 cycle than they were in 1973–6.

The first part of the chapter describes the different policies followed in Europe over the two cycles and the trends recorded, emphasizing, in particular, output, price, and unemployment developments. The second part looks at the major reasons for the similarities and differences in performance in the two cycles. The third part discusses the policy record, stressing the possible longer-term consequences of the recent cycle's swing into restriction. It raises, in particular, the possibility that in a world in which divergent expectations are formulated in different sectors of the economy neither traditional Keynesian measures of reflation nor orthodox monetarist policies of deflation may be able to restore growth and employment. A concluding part briefly summarizes the main arguments and hazards a tentative look at the future.

In principle, the discussion covers the whole of the OECD European area. In practice, however, data limitations and space constraints mean that attention has to focus, more often than not, on the four major countries (France, West Germany, Italy, and the United Kingdom).

Space constraints also impose the frequent use of aggregate statistics (for example for the total of OECD Europe or for the sum of the four major economies) so that much inter-country detail is inevitably ignored or glossed over. While such an approach may provide an illustration of broad trends, it hardly does justice to the great diversity of national experience.

I. Policies and Trends in Two Cycles

Both 1973 and 1979 marked the upper points of medium-term cycles for the world economy even if, in the latter case, this upswing was much less pronounced. On both occasions, a major consequence of the expansion was a rise in commodity prices followed by a sharp increase in the price of oil (itself triggered off more by political events in the Middle East than by economic forces). And each of these two rises in the price of oil had very similar effects on the industrialized countries, both in terms of the initial impact (equivalent to some 2 per cent of the OECD area's GDP[2]) and of subsequent inflation and recession. This is not to say that the 1979-82 cycle was an exact replica of the 1973-6 one. There were differences between the two episodes both in starting-points and in the subsequent development of events. Thus, the synchronization of cyclical movements in the industrialized world was less pronounced in 1979, with the United States partly out of phase with Western Europe and Japan, and the commodity-price increases were very different in their intensity,[3] while subsequent swings in cyclical activity were sharper during OPEC-1 than during OPEC-2. More importantly, slow growth in the period 1973-9, compared to earlier decades, had meant that most countries were facing the 1980s in a much weaker underlying position, exemplified, in particular, by the deterioration in two indicators—much larger budget deficits and much higher rates of unemployment.[4] None the less, observing the broad trends in output, inflation, and unemployment, one is struck by a certain number of parallels (Fig. 1.1).

Policies

The same, however, is less true for the stance of economic policies. Similarities may have prevailed at the outset, but they soon gave way to pronounced differences. In both 1972 and 1978 economic policies had been relatively expansionary in Europe in response to the earlier, 1971 and 1977, slow-downs. But when the oil crises broke out, reactions differed in two important respects. Firstly, Europe met OPEC-1 in dispersed order but responded to OPEC-2 in much more uniform fashion. Secondly, the years 1973-6 were characterized by 'stop-go' policies while 1979-82 saw much greater continuity. During OPEC-1,

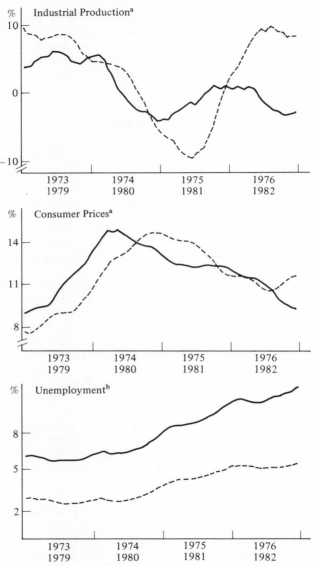

Fig. 1.1: Output, inflation, and unemployment in OECD Europe (Three-month moving averages)

ᵃ Percentage change from previous year.
ᵇ Percentage of the labour force; figures obtained by adding not strictly comparable data for thirteen countries.
Source: OECD data bank.

one major country (Germany) swung initially into a very restrictive stance, two (Italy and the United Kingdom) went into the almost opposite direction, while France followed an intermediate course.[5] These roles were almost reversed through 1974 and into early 1975, with Germany relaxing its stance, while Britain, France, and Italy were forced, to differing extents, into monetary restraint. In 1979–80, by contrast, both fiscal and monetary policies were tightened roughly at the same time in all four major countries and (with only the temporary exception of France from mid-1981 to mid-1982) remained tight throughout the subsequent two years.

Some impression of these different stances is provided in aggregate form in Table 1.1. Though the summary indicators chosen are clearly imperfect, they should suffice to bring out three major features: the less pronounced expansionary posture of 1978 versus 1972, the much sharper move into restriction in 1979–80 compared to 1973–4, and, most importantly, the absence of a swing in policies in 1981–2 in contrast to the shift recorded in 1975. Despite recession in 1981 and virtual stagnation in 1982, monetary policy, if anything, became more restrictive through time and this was also true of fiscal policy—the cyclically adjusted budget balance of the four major countries moved into increasing *surplus* rather than into deficit (as it had done in 1975). And while the blame for rising real interest rates can, to some extent, be laid at the door of developments in the United States, the same is clearly not true for fiscal policy.

The reasons for the difference in policy stance are, of course, well known. At an immediate level, most European governments feared a renewed inflationary outburst in the wake of the oil-price increases, a repetition of the profits squeeze of 1974–5 and the likelihood of substantial exchange-rate depreciation (at least in the so-called 'weaker' countries).[6] In addition, there was the fear that, in the presence of what were perceived as limited energy supplies, any concerted expansionary move would hit an energy ceiling and hence lead to continuing oil-price increases. This was a further factor ruling out any calls for reflationary action of the 'locomotive' or 'convoy' type.

More importantly, however, the move into a more uniform and rigorous stance was influenced by the 'demonstration effect' of earlier post-1973, developments. Looking back at that experience it seemed clear that the two countries which had initially followed the most stringent policies (Germany, but also Japan), had met with the greatest success. Growth in both countries had been relatively rapid after the 1975 recession, inflation had come down to the rates of the 1960s, while currency appreciation seemed to have had little lasting impact on competitiveness and current-account positions. At the other end of the spectrum, the countries which had initially tried to follow

14 ANDREA BOLTHO

TABLE 1.1
Indicators of Policy Stance

	Fiscal policy Four major countries[a]		Monetary policy Eight major countries[b]	
	Fiscal policy impact[c] (percentage of previous year's real GDP)	High-employment budget balance[d] (percentage of nominal GDP)	Real money supply[e] (percentage change from previous year)	Real interest rates[f] (percentage)
	A. 1972 to 1976			
1972	−1.1	−0.1	9.0	1.4
1973	−0.2	−	4.6	0.6
1974	−1.0	−0.2	2.5	−1.2
1975	−2.1	−2.2	−0.4	−1.9
1976	0.8	−1.3	3.0	0.3
	B. 1978 to 1982			
1978	−0.5	−0.3	4.6	2.1
1979	0.4	−	3.4	1.1
1980	0.4	1.0	−0.4	−
1981	−0.5	1.5	−0.3	3.0
1982	−0.3	2.6	(0.3)	3.5

[a] France, West Germany, Italy, and the United Kingdom.
[b] Four major countries plus Belgium, the Netherlands, Sweden, and Switzerland.
[c] Changes in real weighted budget balance: negative change = expansionary effect; positive change = restrictive effect.
[d] Budget balance excluding the effects of built-in stabilizers and assuming that 1973 and 1979 were years of high employment in which the actual and adjusted balances coincided.
[e] Broad definition of money supply deflated by GDP deflator.
[f] Long-term interest rates deflated by consumer prices.
Sources: OECD, *National Accounts of OECD Countries, 1951–1980,* vol. I; 'Budget Indicators', *OECD Economic Outlook—Occasional Studies,* July 1978, and *Economic Outlook* (various issues); EEC, *European Economy,* Nov. 1980 and Nov. 1982; IMF, *International Financial Statistics,* 1981 yearbook and various monthly issues.

more expansionary policies (Britain and Italy, in particular), had witnessed a sharp deceleration in growth, continuing high rates of inflation, and few favourable effects on competitiveness from currency depreciation, while their policies had eventually been forced into severe deflation. If, in the end, restriction was inevitable, then it was probably better to accept its need sooner rather than later.

The precursor of this conversion to a more orthodox stance was France, under the Barre Plan, the latecomer the United Kingdom under the Thatcher government. In between followed many of the other

European countries, with the creation of the EMS as a particularly important landmark for the 'weaker' economies such as Italy.

In both the Barre and Thatcher cases (as earlier in Germany), the conversion had come more from conviction than from necessity. But the perception of how the new policies would succeed differed greatly. Lulled, perhaps, by the relatively painless deflations of Germany and Japan and/or by the optimistic predictions of the 'new' classical macro-economics, British policy-makers did seem to believe that the transition to lower inflation could be bought at the cost of only a small and short recession thanks to the announcement effect of new and *credible* policies—in particular the 'Medium-term Financial Strategy'. No such illusions prevailed on the other side of the Channel. France knew well (and Italy even better) that its labour market was far from being as flexible as the German labour market had been in 1974-5, while Barre, perhaps because of his background as a professor of economics, showed a healthy scepticism for simplistic economic theories. It was accepted that a strict stance was going to be accompanied by high costs in terms of both output and employment. Hence, and in contrast to Britain, deflation was much more gradual and less dogmatic—yet a further example of how the traditional distinction between the ostensibly pragmatic English and the 'ideological' Continentals should, at least in the realm of economic policy-making, be stood on its head.[7]

A further interesting inter-country difference (*vis-à-vis* the earlier period) is provided by Germany and the United Kingdom. As already mentioned, the two countries pursued restrictive and accommodating policies respectively in 1973-4. On the more recent occasion the roles were reversed as Germany, after the mid-1978 Bonn Summit reflation, moved into restriction only very gradually through 1980. The German fiscal package appears to have been relatively successful—growth was sustained without inflation being rekindled as trade-union behaviour remained moderate and the often-feared price-raising sectoral bottlenecks did not appear.[8] In Britain, by contrast, the deflation was clearly overdone. The exchange rate was allowed to appreciate by some 50 per cent in real terms in the two years to early 1981, fiscal policy became increasingly pro-cyclical as the recession worsened,[9] and both the falls in output and increases in unemployment were little different from those in the years 1929-31.[10]

In complete contrast to post-1973 developments, therefore, the two countries which had, in the post-war period, given priority to full employment (France and the United Kingdom), were, by the turn of the 1970s, following policies a good deal more restrictive than those of the country which had traditionally given pride of place to the fight against inflation. It is true that midway through the second cycle French strategies changed as a consequence of the coming to power of a Socialist government, but this expansionary phase was quickly re-absorbed under the pressures of accelerating inflation, worsening competitiveness, and successive devaluations of the currency.

Trends

In the light of this greater overall stringency of policy, one may have expected that activity would have been more depressed than in 1974-5 (the more so as the growth of demand outside Western Europe was less buoyant on the latest occasion), and that inflationary develop-ments would have been more subdued (the more so as commodity prices rose less rapidly at first, and fell more sharply later, than in the previous cycle). Yet a cursory glance at Fig. 1.1 shows that the course of both output and prices was relatively similar in the two cycles. If anything, the performance on the output front may have been slightly more favourable, with less overheating at the outset and with the 1981 recession milder than the 1975 one. The price picture suggests a small improvement—though the inflation peaks were similar, OPEC-2 was superimposed on a higher starting-point and in a climate, almost cer-tainly, of more entrenched inflationary expectations than those that had prevailed in 1973. The second cycle saw, moreover, a distinct improvement in one further important area—income distribution. In contrast to 1974-5, which had seen a very sharp fall in the profit share, real-wage developments in 1980-1 were a good deal more moder-ate, a consequence of greater realism on the part of trade unions in some countries, and of higher unemployment levels in all (Table 1.2).

In two respects, however, performance worsened markedly—there was a sharp rise in unemployment and no recovery. Not only was unemployment much higher in 1982 than in 1976, but its growth accelerated in the second cycle—the rate of unemployment which had risen by 2 percentage points in Europe as a whole between 1973 and 1976, rose by some 4 percentage points in the three years to 1982. And while output recovered strongly in 1976, there was no such re-covery in 1982 and few signs of it in 1983.

II. Why was Performance Different?

This section will try to answer three major questions implicitly raised in the preceding discussion.

(i) Why was the growth of output in 1980-1 more resilient than in 1974-5 despite less favourable 'exogenous' (i.e. world-market and policy) conditions?

(ii) Why did unemployment rise so much more rapidly in the recent cycle despite no worsening in the output trend until 1982 and a better profit performance?

TABLE 1.2
'Real-wage Gap'—Four Major Countries
(Percentage change from previous year)

	'Warranted' real wage growth[a]	Actual real wage growth[b]	Real wage gap[c]
1973	3.8	4.8	1.0
1974	−0.7	2.7	3.4
1975	1.4	2.9	1.5
1976	4.9	1.8	−3.0
1979	2.7	2.3	−0.5
1980	0.3	2.0	1.7
1981	0.2	1.3	1.1
1982	2.1	0.5	−1.6

[a] Growth of output per employee corrected for the income effect of terms-of-trade changes.
[b] Compensation per employee deflated by private consumption deflator.
[c] A negative sign indicates a shift towards non-wage incomes.
Source: OECD, *Economic Outlook* (various issues).

(iii) Why was there no real recovery in output growth from OPEC–2 as there had been from OPEC–1?

Output

Three major factors, linked to household, corporate, and public-sector behaviour, throw light on the absence of a pronounced recession in 1980-1, in contrast to 1974-5. On the household side, the tight policy stance as well as rising unemployment levels meant that real disposable income rose much less rapidly than in the previous cycle. But the effects of this on the growth of output were resisted by a decline in the propensity to save, in contrast to the unexpected rise in saving ratios which took place between 1973 and 1975. The reluctance to see living standards decline was thus a stronger force than the desire to restore real balances or precautionary savings, and real consumer expenditure grew at a rate virtually identical to the one recorded in the previous cycle (Fig. 1.2).

On the corporate side the differences are not to be found in stock-building—in both cycles the patterns of inventory accumulation and decumulation were similar. Surprisingly, however, investment performed much more favourably in the early 1980s than in the mid-1970s despite more restrictive policies, higher real interest rates, and larger margins of spare capacity. This is even more apparent if it is borne in mind that Fig. 1.2 shows the behaviour of total gross fixed capital formation, thus including public-sector investment. Since the latter was flat between 1978 and 1981, as against a 10 per cent rise in the

Indices 1972 Q1 = 100: – – – –
1978 Q1 = 100: ———

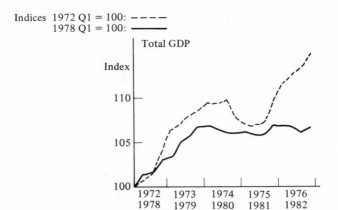

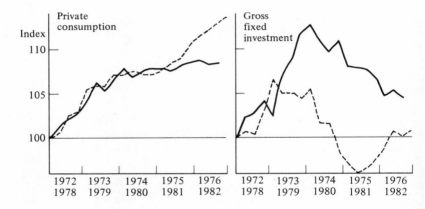

Percentages of constant price GDP 1972–6: – – – –
1978–82: ———

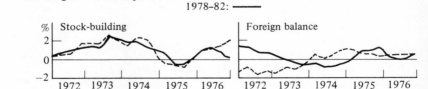

Fig. 1.2: Output and demand components in the four major economies[a]

[a] France, West Germany, Italy, and United Kingdom.
Source: EEC data bank.

three years to 1975, the contrast between the two cycles is even more marked. In view of the stagnation in investment that had occurred in the years 1972 to 1977, some upward spurt was probably inevitable, and it may also have been helped by the better profit–wage configuration that emerged from the second oil shock. But there may be some more important reasons for this relative resilience—in particular, rapid changes in technology and sharp shifts in labour and energy prices.

In a sense, all these three factors are of a trend nature—investment is constantly being carried out incorporating latest technological innovations and allowing economies in the use of labour and raw materials. It is possible, however, that the late 1970s saw some acceleration in the rate at which technical progress was being embodied in new investment, either because innovations themselves were coming on stream at an accelerating rate, or because the pressures of international competition were forcing European producers to match more rapidly best-practice techniques in, say, Japan or the United States. Similarly, it is likely that labour-saving investments were being stepped up in the wake of the sharp shift in income distribution towards wages that had taken place following the first oil shock (as well as in response to the mounting body of legislation which, since the early 1970s, had sharply increased rigidities in the labour market).[11] These trends may have been reinforced, after the second oil shock, by a need to move out of energy-intensive equipment and to shift production into less energy-intensive goods and services.[12]

Finally, policy may also have played a part in moderating the recession despite its generally restrictive stance. The reason for this is to be found in the already mentioned contrast between British and German policies. The switch in the relative position of the two countries meant that, in lieu of a sharp German recession one witnessed on the more recent occasion a sharp British recession and much more moderate German developments, with Germany's current balance swinging into substantial deficit in 1979–81 as against its move into surplus in 1973–5 (Fig. 1.3). This had repercussions on the whole European scene given not only the different weights of the two countries in any aggregate statistics, but also the leading role of Germany for Continental European developments. Taking, for example, the growth of output in those smaller countries most dependent on German import demand (Austria, Belgium, Denmark, the Netherlands, and Switzerland), this slumped in 1975 ($-2\frac{1}{2}$ per cent), but was virtually flat in 1981 ($-\frac{1}{4}$ per cent)—two sets of figures quite similar to those of Germany ($-1\frac{3}{4}$ per cent and $-\frac{1}{4}$ per cent respectively).[13]

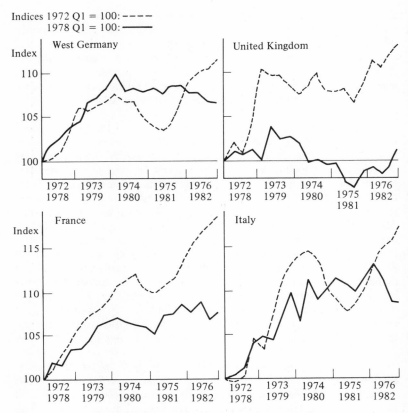

Fig. 1.3: GDP cycles in the four major economies

Source: EC data bank.

Unemployment

Turning to unemployment, the major factor at work seems to have come from the demand side. Demographic trends did make for a sharp increase in the population aged between fifteen and sixty-four in Western Europe over the more recent cycle (over ten million between 1978 and 1982, as against not quite eight million between 1972 and 1976). This was offset, however, by a sharp fall in participation rates so that the increase in the actual labour force was, if anything, smaller than that recorded in the previous cycle when participation rates had remained stable.[14] But the demand for labour fell sharply. While between 1973 and 1976 total employment had remained roughly flat in Europe, it declined by some two and a half million in the three years to 1982, boosting unemployment from just over ten million people to perhaps some sixteen million.

Several factors may explain the developments through OPEC-2—the likelihood that investment took an increasingly labour-saving character, the deceleration in the growth of public-sector consumption (a very labour-intensive item of demand), the diminished scope for countries of immigration (in particular Germany) to send home foreign workers (who do not always appear in the unemployment data of receiving countries). But the most important reason is probably to be found in a change in entrepreneurial behaviour. The recession of the mid-1970s was largely met by a policy of labour hoarding (as indirectly confirmed by the sharp upward jump in youth unemployment over this period, in contrast to the much more modest rise in adult male unemployment). The early 1980s, on the other hand, saw a much greater willingness to dismiss members of the 'permanent' labour force. Changed expectations about the future, rather than sluggish output trends, would seem to be paramount in explaining this.

Traditional views of employment demand suggest that this is sticky in the short run and adapts over the longer term to past changes in output. In the world of the 1950s and 1960s, when past trends were a reasonable proxy for future developments, such a specification could, and did, provide good econometric results.[15] It is unlikely, however, to fit as well in a world in which policies are seen to have switched radically and the expected growth of demand is much less buoyant. Uncertainty clearly existed also in the mid-1970s, but many still foresaw a resumption of relatively rapid growth[16] which made labour hoarding a realistic option. Much less confidence prevailed in the early 1980s so that desired employment levels were set more as a function of future than of past output trends.

The missed recovery

The final, and most important, question concerns the lack, by the end of 1981, of any revival in activity, in sharp contrast to the pronounced acceleration in growth which was recorded in 1976. The lesser depth of the 1981 recession provides only a partial and proximate explanation. For more underlying reasons one must turn to economic policy. As was mentioned earlier, economic policies played no deliberate counter-cyclical role in 1981 (except in France). Such a stance is highly likely to have nipped in the bud any expansionary forces that may have followed the inevitable OPEC-induced slowdown. But the role of policies did not stop there. The strategy followed in 1981 was pursued, and indeed reinforced, in 1982. Partly, this arose from necessity (the dollar's strength made some continuing monetary restraint inevitable), but partly also from conscious design—and, in particular, from the continuing search for lower budget deficits.

In such circumstances, it is no surprise that private-sector reactions should have increasingly paralleled those of the public sector—household saving ratios seem to have declined only marginally in 1982, as precautionary balances were being reconstituted, while private investment, after a positive stock adjustment in 1979–80, fell sharply. Since, in addition, by the close of 1982 there had been no real switch in policies, while demand expectations had worsened further because of a deceleration in the growth of world trade as well as mounting fears of an international financial crisis, the sluggishness of 1982 continued into 1983.

III. An Assessment

The foregoing brief overview of some of the major European macroeconomic trends in the OPEC-1 and OPEC-2 cycles suggests two broad conclusions.

(i) The short-run output and price adaptation of Europe's major economies to the second oil shock was smoother and more successful than in 1974–6;

(ii) The longer-run prospects raised by the continuation of the policy trends initiated during the second cycle are, on the other hand, much more disquieting.

The short-run response

The improved performance of the European economies in 1979–81 relative to 1973–5 was detailed earlier on—there was no overheating at the outset, there was no sharp recession, and there was some price deceleration (interrupted, it is true, in mid-1981, but by an exogenous factor, namely the dollar's sharp revaluation). Policy can take some credit for this. The 'Evident errors of factual judgement regarding: (i) the strength of the underlying cycle when the oil shock occurred; (ii) the effects of the oil shock; (iii) the strength of transmission' of 1973–5 were not repeated.[17] Governments were clearly better prepared on this occasion and lessons had been learnt from the experience of OPEC-1.[18] Moreover, there was greater awareness of the importance of the international transmission of business fluctuations and a greater degree of realism as to what policy could, or could not, achieve in any single country. Not by chance were most of the output forecasts prepared in this period much more accurate than those of 1973–6 (Table 1.3).

This is not to say that there were no errors in policy formulation. It

TABLE 1.3
OECD Secretariat Forecasts for OECD Europe's GDP
(Percentage change from previous year)

	1974–6			1980–2		
	Forecast	Actual	Error[a]	Forecast	Actual	Error[a]
1974/80	$4\frac{3}{4}$	2.1	2.6	$1\frac{1}{2}$	1.4	0.1
1975/81	$2\frac{1}{4}$	−1.9	4.1	$\frac{1}{4}$	−0.3	0.5
1976/82	2	4.2	2.2	$1\frac{1}{2}$	0.6	0.9

Note: The forecast values are those published in the preceding year's December issue of the OECD *Economic Outlook*; the 'actual' values are those published in the succeeding year's December issue.

[a] Irrespective of sign.

Source: OECD, *Economic Outlook* (various issues).

is clear that United Kingdom policies, for instance, turned out to be far too restrictive, partly because they underestimated both the strength of the pound and its subsequent effects on the economy. And the French attempt at 'Socialism in one country' between mid-1981 and mid-1982 overestimated the capacity of a medium-sized economy to go against the general trend. But if one takes the European 'loco-motive'—Germany—it would seem that its policy reactions were moderate, compared to the sharp monetary squeeze of 1973–4, and that cyclical developments were largely under control. A modest recession seemed necessary to the authorities in order to curb infla-tionary expectations and a modest recession was engineered. Success in Germany meant that most other European countries were less subject to powerful external deflationary forces. And German member-ship of the EMS meant also that they were less subject (until the dollar appreciated) to simultaneous and powerful external inflationary forces (over and above those coming from OPEC), via depreciations of their currencies *vis-à-vis* the DM.[19]

The longer-run dilemma

But these short-run successes seem to have given way to longer-run failures. No resumption of rapid growth took place in 1982–3 as neither household savings (which were down to their 1969 level in 1982), nor business investment (which may have nearly completed its adjustment to changed input prices), could be expected to stimulate activity. Indeed, the prospects of continuing semi-stagnation in output and relentless rises in unemployment levels through most of the 1980s cannot be excluded.[20] The major problem seems to lie in the continua-tion of a deflationary strategy in each individual country whose ultimate aim is clearly desirable (a resumption of non-inflationary growth), but whose workings may have postponed the achievement of that aim.

A very simplified presentation of this policy stance in most major countries could be based on three propositions. The first one is that any programme of reflation designed to sustain demand is likely to sustain inflation and inflationary expectations instead. The transmission mechanism may work via expectations in product and labour markets, or via exchange-rate falls engendered by financial-market reactions, or through some mixture of the two—either way, the end results are likely to be higher prices and nominal interest rates. The second proposition is that rapid and variable rates of inflation are inimical to growth. In particular, business investment is depressed by high nominal rates of interest and tax systems that have not fully adjusted to inflationary conditions, private consumption is reduced by the losses in real wealth that households suffer from falling financial-asset values, and both corporate- and personal-sector spending are discouraged by the uncertainty that inflation generates. The third proposition is, thus, that growth can only be restored if inflation and inflationary expectations are brought under control. In addition, it is also felt that a private-sector upswing will require not only low inflation and low interest rates, but also a shift of income towards profits and a slimming of an overgrown public sector which dampens private initiative directly (because of a plethora of regulations and high marginal tax rates) and indirectly (because it pre-empts scarce resources). The return to low inflation, the restoration of adequate profitability, and the reduction in the size of the public sector can only be obtained by a restrictive policy whose duration will be inversely related to the degree of flexibility in the economy and, in particular, in the labour market. Reflation is not only impotent, since private-sector reactions would nullify its effects in a relatively short time-span, but also positively harmful since it would make the indispensable future adjustment more painful.

There is clearly some truth in this very summary and inevitably highly over-simplified view of the present orthodoxy. Thus, the idea that high nominal interest rates and unfavourable tax rules reduce corporate investment is very plausible,[21] while empirical work has shown that rapid rates of inflation lowered private consumption in the later 1970s in all the four major European countries.[22] Turning to the economic policy side, the 'Lucas critique,[23] which argues that private-sector behaviour is likely to vary as policies change, thus (possibly) impairing their effectiveness, is, by now, largely accepted. Indeed, recent experience (for example in France) has shown how the effects of reflationary packages can be frustrated by unfavourable expectations of the ultimate impact of such policies held by financial markets.

The third proposition, however, poses greater difficulties. If the world approximated to the model of the rational expectations theorists, then, indeed, lower prices and interest rates would generate a spontaneous upswing, back to the 'natural' rates of unemployment and output growth. But economies are not necessarily as self-stabilizing as assumed by the new classical macroeconomics. In particular, the overwhelming body of econometric research suggests that investment is primarily determined by expected sales rather than by interest rates. And though profits are, no doubt, also important, business is likely to be influenced more by the *future rate of profit* (itself largely a function of expectations), than by the *past share of profits* (the variable which governments are at present trying to boost). Turning to consumption, theoretical considerations suggest that falling prices (or, rather, decelerating rates of inflation) not only take time to materialize, but need not have favourable effects on household spending: 'The forces which lower money wages and prices are slow and weak, and those which translate deflation or disinflation into greater real demand are uncertain.'[24]

If there is any truth in what has been said so far, there may be a dilemma for policy. An expansionary stance may have rapid effects on the price level, for example via exchange-rate depreciation and rising inflationary expectations. It should also have positive effects on output, via higher public expenditure, lower taxes, or rising net exports. But these take time to come through—there are lags in the implementation of government policies, in the reactions of households to higher disposable incomes, and, most importantly, in the responsiveness of trade flows to greater competitiveness. The much-quicker-acting unfavourable impact of higher inflation on demand could rapidly nullify any such slow-working multiplier effects on activity.

The alternative policy stance of continuing restriction has also a number of unfavourable consequences. Restrictive policies may be slow working in their effects on inflation and on inflationary expectations. The reasons for this can be numerous and are well known. An example often quoted in connection with the United Kingdom, is the likelihood that various markets adjust at different speeds to 'news'. Thus, while in some markets, in which 'rational' expectations prevail, the adjustment to new policy rules may be very rapid, in the labour market, in particular, expectations may be formed differently, thereby imparting greater sluggishness to the disinflation process.[25] Alternatively, inflation may not decelerate because a 'game' situation develops (and pre-1981 France could provide an example of this).[26] The authorities implement a non-accommodating policy, which should lead to lower wages, but workers, in the light of past experience, anticipate a shift to an accommodating stance as unemployment rises and/or a general election approaches. In either case, the path to lower inflation is slower than expected, involves higher unemployment, and requires continuing restriction.

Such restriction, in turn, may have cumulative effects on aggregate demand, as enterprises revise their forecast sales and households lower their permanent income expectations in the light of announced government policies.[27] Just as agents may eventually take systematic policy rules of accommodation into account when setting their prices or wage claims, so agents may equally take systematic rules of non-accommodation into account when deciding on their spending plans. This is particularly true for investment, a component of demand for which in a climate of uncertain expectations 'there will always be the temptation to postpone and keep on postponing decisions'.[28]

Finally, the investment shortfall creates a difficulty for any future recovery, be this spontaneous or policy-induced, since it is likely to depress the potential output ceiling. A more rapid growth of demand in the future could spark off price rises in particular sectors (including oil and commodities, since the investment shortfall is hardly limited to Europe). Even if one discounted the possible reappearance of cost-push pressures, inflation could none the less re-emerge from the demand side and nullify the effects of earlier government measures.

An 'expectations trap'?

The policy dilemma just sketched would thus seem to arise primarily from the different processes of expectations formation in different sectors of the economy and, particularly, in the financial and in the industrial (or 'real') parts of the corporate sector. Expansionary policies could well lead to runs on currencies and/or higher interest rates, as the financial sector, imbued with monetarist orthodoxy, expects inflation to accelerate. Yet restrictive policies could affect the much more Keynesian expectations of the industrial sector. The problem lies not primarily in the different speeds of adjustment of various markets to changes in policy—this difficulty plays a role in so far as it prolongs the period of disinflation—but rather in the opposite reactions of different sectors to announcements of policy changes.

As just sketched, this view implies that agents in financial markets assume monetarism to be correct, while industry holds a Keynesian view of the world. The former need not be true. Financial markets may act on the expectation that governments will behave as though monetarism were correct. If this was the case, then an announced and credible change in policy stance could dispel some of the unfavourable price-raising expectations. Yet such an interpretation of financial-market behaviour seems, on balance, unlikely. Adoption of, and adaptation to new policies are lengthy processes. It took ten to fifteen years for Germany or Italy, for instance, to accept Keynesian demand management views, and it took some ten to fifteen years before Keynesian measures were thought to be losing effectiveness in, for example, Britain or France. Similarly, it has taken a long time for monetarism to become an accepted 'general theory' outside the academic world and it may take a long time (and the pressure of events, rather than changes in policies), for it to be abandoned by market participants.

The implication of what has been said so far is that economic policy may at present be impotent. The new classical macroeconomics has, of course, already reached this result, starting from the premise that the private sector of the economy is self-stabilizing. The conclusion here is similar, but the premise is exactly the opposite one— it is the existence of a *non* self-stabilizing private sector within which different forms of expectations are held that leads to policy impotence. Financial-market expectations frustrate any attempted reflation. But industrial-sector expectations react negatively to policies of deflation. In the process inflation decelerates (slowly), but activity does not revive (with profits remaining low and budget deficits high). In other words, Western Europe may be caught in what could be called an 'expectations trap'[29]—the idea that the public sector frames its stance in the light of its perception of the short-run reactions of the private financial sector to policy changes, while the private industrial sector bases its longer-run spending decisions on what it perceives the stance of macroeconomic policies to be. Policies are a function of expectations, but expectations are also a function of policies.

Conclusions

The three main arguments developed in this chapter have been that:

(i)   Europe's economic policy performance during the second oil shock was more successful in the short run than that of 1973–5, largely because of a more appropriate policy stance in the area's 'locomotive' economy—West Germany;

(ii) The longer-run outcome was probably negative since a policy posture suitable for a cooling-off period was not reversed, thereby preventing a resumption of growth even of the modest kind that occurred between 1975 and 1979;

(iii) To some extent, however, such an outcome may have been inevitable, at the level of any single economy, given the nature and importance of expectations, particularly in the financial sector; what is called the 'expectations trap' may stop individual countries from returning to full employment in the foreseeable future.

Coping with such an 'expectations trap' could be a good deal more difficult than it was to cope with Keynes's 'liquidity trap'. At the time, this could be circumvented by overcoming the resistance to budget deficits and running an expansionary fiscal policy. What are required in the 1980s are policies that, at one and the same time, rekindle growth and curb the inflationary expectations generated by any programme of reflation, via both currency depreciation and labour-(or product-)market price escalation. Two courses of action, at least, would thus seem necessary—forms of incomes policies at the domestic level in order to dampen the chances of wage acceleration, and co-ordination of reflation at the international level to minimize the danger of sudden exchange-rate lurches (with such reflation probably having to be substantial if it is to overcome the inertia of pessimistic expectations). The adoption of either course of action, let alone of both, seems fraught with great difficulties in view of the glaring gaps in attitudes between the four major European countries (as well as the United States and Japan), and between the social partners within these countries. In the 1930s, the problem was merely that of debunking a shibboleth (and even that turned out to be quite difficult); in the 1980s it could be that of accepting partial losses of sovereignty at the international level and of union power at the domestic level— clearly very major and unlikely steps.

Barring any such changes in attitudes and policies, the question could be asked whether other forces may exist that could pull Europe out from semi-stagnation. After all, disequilibrium situations like the present one do not persist for ever and markets do ultimately clear. Indeed, in earlier periods of its history, capitalism had been confronted with prolonged periods of low growth to which policy could provide no answer (largely because governments did not assume a demand management role at the time), yet cyclical downswings did give way to subsequent recoveries and to the restoration of full-employment conditions, at least in the urban sector of the economy. At times such recoveries may have been due to purely exogenous forces, for example wars, gold discoveries, or colonial adventures,[30] but there were also instances of more endogenous, investment-led upswings.

An eclectic view of such historical adjustment periods (which borrows from both Marx and Schumpeter), suggests that a number of conditions needed to be fulfilled for such upswings to occur:

(i)   The reappearance of a 'reserve army of the unemployed', to-gether with falling prices and wages;
(ii) The accumulation of a backlog of unexploited innovations made possible by a continuous progress in knowledge;
(iii) The scrapping of significant segments of the capital stock, thus

generating potential demand for new investment;

(iv)   The emergence of Schumpeterian entrepreneurs ready to venture into risky projects by seizing the opportunities provided by ongoing technical progress, scarce capital, and abundant labour.

A cursory reading of this summary list shows that several of the conditions listed are beginning to be fulfilled in Western Europe at present. The rise in unemployment is increasingly affecting not only youths and women but also prime-aged males, while labour markets are reacquiring some degree of flexibility. Wages and prices may not be falling (that would be too much to expect), but inflation is clearly decelerating and inflationary expectations are probably declining. Technical progress would seem to be advancing, while capital equipment has certainly been, and is being scrapped in the wake of low growth and relative price shifts. The appearance of Schumpeterian entrepreneurs may seem more problematic—indeed, if one accepts the Galbraithian view that we live in a world of oligopolies, they probably no longer exist. Yet their re-emergence cannot be excluded. Technological innovations on the one hand (in particular the microchip), more diversified demand patterns on the other, combine in making possible a revival of smaller-scale production. This is strongly suggested, for instance, by trends in Japan, where for a decade now large-scale firms' employment has been rapidly declining in favour of smaller establishments. Small need not be beautiful, but it could be both feasible and inexpensive.

Such optimistic reflections need, however, to be tempered. Even if the various trends just sketched are indeed establishing themselves —something which is far from certain—their consolidation could take a long time. In particular, trade unions and welfare states provide, often socially desirable, obstacles to what would otherwise be a quicker labour-market adjustment. In other words, a spontaneous revival could occur eventually in our market economies, but its timing might tend to be shifted into the late 1980s. The present strategy would then be vindicated, but it is an open question whether it can be politically feasible in our democratic societies. The reaction to mounting unemployment since the mid-1970s has so far been largely muted, but this passive response to increasing social difficulties and economic hardship may well give way one day to much more open forms of discontent. Policy-makers may have learnt some lessons from the first oil shock, but may, in the process, have forgotten some lessons from the 1930s.

Notes and Sources

* The author would like to thank his friend and colleague Chris Allsopp for numerous suggestions and continuous encouragement, and he is grateful to Luigi Spaventa and David Worswick for helpful comments (which is in no way to imply any responsibility for the views expressed or for any errors and omissions).

[1] They have often been labelled OPEC-1 and OPEC-2 and this shorthand notation will at times be used in what follows.

[2] OECD, *Economic Outlook*, July 1980, p. 114.

[3] *The Economist*'s (dollar) index of non-oil commodity prices showed a peak year-to-year growth rate of 85 per cent in August 1973, but of barely 30 per cent in July 1979.

[4] For OECD Europe as a whole, general government net lending had moved from rough balance in 1973 to $-3\frac{1}{4}$ per cent of current price GDP in 1979, while unemployment had risen from 3 to $5\frac{1}{2}$ per cent of the labour force.

[5] For a careful account of policies in Europe between 1972 and 1977, see L. Izzo and L. Spaventa, 'Macroeconomic Policies in Western European Countries: 1973–1977', in H. Giersch (ed.), *Macroeconomic Policies for Growth and Stability*, J. C. B. Mohr, Tübingen, 1980.

[6] OECD, *Economic Outlook*, Dec. 1981, p. 6.

[7] An alternative, and much more political, interpretation of the two countries' position is also possible, however. In both France and the United Kingdom, the real, ultimate aim of restrictive policies may have been that of weakening the power of trade unions and re-establishing some of the old 'rules of the game' of a market economy. But the danger of greater political instability in France meant that this aim could not be pursued as radically as it was in Britain. In such an interpretation, the claims that disinflation can be painless must be seen as merely a smoke-screen since, in fact, a major recession is an indispensable part of the strategy.

[8] Simulations carried out on the Hamburg University model of the economy, suggest that fiscal policy boosted output growth by some $2\frac{1}{2}$ to 3 per cent between 1978 and 1980, while wage moderation dampened consumer-price inflation by half a percentage point over the same period; U. Sander, 'Die Rolle der Fiskal- und Lohnpolitik in den beiden Ölkrisen', *Sysifo Studien* (Universität Hamburg), No. 2, July 1982.

[9] EEC estimates of the cyclically adjusted budget balance show that (if one assumes 1979 to have been a year of high employment, as is done in Table 1.1), this recorded surpluses equivalent to $1\frac{1}{4}$, $4\frac{1}{2}$, and $6\frac{1}{2}$ per cent of GDP in 1980, 1981, and 1982 respectively—a move into deflation probably sharper than the one pursued by the orthodox Treasury at the time of the Great Depression (R. Middleton, 'The Constant Employment Budget Balance and British Budgetary Policy, 1929–39', *Economic History Review*, May 1981). And such figures, in an underlying sense, underestimate the tightness of fiscal policy, not only because they are not adjusted for inflation, but also, and more importantly, because they ignore the deflationary effects of the oil-price increase. In an energy self-sufficient United Kingdom, this increase is akin to a rise in indirect taxation since the higher profits of British oil producers accrue in large measure, if with a lag, to the Treasury itself via taxation on North Sea oil companies. In such circumstances, not offsetting the price increase by, for instance, a reduction in VAT or in payroll taxes, represents to all intents and purposes a further shift into restriction, equivalent in 1980 to perhaps 2 per cent of GDP.

[10] For a very complete survey of British trends and policies in this period, see W. H. Buiter and M. Miller, 'The Thatcher Experiment: The First Two Years', *Brookings Papers on Economic Activity*, No. 2, 1982.

[11] F. Bernabè, 'The Labour Market and Unemployment', in A. Boltho (ed.), *The European Economy: Growth and Crisis*, Oxford University Press, Oxford, 1982.

[12] It has often been claimed that such a need must already have arisen after the first oil shock. Yet, on reflection, this was probably unlikely. It should not be forgotten that in the mid-1970s real energy prices to final users did not rise very rapidly (OECD, *Economic Outlook*, Dec. 1981, p. 51), while real oil prices were declining on world markets. At the same time, the demand for energy-intensive products may well have risen rather than fallen in view of the shift in purchasing power towards OPEC. Thus, European demand (largely non-tradable at the margin) was curtailed, while OPEC import demand (by definition entirely tradable and of an energy-intensive nature) rose. Following the second oil shock, however, the growth of OPEC imports was less buoyant, real energy prices to final users rose much more rapidly and were, in addition, expected to remain high or even rise over the medium term.

[13] Ireland, conversely, which in the early 1980s was still sending over 40 per cent of its exports to the United Kingdom, fared relatively worse in the second cycle.

[14] Since these falls in participation rates are likely to reflect a 'discouraged worker' phenomenon, the trends in the second period almost certainly mask a much larger increase in 'real', or underlying, unemployment.

[15] F. Brechling and P. O'Brien, 'Short-run Employment Functions in Manufacturing Industries: An International Comparison', *Review of Economics and Statistics*, Aug. 1967.

[16] See, for instance, the optimistic medium-term projections contained in the OECD's 'Growth Scenario' for the second half of the 1970s: OECD, *Economic Outlook*, July 1976.

[17] Izzo and Spaventa, op. cit., p. 101.

[18] It may be interesting to speculate whether the much greater political stability of the Western world as a whole in this period may also have helped, in contrast to the turmoil of 1974. It will be remembered that at the time political problems were besetting all the OECD's five major economies. President Nixon was under impeachment because of the Watergate scandal and Prime Minister Tanaka on account of business malpractices; Chancellor Brandt was forced to resign in the wake of the Guillaume affair; President Pompidou died unexpectedly; while Britain went through two general elections in quick succession. There was nothing comparable to this 1974 political vacuum in 1979–80.

[19] The views just expressed assume, implicitly, that exchange-rate changes may work asymmetrically—DM appreciation does little to stimulate German import demand (unless accompanied by expansionary policies), while pound, lira, or French franc depreciation stimulates inflation well before it encourages export growth (and hence forces governments into restrictive measures).

[20] A mid-1982 five-year joint forecast by six major European research institutes foresaw only a 2 to $2\frac{1}{2}$ per cent annual growth rate between 1982 and 1987. Even this figure may be on the high side since it was based on the assumption of a revival in United States activity and no collapse in Third World demand. It, moreover, made no allowance for the possibility of any mid-period slow-down or recession; Economist Intelligence Unit, *The Major European Economies, 1982-1987*, Special Report No. 127, London, 1982.

[21] See, for instance, J. S. Flemming, 'The Cost of Capital, Finance and Investment', *Bank of England Quarterly Bulletin*, June 1976, and M. Feldstein, 'Inflation, Tax Rules and the Accumulation of Residential and Non-residential Capital', *Scandinavian Journal of Economics*, No. 2, 1982.

[22] EEC, *European Economy*, Mar. 1980, pp. 39–41.

[23] R. E. Lucas, Jr, 'Econometric Policy Evaluation: A Critique', in K. Brunner and A. H. Meltzer (eds.), *The Phillips Curve and Labor Markets*, Carnegie–Rochester Conference on Public Policy, vol. 1, North Holland, Amsterdam, 1976.

[24] J. Tobin, *Asset Accumulation and Economic Activity*, Basil Blackwell, Oxford, 1980, p. 19.

[25] For a model showing what implications this can have for prices and output trends, see D. A. Peel and J. S. Metcalfe, 'Divergent Expectations and the Dynamic Stability of Some Simple Macro Economic Models', *Economic Journal*, Dec. 1979.

[26] L. Calmfors, 'Long-run Effects of Short-run Stabilization Policy—An Introduction', *Scandinavian Journal of Economics*, No. 2, 1982.

[27] It is true that ultimately such policies may imply lower taxes or interest rates, but this will only occur at some uncertain future date while, in the meantime, unemployment is rising.

[28] G. L. S. Shackle, 'Expectations and Employment', *Economic Journal*, Sept. 1939, 444.

[29] This expression was first suggested to the author by Michael Emerson.

[30] E. Mandel, *Long Waves of Capitalist Development: The Marxist Interpretation*, Cambridge University Press, Cambridge, 1980.

2

Stagflation in the EC Countries 1973–1981: A Cross-sectional View

MICHAEL BRUNO

The Common Market economies, like the rest of the industrial world, have since 1973 undergone a process of severe stagflation. Waves of accelerated inflation were accompanied by a gradual increase in unemployment. At the same time all countries exhibited a sharp slowdown in productivity growth. During the period 1973–81 as a whole the average CPI (Consumer Price Index) in the EC has been increasing at a rate of 11 per cent, which is three times the inflation rate during most of the sixties and is double the inflation of the pre-OPEC period, 1967–73. By 1982 total EC unemployment came close to 9 per cent compared to about 2.5 per cent in the early 1970s, while labour productivity grew only at about 2 per cent on average in 1973–81 compared to more than double that rate during the 1960s.

Our understanding of these unprecedented developments is only gradually improving as time passes, experience accumulates, and extensive theoretical and empirical research gets under way. While there are still quite a few remaining puzzles, especially concerning the issue of the productivity slow-down, more is known now on the process and its prime movers than was known in 1975 or 1976. Macroeconomic theory has been extended to take account of the role of supply shocks and the empirical study of comparative cross-country response has greatly benefited from the systematic computerized publication of comparable and updated time-series data by major international institutions such as the OECD, IMF, and the World Bank (IBRD).

The approach taken here is largely based on theoretical and empirical work that I have been doing over the last few years, in part carried out jointly with Jeffrey Sachs of Harvard University. There is considerable work going on by other researchers, taking similar or differing points of view, and I shall hardly do justice to other contributions in a paper like this. With a non-technical audience in mind, the paper will attempt to concentrate on broad-brush descriptions of the main phenomena rather than go into great technical detail.

The main argument is that an increase in the real cost of material and energy inputs pushes back the aggregate supply schedule of final goods. This supply-side shock will be more aggravated the more rigid the real cost of labour tends to be, since profits will be squeezed and both short-run as well as long-run output supply will be reduced and prices will be increased. The adjustment process is further compounded by the contraction in aggregate demand. The latter is partly caused by the real income effects of the worsening terms of trade and partly exacerbated by contractionary monetary and fiscal policy which was followed by most countries in response to the supply shocks, for fear of inflation and balance-of-payments deficits. It is thus difficult to disentangle that part of unemployment and productivity slow-down caused by real factor price increases from that which follows more conventional Keynesian, cyclical arguments, although it is clear that both types of phenomena were at work. Another factor making for differential acceleration of inflation rates is the role of exchange rates in the adjustment process. This will only be mentioned briefly here.

The first section of the paper looks at the empirical data for the EC region with emphasis on the two main stagflation upheavals, 1973–5 and 1979–81. This is followed by a brief theoretical digression on the interaction of aggregate demand and aggregate supply under input price shocks. Section III reports some empirical estimates of output and labour demand and the role of changes in terms of trade, in monetary policy, and in real wages. This is followed in Section IV by some inflation-rate equations with emphasis on the role of domestic import prices, exchange rates, and wage adjustment in determining differential inflation rates by country. We end with a brief discussion of policy issues and open questions.

I. Empirical Background

A useful starting-point for the study of stagflation is to look at inflation and unemployment within a two-dimensional chart of the kind that has traditionally formed the framework for study of the Phillips curve. Fig. 2.1A charts EC unemployment rates against the rate of inflation, while Fig. 2.1B replaces the horizontal axis with unutilized capacity for the manufacturing sector (for six large OECD countries). The 1960s still seemed to conform, more or less, to the view that there is a fairly stable trade-off between inflation and unemployment. Over the business cycle industrial economies could be expected to move from recession, high unemployment, overcapacity, and relative price stability, into boom, or full (or overfull) employment of resources, accelerated inflation, with relative regularity of timing as well as trade-offs. The 'perversities' started at around 1972–3, when a very sharp acceleration occurred in inflation followed by a considerable increase

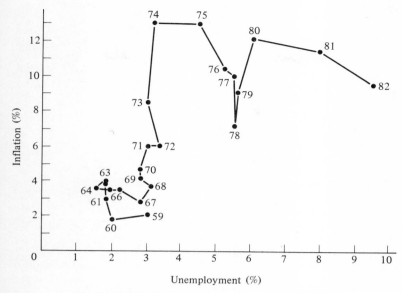

Fig. 2.1A: EC inflation and unemployment 1952–1982

Source: OECD, 'Historical Statistics of the Main Economic Indicators'.

in unemployment. There followed a period from 1975 to 1978 (or 1979) during which inflation decelerated and unemployment continued to increase, more in line with a conventional Phillips-curve trade-off. Then came a new 'perverse' shift from 1978 to 1979 and 1980, followed by like another Phillips-type contractionary phase. Inspection of the curve in Fig. 2.1A reveals the considerable similarity of the four-year sequence 1972-3-4-5 with that of 1978-9-80-1, as well as the fact that outside these two periods the old quasi-regularity seems to hold. One naturally connects these two sub-periods with OPEC-1 and OPEC-2 respectively. During both sub-periods the real price of oil rose substantially and so did the relative prices of other industrial raw materials and food.

Table 2.1 sets out the aggregate performance of the EC region in terms of the key variables, broken down by relevant sub-periods. Individual country data for the change in some of these variables in 1973-5 and 1979-81 appear in Table 2.2.[1]

We note the sharp fall in the growth of output and labour productivity in 1973-5, partial revival during 1975-9, and renewed slump in 1979-81 (see rows 1 and 2 in Table 2.1). The two slump periods,

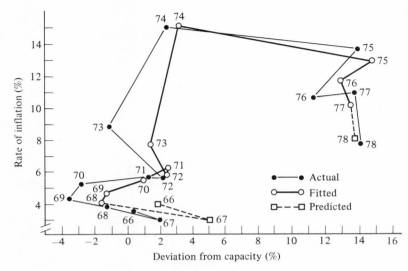

Fig. 2.1B: Inflation and rate of deviation from capacity (six major industrial countries) 1966–1978

Source: Bruno (1980).

TABLE 2.1

Selected Macroeconomic Variables, Aggregate EC, 1960–1981, by Sub-period (Percentage rate of change)

	1960–7 (1)	1967–73 (2)	1973–5 (3)	1975–9 (4)	1979–81 (5)
1. GDP	4.4	5.0	−0.3	3.6	−0.3
2. GDP per employee	4.3	4.7	0.7	3.1	0.9
3. Rate of unemployment (end-of-period level)	2.6	2.8	4.2	5.3	7.6
4. Investment	5.5	5.2	−4.2	3.0	1.2
5. Real money supply	5.1	8.1	−0.5	2.9	−4.4[b]
6. Consumer prices	3.4	5.5	13.0	9.2	11.9
7. Import prices (lagged)[a]	1.1	2.9	23.8	6.5	12.8
8. Relative import/export prices (lagged)[a]	−0.5	−0.4	8.1	−1.1	2.1
9. Real wages	–	4.6	5.2	3.5	2.7

[a] These data are given at one year's lag, for example in column (3) the data are for 1972–4.
[b] 1979–80.
Sources: OECD, *Historical Statistics, 1960–1980*, Paris, 1982; and OECD, *Economic Outlook*, July 1982 (for 1981 data).

TABLE 2.2

Change in Growth Rates, Selected Variables, during OPEC-1 and OPEC-2

	Acceleration in 1973–5[a]					Acceleration in 1979–81[b]				
	Un-employ-ment	Infla-tion	Relative import prices	Real money supply	Real wage	Un-employ-ment	Infla-tion	Relative import prices	Real money supply	Real wage
		$\Delta \dot{p}_c$	$\Delta(\dot{p}_n - \dot{p}_x)_{-1}$	$\Delta \dot{m}$	$\Delta \dot{w}_c$		$\Delta \dot{p}_c$	$\Delta(\dot{p}_n - \dot{p}_x)_{-1}$	$\Delta \dot{m}$	$\Delta \dot{w}_c$
	(1)	(2)	(3)	(4)	(5)	(6)	(7)	(8)	(9)	(10)
France	1.5	6.9	8.1	-1.8	1.7	1.7	3.8	3.5	-2.8	-2.8
Germany	2.8	2.2	6.4	1.2	-2.4	1.1	1.9	5.3	-9.0	-1.9
Italy	-0.4	13.1	12.9	-20.8	-0.6	0.8	4.9	4.0	-15.7	-2.4
UK	1.5	13.1	12.0	-6.4	-1.5	5.6	1.5	-1.7	-5.6	1.5
Belgium	2.3	8.3	1.1	4.3	1.5	2.5	0.8	1.0	-5.6	0.6
Denmark	–	5.8	7.1	1.5	1.4	–	2.1	6.8	-0.8	0.1
Netherlands	1.7	3.6	3.2	1.6	1.2	3.3	0.7	2.6	-6.0	-3.0
Average 7 EC	1.6	7.6	7.4	-4.1	0.2	2.5	2.2	2.5	-4.6	-1.1
US	3.5	5.2	8.7	-7.0	-2.9	1.8	4.2	6.4	-6.5	-5.8
Japan	0.6	11.5	17.9	-20.4	-4.2	0.1	0.3	20.7	-5.6	-2.5
Total OECD	2.0	7.0	6.6	–	–	1.7	3.0	4.7	–	–

Notes: Unemployment—change during period. Other variables—rate of growth in 1973–5 compared with 1967–73; 1979–81 compared with 1975–9. Real wage—nominal wage (IMF, IFS data) deflated by consumer prices. Col. (10) is the difference between 1978–81 and 1975–8 except for US and Denmark (1978–80). Real money supply—M, deflated by consumer prices.
    a Change in growth rates compared to 1967–73.
    b Change in growth rates compared to 1975–9.
    Sources: Same as for Table 2.1 except for wages.

1973–5 and 1979–81, which were also marked by peak inflation rates (for differences among countries see Table 2.2), followed upon a substantial increase in the relative import/export price (shown in row 8 of Table 2.1).[2] During the period up to 1972, and again during 1975–9 this relative price was falling.

Table 2.2 shows the acceleration in unemployment and inflation for seven EC countries as well as for the US, Japan, and the OECD total. We note the fact that EC unemployment rose by less than that of the US (and the OECD total) during OPEC-1, but rose faster during OPEC-2. In between, during 1975–9, the US unemployment rate had been falling while that of the EC continued to rise. Employment, as we shall see, was closely related to output performance, which in turn was closely related to monetary policy and negatively affected by the relative price of raw materials. During the two slump periods both factors were strongly operative, as the relevant columns ((3), (4), (8), (9)) of Table 2.2 show. Finally we note the differences among countries in real-wage behaviour, shown in columns (5) and (9) for the two respective periods. The existence of real-wage rigidity or flexibility can be learnt from the acceleration or deceleration of real wages after an input-price shock.[3] Judged by this measure, all EC countries seemed to have been more rigid than either the US or Japan at least during the first oil crisis. Greater flexibility seems to have marked the second episode (consider France, Germany, Italy, and the Netherlands), but when one compares real-wage performance with that of labour productivity (compare rows 2 and 9 in Table 2.1), it is clear than even at the time of OPEC-2, real wages on average continued to grow faster than labour productivity. The important role of wages in a country's response to a supply shock will be discussed further below.

Another aspect of the same phenomenon is the sharp profit squeeze (for which no separate data are shown here). This partly explains the large drop in investment after OPEC-1 (see row 4, Table 2.1) and a more moderate slow-down in investment after OPEC-2.

The basic data briefly discussed here suggest the potential importance of both cost-push as well as demand-squeeze arguments for the explanation of the macroeconomic developments within countries. Before returning to some numerical estimates we digress into a brief theoretical discussion of the role of material inputs within an aggregate supply and demand framework.

II. Aggregate Supply and Aggregate Demand in the Short Run

A macroeconomic framework within which the effects of input-price shocks can be analysed requires the explicit incorporation of raw

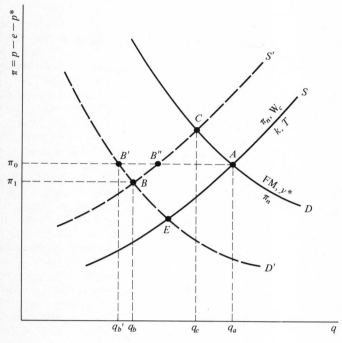

Fig. 2.2

materials (n) as a separate factor of production along with the conventional labour (l) and capital (k) inputs in the production of final goods (q). The determination of output and prices in a system like this can be described in terms of aggregate supply (S) and aggregate demand (D) schedules, as drawn in Fig. 2.2.[4] Along the horizontal axis we measure gross output quantity of final goods and along the vertical axis the price of these goods (p) relative to the domestic price of a competitive basket of goods, $p^* + e$, where p^* represents the world price of final goods and e the exchange rate. The relative price measured along the vertical axis in Fig. 2.2 will be denoted by π ($= p - p^* - e$). This relative price is also the reciprocal of what is sometimes termed the 'real exchange rate'.[5]

Two other relative prices play a major role in accounting for aggregate shifts in this system. One is the relative world price or real cost of material inputs ($\pi_n = p_n^* - p^*$), where p_n^* is the nominal world price of materials. The other is the real cost of labour, w_c ($= w - p_c$, where w is the nominal wage and w_c is measured in the units of some final basket of goods, p_c, here consumption goods).

The aggregate supply of goods in the short run can be described as an upward-sloping curve, S, where the productive capacity (represented here by capital stock, k), the level of technology or total factor productivity (T), and the real cost of the two variable factors of production, materials and labour (i.e. π_n and w_c, respectively), are held constant. The curve S is nothing but a marginal short-run cost schedule which assumes rising marginal costs of production with an increase in output. Below a certain output level, as capacity becomes underutilized, the supply curve may be horizontal, while above a certain output level S may become fairly steep as full employment of all factors in the economy is reached. Under fairly reasonable assumptions it can be argued that an increase in the real cost of either materials (π_n) or labour (w_c) will shift the supply curve (S) up and to the left while an increase in the capital stock (k) or in total factor productivity (T) will in the long run shift S down and to the right.[6]

The curve D marks the aggregate demand schedule for this economy. Other things being equal, the demand for final goods (such as consumer goods or exports) rises with a fall in the relative final goods price (π). What are those 'other things' that are held constant when the downward-sloped aggregate demand curve is drawn? One is the relative price of materials (π_n) which affects demand through real income and wealth, and not only on the supply side. When the real price of materials such as oil rises, a net importer of such goods suffers a real income loss while a net exporter (such as OPEC) benefits. For a typical EC country a rise in the real cost of material inputs shifts the aggregate demand schedule to the left (this is why π_n is placed on the left-hand side of D in Fig. 2.2). A real rise in real world income (y^*), which affects export demand, or expansionary domestic fiscal and monetary policy (briefly denoted by FM in Fig. 2.2), which affects domestic demand for consumption and investment goods, will each shift the D curve up and to the right.

We can now use this framework to analyse the output and price effects of rising material prices as well as the derived effects coming from the policy response to such input-price shocks. The first impact of rising input prices is a leftward shift of the aggregate supply curve (from S to S')—rising costs of material inputs reduce profits and the output that producers will be willing to supply at each given relative price level. Suppose for a moment that there is sufficient compensatory expansionary policy on the demand side to neutralize the contractionary effect of rising material prices on real income, so that the demand curve (D) stays put. In this hypothetical case, with everything else (including real wages) held constant, rising material prices cause a move of the economy from the equilibrium point A to a new equilibrium point C. There is a fall in output and a rise in prices, which are the essence of a stagflationary impact effect. Such supply shock is in marked contrast to a shift in aggregate demand, with S held constant, where prices and output tend to move together (compare, for example, the points A and E). Note that a similar effect would be observed if there is an autonomous real wage push, exceeding productivity growth.

The size of the supply shock depends on what happens to real wages. If real wages are downward flexible, thus mitigating the squeeze on profits, this in itself may impart a compensatory rightward shift in the S curve. If wages are rigid, or rising, relative to productivity (T), the leftward shift in S, for a given upward push on material prices, will be more pronounced. The associated profit squeeze which hampers investment depresses capital growth (the change in k), which may further strengthen the supply shock in the medium and long run.

Consider the demand side now. Other things being equal, a rise in π_n, we have argued, depresses real income and demand for a net importer, thus shifting the D schedule leftward and imparting further downward pressure on output (and employment). Contractionary demand-management policy (a fall in FM) and the mutual interaction of falling incomes in export markets of other industrial countries (reducing y^*) cause a further contraction of aggregate demand.

Suppose D shifts to D'. A new equilibrium in the commodity market, given the configuration of Fig. 2.2, will be at the point B, output having fallen further to q_b and the final-goods relative price also falling in this case (a real depreciation) from π_0 to π_1.[7] The price *level* need not fall, however, since this also depends on what happens to world prices of final goods (p^*) and to the exchange rate (e). If π is downward rigid then production may actually take place at B' (a further fall in demand and output to $q_{b'}$), where a disequilibrium between supply and demand (potential excess supply of $B'B''$) may for a time persist.

A system like this can be used to write down the determinants of gross output in a subsector like manufacturing or for the determination of total final expenditure in the aggregate economy in which case n will represent imported inputs. Gross output can be expected to be negatively related to π_n and w, and positively related to all other demand and supply factors (FM, y^*; k, T). An analogous relationship can be written down for GDP (which is the output of final goods, net of material inputs) as the dependent variable. Likewise, a labour-demand schedule can be derived, depending on whether producers are maximizing profits on their nominal supply schedule or whether production is effectively constrained on the demand side (cf. the earlier example of the point B' in Fig. 2.2). The system must be further complemented by specification of a dynamic adjustment process for prices when the commodity market is out of equilibrium and for slow adjustment of wages when the labour market is in disequilibrium. Two other important adjustment processes must be specified: one for the exchange rate (e) when floating (a function of monetary policy and current-account imbalances), the other for investment and the capital stock (k) (a function of profits etc.). The approach taken here will be more limited.[8] We shall confine ourselves only to an output and employment adjustment relation on the one hand and a price adjustment relationship on the other, taking the adjustment of the capital stock, the real exchange rate, and the real wage as given from outside the realm of our discussion. This obviously has some drawbacks (mainly from an econometric point of view), but it also helps to simplify the analysis and confine the discussion to the main issues of this paper.

An earlier cross-sectional study for sixteen OECD countries (Bruno 1980) showed the importance of both supply-side factors (primarily the relative price of imports) as well as demand-side factors (primarily real money balances) in accounting for manufacturing output behaviour in the OECD countries. Likewise we derived an equation for the rate of inflation as a function of the rate of change of import prices (also allowing for the separate role of world prices and the exchange rate) and the rate of change of wages (which in turn was expressed as a function of lagged inflation and unemployment). An attempt to include some separate measure of commodity-demand pressure in the price equation failed, which may be consistent with a relatively flat aggregate-supply curve. In the latter case shifts in aggregate demand mainly affect output and not prices, while prices are mainly driven by cost-push factors.

The pairs of output and price equations pooled over a cross-section of countries and time series gave a reasonably good explanation for the curve drawn in Fig. 2.1B. The cross-sectional regression run for the period 1968–77 together with out-of-sample predictions to 1978 and back to 1966 gave a reasonably good account of average movements for the period covered, just before OPEC–2 set in. In the next section we shall look afresh more specifically at the performance of EC countries, consider aggregate GDP as well as employment rather than the output of the manufacturing sector only, and extend the period of analysis up to 1980–1.

III. Output and Employment in the EC

One attempt to account for the aggregate EC GDP performance in the 1970s is represented by the first row of Table 2.3. This regression was

TABLE 2.3

Selected Aggregate GDP Growth Regressions, EC Countries, 1962-1980[a]

	Constant	Change in import/export price	Change in real money supply		Statistics			No. of observations
			Domestic	US				
		$(\dot{p}_n - \dot{p}_x)_{-1}$	$(\dot{m}_{-1})$	$(\dot{m}^*_{-1})$	$\bar{R}^2$	DW	ρ	
	(1)	(2)	(3)	(4)	(5)	(6)	(7)	(8)
1. Aggregate	4.01 (0.39)	−0.38 (0.08)	—	0.18 (0.09)	0.65	1.67	0.36 (0.28)	19
2. Average over 7 country regressions[b]	3.05	−0.26	0.18	—	—	—	—	133
3. Pooled cross-section	3.08 (0.02)	−0.24 (0.05)	0.19 (0.03)	—	0.35	1.97	0.13 (0.09)	133
4. Pooled with country intercepts	—	−0.24 (0.05)	0.18 (0.03)	—	0.36	1.84	—	133
5. Pooled	3.12 (0.02)	−0.08 (0.05)	0.14 (0.03)	0.20 (0.04)	0.45	1.92	—	133

a Parenthesized numbers below coefficients are estimated standard errors.
b The countries are France, Germany, Italy, the UK, Belgium, Denmark, and the Netherlands.

run over the aggregate EC data and shows a very strong negative relationship between the rate of growth of GDP and the previous year's rate of growth of import prices relative to export prices ($\dot{p}_n - \dot{p}_x$). Its role probably incorporates both demand-side and supply-side factors and possibly also the policy response to these sharp increases in relative import prices. The second factor included in this equation is the real money supply, lagged one year, but not that of the aggregate EC region (which did not show as significant in this particular regression) but rather that of the US (!). Its role may represent the general squeeze or expansion in world money markets following upon such changes in the US or else the implied effect of US economic activity on world export markets.

We have also run individual country regressions of GDP growth in which both import prices and the country's own lagged real money supply feature as the prime movers of changes in GDP growth. In almost all cases the negative coefficient of the relative import price and the positive coefficient of money are highly significant. Adding a real-wage variable ($\dot{w} - \dot{p}_v$) one gets a negative coefficient but it is usually statistically insignificant (with Germany as a clear exception; see also subsequent discussion). A weighted average of these seven individual equations, with the real wage left out, is given in equation 2 of Table 2.3. Here the money supply is the country's own weighted money supply and not that of the US as in equation 1.

Pooling the time series of these seven countries into one regression (with $19 \times 7 = 133$ observations) one obtains a very similar equation (see 3 in Table 2.3) in spite of the fact that this is not weighted by country size. When one allows for additional separate country effects these coefficients remain virtually unchanged (see equation 4). Finally, when the US lagged real money supply is also included, the effect of relative import prices is substantially reduced. These two variables were highly negatively correlated over the world contractionary and expansionary phases, much more than the other two pairs of explanatory variables.[9]

There is evidence for the claim that of these two major exogenous factors raw material prices were mostly responsible for the contractionary phase in the first slump (1973-5) while the US monetary squeeze played a relatively more important role in the second downturn (1979-81).

Table 2.4 gives a selection of employment growth regressions in which the main explanatory variable is the GDP growth rate, both concurrent and lagged. The first equation, run over the aggregate data for the more limited period 1967-80, suggests a total elasticity of about $\frac{1}{2}$ (consisting of 0.29 for concurrent and 0.19 for lagged GDP growth). The effect of lagged GDP is reduced somewhat when the

TABLE 2.4

Selected Aggregate Employment Growth Regressions, EC Countries, 1962-1980

| | Constant | GDP growth | | Change in relative wage | | Statistics | | | No. of observations |
| | | Concurrent $(\dot{v})$ | Lagged $(\dot{v}_{-1})$ | $(\dot{w}-\dot{p}_c)$ | $(\dot{w}-\dot{p}_n)$ | $\bar{R}^2$ | DW | ρ | |
	(1)	(2)	(3)	(4)	(5)	(6)	(7)	(8)	(9)
1. Aggregate 1967-80	−1.60 (0.61)	0.29 (0.05)	0.19 (0.05)	—	—	0.68	2.13	0.87 (0.15)	14
2. Aggregate 1962-80	−1.38 (0.46)	0.28 (0.06)	0.14 (0.06)	—	—	0.46	2.32	0.70 (0.20)	19
3. Aggregate	−1.07 (0.60)	0.27 (0.06)	0.14 (0.06)	−0.07 (0.08)	—	0.45	2.27	0.69 (0.08)	19
4. Aggregate	−1.60 (0.54)	0.38 (0.19)	0.15 (0.05)	—	−0.03 (0.02)	0.49	2.21	0.80 (0.17)	19
5. Pooled cross-section[a]	−0.78 (0.24)	0.23 (0.03)	0.12 (0.03)	−0.05 (0.03)	—	0.35	2.01	0.39 (0.00)	133
6. Pooled with country intercepts[a]	—	0.23 (0.03)	0.12 (0.03)	−0.04 (0.03)	—	0.37	1.97	0.32 (0.09)	133

[a] Seven EC countries are included.

period is extended back to 1962 (regression 2). The negative intercept of these regressions probably represents two important factors that were left out: capital-stock growth[10] and technical progress, representing a secular decline in employment requirements. For a given level of gross output (or total expenditure in the case of the aggregate economy) cost-minimized labour demand may also depend on the relative wage. This may or may not show in a regression in which GDP, rather than the growth in output, appears as the argument. Regressions on the aggregate data (equations 3 and 4 in Table 2.4) turn out negative but insignificant coefficients. Individual country regressions that were run in level form give very similar orders of magnitude for the coefficients on v and v_{-1} and sometimes (for example for the UK and Belgium) suggest an additional negative coefficient for the relative wage ($w - p_v$) which borders on significance (with an elasticity of the order of 0.05 to 0.06). The pooled seven-country cross-sectional regression in Table 2.4 (equations 5 and 6) bears this out.

Sometimes a broader cross-section of average-country growth rates may give a better overview of the main forces at play and the relevant orders of magnitude. Consider the change in the average growth rate of employment between the periods 1960–73 and 1973–80 for a broader sample of nineteen OECD countries (of which fourteen are European[11]). The following regression was obtained:

$$\Delta \dot{l} = -0.906 + 0.524 \Delta \dot{q} - 0.300 \Delta(\dot{w} - \dot{p}_n) + 0.708 \Delta \sigma_v. \quad (\bar{R}^2 = 0.54.)$$
$$\phantom{\Delta \dot{l} = } (0.707) \ (0.169) \quad\ \ (0.079) \qquad\ \ (0.336)$$

The change in employment growth ($\Delta \dot{l}$) here depends on the change in the growth of aggregate national uses ($\Delta \dot{q}$) with an elasticity of about 0.5 (cf. the sum of the coefficients on GDP in the equations of Table 2.4). It also depends very significantly on the change in growth of relative wage to import prices ($\Delta(\dot{w} - \dot{p}_n)$), with an elasticity of 0.3. The third argument in the regression is the change in the variability of growth ($\Delta \sigma_v$), measured in terms of the mean standard deviation of GDP growth rates before and after 1973. For given average output growth, greater output fluctuations around the mean trend make for higher employment levels (and therefore lower labour productivity). Because labour is in part a quasi-fixed factor and because of the role of uncertainty, such dependence makes considerable theoretical sense. It is also consistent with the argument that productivity lost in a slump may not be fully regained during an upturn (see Dickens 1982).[12] All EC countries exhibited greater output fluctuations after 1973, but in varying degrees. On average this factor by itself is estimated by the regression to have accounted for a 0.4 per cent growth rate for EC employment over and above what it would otherwise be. The output slow-down, in comparison, explains a drop in employment growth of 1.4 per cent. The fact that the average EC employment growth rate none the less dropped only very slightly between 1960-73 and 1973-80[13] may be accounted for by the fall in relative labour to raw material costs.

Equations like those given in Table 2.4 may be representative of labour demand when output is constrained on the demand side (recall the discussion of the case in which the economy is at a 'Keynesian' point B' in Fig. 2.2, with short-run excess supply in the commodity market). If output is supply determined, profit maximization (and not only cost minimization) may be assumed and a conventional labour-demand schedule incorporating only supply-side factors (the real cost of materials and labour, and the quantity of capital) can be derived. An example of such an equation for German aggregate employment during 1961-80 (in logarithmic level form) is the following:

$$l = 3.84 + 0.006t + 0.70l_{-1} - 0.21(w - p_c)_{-1} - 0.18(p_n - p_c)_{-1}.$$
$$(2.99) \quad (0.005) \quad (0.31) \quad\quad (0.12) \quad\quad\quad (0.07)$$

$$(\bar{R}^2 = 0.83, \sigma = 0.32.)$$

This equation allows for lagged adjustment of labour (l_{-1}). Both the real wage and real import costs (here deflated by consumer prices) are negative and significant. Time (t) also appears as a proxy for the net effect of capital and technical progress, which should here be positive (but is statistically insignificant). Similar regressions for other EC countries generally yield a significantly negative coefficient for the real import price and a negative, statistically insignificant, coefficient for the real wage. The latter variable often evades this type of single-country time-series regression.[14] None the less, there are good reasons to believe that varying degrees of real-wage rigidity account for at least part of the variation in employment performance of EC and other European countries during the last decade.

IV. The Inflationary Process

There are various ways in which a price determination process can be described, which is consistent with the theoretical discussion of supply and demand factors given in Section II. Important elements in the inflationary process are changes in the variable costs, consisting of changes in nominal wages $(\dot{w})$ and in the domestic cost of materials $(\dot{p}_n)$. If we add another variable to take account of demand pressure (d) and assume that lagged inflation also plays a role (on account of lagged adjustment or an adaptive expectation-formation process) we can write down the rate of inflation $(\dot{p})$ in the form[15]

$$\dot{p} = -\alpha_0 + \alpha_1 \dot{w} + \alpha_2 \dot{p}_n + \alpha_3 \dot{p}_{-1} + d$$

where one assumes $\alpha_1 + \alpha_2 + \alpha_3 = 1$. The negative intercept (α_0) stands for autonomous shifts in productivity and capacity which mitigate the rate of inflation.

One may then append a wage-determination process to explain $\dot{w}$ and an equation for exchange-rate formation (under floating exchange rates) to account for the translation of import prices from foreign $(\dot{p}_n^*)$ to domestic $(\dot{p}_n = \dot{p}_n^* + \dot{e})$ import prices. Instead we here look at real wages and real exchange rates as given and rewrite the above equation as follows:

$$\dot{p} - \dot{p}_{-1} = -\alpha_0 + \alpha_1 (\dot{w} - \dot{p}_{-1}) + \alpha_2 (\dot{p}_n - \dot{p}_{-1}) + d.$$

When rewritten in this form the acceleration in inflation $(\dot{p} - \dot{p}_{-1})$ is viewed as a function of a real wage and a real import price rate of change[16] in addition to the previous demand variable (d). For a measure of demand pressure we use relative deviations of GDP from capacity (u) where the latter is crudely corrected for productivity and terms-of-trade changes after 1973.[17] For inflation the CPI change $(\dot{p}_c)$ of respective countries is used, and for $\dot{p}_n$ the import deflator, as before.

Table 2.5 lists regression results, based on this equation, for eight EC countries (Ireland is included here) as well as for the US and Japan. The coefficients for both relative cost variables are usually significant while the excess capacity variable tends to be positive but insignificant for the EC countries but quite high and significant for the US and Japan. For the EC group, at least, the cost-push part of the price adjustment process seems to account for the bulk of the price acceleration. The pooled cross-section regressions given at the bottom of Table 2.5 show the overall regression to be insensitive to either exclusion of the capacity variable (regression 3) or the allowance for differences in intercepts among countries (regression 2).[18] When one considers the average performance of the pooled regression (regression 1) over sub-periods, it turns out that there is a slight overprediction of inflation in the 'Phillips trade-off' periods 1967-73 (by 0.4 percentage points) and 1976-9 (by 0.2 per cent), and a slight underprediction during the supply-shock periods 1973-5 (by 0.1 per cent) and 1979-81 (by 0.4 per cent). Within the latter period, the prediction for 1981 (11.1 per cent compared with 10.1 per cent actual inflation, a slight overestimate), is an out-of-sample prediction for the model. The direction in which errors go may be an indication of the fact that we have not fully accounted for the respective roles of excess demand and excess supply in these various sub-periods.

When one leaves out the wage variable and regresses the inflation rate itself on lagged inflation, share-weighted import prices, and capacity

(u_{-1}), the following equation is obtained:

$$\dot{p}_c = (\text{country intercept}) + 0.663\dot{p}_{c-1} + 0.175\dot{p}_m + 0.190u_{-1}.$$
$$\phantom{\dot{p}_c = (\text{country intercept}) + } (0.049) \phantom{\dot{p}_{c-1} +} (0.020) \phantom{\dot{p}_m +} (0.089)$$

$$(\bar{R}^2 = 0.82, \text{DW} = 1.93.)$$

We note that the coefficient for lagged inflation is somewhat higher than that implied by the pooled regressions of Table 2.5 (which is 0.56) and the coefficient of the capacity variable is considerably higher and significant. The above equation may be regarded as a reduced form in which wage adjustment is proxied in part by capacity utilization (which is negatively correlated with unemployment) and partly by lagged inflation, as it would be under an augmented Phillips curve.

Consider the following rough numerical exercise. Let us apply the elasticities of regression 1 in Table 2.5 to the components of inflation acceleration between 1967–73 and 1973–5 as they can roughly be derived from Table 2.1. The real-wage factor, net of the productivity factor, gives an average inflation acceleration of $(12.7 \times 0.19) - 0.8 = 2.9$ per cent, while the import-price factor gives an inflation acceleration of $18.3 \times 0.16 = 2.9$ per cent. While this gives only a rough measure (the sum, 5.8 per cent, does not add up to the actual inflation acceleration of 7.5 per cent), it shows that both cost factors were, on average, more or less equally important in the inflationary process under OPEC-1. For OPEC-2 a similar rough calculation shows the sluggishness of the real wage to be a much more important factor in inflation acceleration than the rise in import prices.[19]

A similar exercise can be applied to the mean differences among countries (see Table 2.2) to see how differences in real-wage adjustment and in import-price behaviour can account for different inflation profiles. Differences in import-price behaviour, mainly on account of differential exchange-rate movements, were particularly important. When one reruns the regressions putting in foreign import prices $(\dot{p}_n^*)$ and real exchange-rate movements (here measured by $\dot{e} - \dot{p}_{c-1}$) the resulting separate elasticities for these two components are both almost identical to the one obtained for the combined relative price variable.[20] For example, given an elasticity of 0.15, a 25 per cent rate difference between an appreciating country and a depreciating country may account for a difference in inflation acceleration of close to 4 per cent. For example, the relatively low inflation profile for Germany can be ascribed to a combination of real appreciation and a relatively flexible real wage.

Here, as in the case of employment performance, estimates can be checked against a broader OECD sample. When one estimates pooled regressions for twelve small countries (including ten European countries)

TABLE 2.5
Inflation Acceleration Equations, 1961–1980

	Constant (1)	Real wage $(\dot{w} - \dot{p}_{c-1})$ (2)	Real import price $(\dot{p}_n - \dot{p}_{c-1})$ (3)	Capacity utilization (u_{-1}) (4)	Statistics $\bar{R}^2$ (5)	DW (6)	ρ (7)	No. of observations
France	−1.22 (0.91)	0.377 (0.169)	0.128 (0.035)	−0.078 (0.287)	0.65	1.73	0.249 (0.275)	20
Germany	0.72 (0.29)	0.221 (0.055)	0.077 (0.038)	0.140 (0.099)	0.56	2.15	—	20
Italy (1967–80)	−0.44 (0.92)	0.146 (0.111)	0.206 (0.045)	0.058 (0.227)	0.70	1.41	0.094 (0.511)	14
UK	−0.86 (0.59)	0.585 (0.136)	0.081 (0.076)	0.109 (0.428)	0.63	2.52	—	20
Belgium	−1.14 (2.78)	0.277 (0.049)	0.172 (0.029)	−0.002 (0.089)	0.89	2.31	—	20

Denmark	-0.50 (0.73)	0.204 (0.146)	0.203 (0.065)	0.335 (0.226)	0.51	1.89	—	20
Netherlands	-0.51 (0.55)	0.204 (0.094)	0.096 (0.065)	-0.125 (0.230)	0.26	2.67	—	20
Ireland	-1.03 (0.84)	0.423 (0.105)	0.183 (0.060)	0.177 (0.245)	0.68	1.76	0.223 (0.300)	20
US	-0.07 (0.07)	0.382 (0.140)	0.133 (0.030)	0.253 (0.123)	0.77	2.01	0.735 (0.244)	20
Japan	-0.43 (0.87)	0.042 (0.097)	0.200 (0.049)	0.424 (0.266)	0.56	2.17	—	20
Pooled EC regressions[a]								
1. 8 EC countries	-0.78 (0.20)	0.289 (0.036)	0.155 (0.019)	0.071 (0.067)	0.60	2.15	—	154
2. With country intercepts	—	0.313 (0.038)	0.152 (0.019)	0.091 (0.077)	0.62	2.26	—	154
3. Without capacity variable	-0.79 (0.20)	0.296 (0.036)	0.157 (0.019)	—	0.59	2.17	—	154

[a] The first eight countries are included here.

and seven large (including four European) countries for the same period, 1961–80, the results for the small countries at least are virtually the same as before, while the capacity variable comes out more significant.

Twelve small OECD countries:

$$\dot{p}_c - \dot{p}_{c-1} = -0.71 + 0.269(\dot{w} - \dot{p}_{c-1}) + 0.155(\dot{p}_n - \dot{p}_{c-1}) +$$
$$(0.17)\ (0.030)(0.019)$$
$$+\ 0.095u_{-1}.$$
$$(0.048)$$
$$(\bar{R}^2 = 0.52,\ DW = 2.41.)$$

Seven large OECD countries:

$$\dot{p}_c - \dot{p}_{c-1} = -0.32 + 0.163(\dot{w} - \dot{p}_{c-1}) + 0.176(\dot{p}_n - \dot{p}_{c-1}) +$$
$$(0.20)\ (0.037)(0.017)$$
$$+\ 0.169u_{-1}.$$
$$(0.075)$$
$$(\bar{R}^2 = 0.57,\ DW = 2.20.)$$

The relatively low coefficient for wages in the second equation can mainly be ascribed to the inclusion of Japan in this sample.

V. A Summing-up

We can now pull together the main ingredients of the empirical analysis and look again at the broad features of aggregate unemployment and inflation developments over the last fifteen years. For this purpose we substitute one of the GDP equations (equation 2, Table 2.3) into one of the employment equations (equation 3, Table 2.4) to calculate the 'predicted' aggregate employment growth as a function of twice-lagged terms of trade and real money:

(a) $\dot{l} = 0.18 - 0.070(\dot{p}_n - \dot{p}_x)_{-1} - 0.036(\dot{p}_n - \dot{p}_x)_{-2} -$
$$-\ 0.07(\dot{w} - \dot{p}_c)_{-1} + 0.049\dot{m}_{-1} + 0.025\dot{m}_{-2}.$$

The resulting employment levels are then related to the given labour force and the predicted change in the unemployment rate by subperiod is computed as shown in Table 2.6 (column (2)). The comparison with actual growth in unemployment is given in column (1). Similarly, we apply the following price adjustment equation (equation 1, Table 2.5).

TABLE 2.6
*Predicted and Actual Inflation and Unemployment,
Average by Sub-period*

	Increase in unemployment		Acceleration of inflation rate	
	Actual (1)	Predicted (2)	Actual (3)	Predicted (4)
1967–73	0.2	0.0	2.1	2.3
1973–5	1.5	1.3	7.5	7.2
1975–9	1.1	2.2	−3.8	−3.5
1979–81	2.4	1.4	2.7	2.1
Total increase				
1967–81	*5.2*	*4.9*	*8.5*	*8.1*

Notes: Actual numbers refer to aggregate EC (source: see Table 2.1). Predicted numbers are based on equation 2, Table 2.3 (GDP); equation 3, Table 2.4 (employment); and equation 1, Table 2.5 (inflation). Deviations from average eight-country rates were applied to aggregate EC inflation, as above.

(b) $\quad \dot{p}_c - \dot{p}_{c-1} = -0.78 + 0.29(\dot{w} - \dot{p}_{c-1}) + 0.16(\dot{p}_n - \dot{p}_{c-1}) +$
$\quad\quad + 0.07 u_{-1}.$

The resulting estimate of mean acceleration by sub-period (comparing average period inflation rates, predicted as well as actual) are shown in columns (4) and (3) of Table 2.6, respectively. Inflation, of course, shows a very close fit to the data. This is probably not so surprising in view of the fact that we take import prices, wages, and each period's lagged inflation as given.[21] For unemployment we find a good prediction for 1973–5 (and before), while there is an over-prediction of 1 per cent in 1975–9 and under-prediction by the same amount in 1979–81, part of it in 1981 itself (the 1981 level is an out-of-sample prediction).

Looking at the ingredients of the labour equation used, one can trace the main source of the error, particularly in the last period, to an overestimate of GDP. Inclusion of some world-slump variable (such as the US money supply—see earlier discussion) would partly correct for that. Also, by concentrating only on the real money supply we have ignored the role of domestic fiscal policy during these periods. While both OPEC-1 and OPEC-2 periods represent the stagflationary effects of a supply shock, it seems that in the more recent phase the demand-side effects have probably dominated.

At this point we may go back to Fig. 2.1A and underline the common qualitative features of the development during the four-year sequences 1973–6 and 1979–82. The real shock in oil and other raw material prices was confined to a two-year period in each case (1973–4 and 1979–80). This has a depressive effect on GDP and employment (see equation (a) above) and gives an accelerating push to inflation (equation (b)), which wears out after the lagged responses have worked themselves through.[22] By this time (1976 and 1981) the contractionary monetary policy takes on a dominant role up to the subsequent revival (1977 and 1982(?)). At this point the fall in real input prices also starts affecting the two variables, and particularly attenuating the rate of inflation. Obviously, countries have differed in the extent of the rise in unemployment and particularly in the size of the inflation peaks, depending on real-wage and real exchange-rate behaviour. Both of the latter were not separately accounted for in the present paper and in this respect as well as in a few others our empirical analysis is certainly lacking. The connection between institutional wage-fixing arrangements, union power, and real-wage behaviour is one such link, and the relationship between the current account, monetary policy (at home and abroad), and the exchange rate is another. Also, we have ignored the second-round effects on investment.

We conclude by mentioning some of the possible policy conclusions that could be derived from this type of analysis. Turning first to the supply-side factors we note again the key role that real input prices have played in the upswings and downswings of industrial countries during this last decade. If our earlier argument concerning the relationship between output, output variability, and productivity slowdown is right, there seems little doubt that a smoother growth in real energy and raw material prices in world markets would make for overall welfare improvement since some of the extreme gyrations and losses of productivity would be avoided. This calls for support of commodity-price stabilization policies on a world scale. If fluctuations in real input prices could be smoothened, it is possible that countries could also pursue a more expansionary policy on average. However, the key role played by real wage costs shows how crucial an incomes policy is both for the direct promotion of labour-using production policies and for the attenuation of inflationary pressure without which a more expansionary policy might lead to more inflation.[23] Finally, inter-country linkages, both through monetary policy, export markets, and joint demands on the markets for oil and raw materials, underline the importance of co-ordinated expansion policies among industrial countries.

The main lesson that can perhaps be learnt for macro-policy from the developments of the last decade is that the traditional separation of short-term demand management and real structural adjustment issues seems no longer valid. They should be handled within the same policy framework.

Notes and Sources

* This paper is based on research carried out at the Maurice Falk Institute for Economic Research in Israel and at the National Bureau for Economic Research in Cambridge, Mass. Carlos Bachrach has provided skilful research assistance. Financial support by the National Science Foundation and the Ford Foundation is gratefully acknowledged. I would likewise want to thank DRI (Data Resources Inc.) for access to their excellent computer system.

[1] The EC total in Table 2.2 is a simple average over countries while the numbers in Table 2.1 are weighted by country size.

[2] The import prices are shown lagged one year, i.e. the number shown for 1973–5 is the mean change during 1972–4, etc., as the effect on output tends to come at a year's lag.

[3] For a more detailed discussion of this issue see also Sachs (1979) and Grubb, Jackson, and Layard (1981).

[4] For a detailed analysis see Bruno and Sachs (1982).

[5] We here define variables in terms of their logarithms and therefore the product of the exchange rate and the world price, which is the domestic price of the world good, will be the sum of the logarithms $(p^* + e)$ and the ratio of the two prices is the difference of the logarithms $(p - (p^* + e))$.

[6] The various parameters are thus marked on the respective sides of the curve S in Fig. 2.2.

[7] When both S and D contract the outcome for π may obviously go either way.

[8] For a broader discussion and some empirical illustration for the UK, see Bruno and Sachs (1981, 1982).

[9] The correlation coefficients for the three variables, over the pooled cross-section (ordered as in Table 2.3) are: $R_{13} = -0.56$, $R_{12} = -0.20$, $R_{23} = 0.38$.

[10] The slow-down in capital-stock growth is, of course, not captured in this way, but its effect on employment growth at given GDP growth is likely to be relatively small.

[11] In addition to eight EC countries these include Austria, Finland, Norway, Spain, Sweden, and Switzerland.

[12] When one regresses employment growth on changes in output growth, allowing for different adjustment coefficients in a deceleration or acceleration phase, three EC countries (UK, France, Italy) tend to show more sluggish adjustment for a deceleration and only one country (Belgium) shows the converse.

[13] The average drop in aggregate employment growth is from 0.3 per cent to 0.2 per cent. Unemployment, of course, grew much faster as the labour force was growing more rapidly in the 1970s.

[14] In earlier joint work, Sachs and I have obtained significant real-wage effects in manufacturing-sector employment for the UK, Germany, and Japan (1982). More recently, Jeff Sachs has obtained new aggregate employment regressions for OECD countries, using BLS (Bureau of Labour Statistics) labour compensation data and a somewhat different specification, in which real wages appear negative and highly significant for a larger number of countries.

[15] A more detailed rationalization of this equation is given in Bruno (1980). We have here left out export prices which may play an independent role. For a recent application to OECD data of a similar equation see Turner (1982).

[16] Strictly speaking, $\dot{w} - \dot{p}_{-1}$ is not the change in the real wage but rather the excess of nominal wage growth over *past* inflation, which may or may not represent expected inflation.

[17] The trend growth rate from 1972 to 1978 was used as a reference measure of capacity after 1972.

[18] The UK shows a positive deviation from the average intercept of -0.8 and the other countries vary between 0 and -0.7 per cent below this intercept.

[19] The role of real wages is 2.4 per cent while that of input prices amounts to 0.5 per cent. Here the sum (2.9 per cent) is close to the actual acceleration number ($11.9 - 9.2 = 2.7$).

[20] In a separate pooled regression, comparable to regression 2 in Table 2.5, the estimated coefficients are 0.150 and 0.157 (with estimated standard errors of 0.020 and 0.024), respectively. In individual-country regressions the differences are somewhat larger but they go both ways and are not significant.

[21] When this last factor is computed recursively from the regression rather than from actual numbers one gets a prediction which is almost as good.

[22] A convenient way of looking at the price equation (b) is to consider the case in which the real wage and productivity shift cancel out. Ignoring the capacity term we then have $\dot{p}_c - \dot{p}_{c-1} = 0.16(\dot{p}_n - \dot{p}_{c-1})$ or $\dot{p}_c = 0.84\dot{p}_{c-1} + 0.16\dot{p}_n$. It is easy to see how a one-time shock to $\dot{p}_n$ gives peak inflation and a gradual deceleration afterwards.

[23] This last statement does not necessarily follow from the empirical model used here. Capacity use has been shown to affect inflation only weakly, and the effect of unemployment on real-wage behaviour has not been explicitly analysed in this paper.

References

Bruno, Michael (1980), 'Import Prices and Stagflation in the Industrial Countries: A Cross-Section Analysis', *The Economic Journal,* 90, Sept., 479–92.

Bruno, Michael and Sachs, Jeffrey (1981), 'Supply Versus Demand Approaches to the Problem of Stagflation', in H. Giersch (ed.), *Macroeconomic Policies for Growth and Stability*, Kiel, Institut für Weltwirtschaft, pp. 15–60.

Bruno, M. and Sachs, J. (1982), 'Input Price Shocks and the Slowdown in Economic Growth: The Case of UK Manufacturing', *Review of Economic Studies,* XLIX, 679–705.

Dickens, William T. (1982), 'The Productivity Crisis: Secular or Cyclical?', *Economics Letters* IX, 37–42.

Grubb, D., Jackman, R., and Layard, R. (1982), 'Causes of the Current Stagflation', *Review of Economic Studies*, XLIX, 707–30.

Sachs, Jeffrey (1979), 'Wages, Profits, and Macroeconomic Adjustment: A Comparative Study', *Brookings Papers on Economic Activity,* No. 2, 269–319.

Turner, P. (1982), 'International Aspects of Inflation', OECD.

3

Wages, Unemployment, and Incomes Policies

D. GRUBB, R. LAYARD, and J. SYMONS

Europe has the highest level of unemployment since the Second World War, but there is little agreement about why this is so. In this chapter we shall offer a rather simple analysis, which consists of two propositions.

(i) The main reason unemployment is high is that governments fear the effects on inflation if unemployment were lower. To support this argument, we estimate in Section I wage and price equations for nineteen OECD countries, and show that equations estimated up to 1980 predict quite well for 1981 and 1982. Thus inflation is coming down roughly as predicted by the equations. This is not of course the same as saying that governments have chosen to produce the exact levels of unemployment which we currently have. But governments do constantly say they cannot reflate without abandoning their inflation targets. We pass no judgement on whether their inflation targets are right, but we do offer support for the view that it would be impossible to reflate without a worse inflation performance (unless one had more effective incomes policies). In this sense we see the fundamental medium-term problem as being that the NAIRU (non-accelerating inflation rate of unemployment) is high. And in the medium term it is the NAIRU that determines the level of employment.

(ii) So what becomes of the theory that the real (product) wage determines the level of employment? There is no inconsistency. For given technology, capital, and real prices of materials, the real wage is indeed the proximate determinant of the level of employment. And the real wage is in the short term the product of recent events. But in the medium term, with steady growth of money national income, employment must converge on the NAIRU and the real wage will adjust to its corresponding level.

To test the theory that a high real wage reduces employment, we estimate in Section II standard neo-classical labour-demand functions for six OECD countries, allowing for appropriate lags between real wages and jobs and for the job consequences of the price of materials. The estimated real-wage effects are almost always significant. Adding in variables which affect aggregate demand directly does not improve the explanation significantly. Given this, the view that there is a real-wage problem has great force. But the prime issue is how to change the real wage, if in the medium term it takes whatever value is consistent with the NAIRU. The answer is that the real-wage problem can only be dealt with if one is simultaneously dealing with the NAIRU. This leads to our third point.

(iii)   The most obvious way to deal with the NAIRU is by better incomes policies. The way forward is bound to differ from country to country. Some countries may be able to take advantage of centrally co-ordinated bargaining arrangements. But in others, including Britain, this is not possible and only a more decentralized form of incomes policy has any hope. The best approach would be a tax-based incomes policy, in which firms paid a tax on any excess growth in hourly pay above a national norm. Such a scheme is discussed in Section III of this chapter.

I. The Wage-Inflation Constraint

Our first proposition is that governments could afford to reflate if it were not for the effects of tighter labour markets on the level of wage inflation. The constraint is not always seen this way. Some naïve monetarists see the constraint as a financial one—with higher deficits or money growth leading to higher inflation. But, as many monetarists admit, financial factors cannot of themselves determine how a given money income is divided between real output and prices. Thus, to understand both inflation and employment, we need an independent theory of price formation and hence of wage formation.

In this section of the chapter we analyse the equations determining wages and prices in order to isolate the variables that affect the NAIRU.[1] We do not attempt to explain the year-to-year movements of unemployment, which depend also on the demand side of the economy. But we are able to identify the sources of the main dilemma facing policy-makers—that is, the determinants of the NAIRU in the inflation constraint. We shall conclude that increased import prices, lower productivity growth, and reduced willingness to work are responsible in roughly equal measure for the rise in the NAIRU. We have not been able to find evidence of effects of increased militancy in the labour

market. It will also emerge that recent history is consistent with the
past history of wage and price relationships; thus it would seem reasonable to suppose that current world unemployment results from the
declared aim of most world leaders that priority must be given to the
fight against inflation.

We first estimate a wage equation, consisting of a Phillips curve
determining the rate of growth of real wages, modified to allow for
some nominal inertia in wages. Thus we explain the rate of money-
wage inflation by the current rate of price inflation and last year's
rate of wage inflation (the coefficients on these two being constrained
to add to unity), plus the log of the unemployment rate and a time
trend. We then estimate a price equation in which price inflation is
explained by current and lagged wage inflation, current and lagged
import-price inflation, trend productivity growth, and the unemployment rate.[2] And we then use these two equations in order to see what
relationship is implied between the level of unemployment and the
rate of change of wage inflation.[3]

The wage and price equations are estimated for nineteen OECD
countries on annual data for 1957–80.[4] The results are shown in Tables
3.1 and 3.2, with the average residual errors being shown in Table 3.3.
The wage equation shows a negative effect of unemployment on wages
in all countries—significantly so in most. And the average residuals
are not particularly out of line in 1981 and 1982. In this sense unemployment seems to be doing to wages what one would expect of it.
This is because we have measured the pressure of demand by the log
of unemployment. In earlier work we had found that the simple unemployment rate was the best explanatory variable for wage inflation,
but such equations estimated to 1980 tended to over-predict the fall
in inflation in 1982. Equations using the log of unemployment did
much better.[5] Thus there is some evidence of diminishing returns to
higher unemployment in terms of its effects on the inflation rate.[6]
This may not have been fully anticipated when governments embarked
on the current round of deflation.

Turning to the price equation, the results are shown in Table 3.2.[7]
The equation somewhat under-predicts price inflation for 1981 and
1982, which could reflect efforts to restore profits or further falls in
underlying productivity growth.

Accounting for the higher NAIRU

We can now put the price and wage equations together to look at
the (reduced form) relationship between the change in the rate of
wage inflation and the variables which determine it. Table 3.4 shows
the predicted effects of these variables in each year from 1957 to 1982.
It shows (weighted) average figures for eight EC countries of both

TABLE 3.1

Wage Equation (using Unemployment) 1957–1980

Country	Constant/100	$\dot{p}$	$(\log U)/100$	$t/100$	(SE)100	R^2	DW
Belgium	−11.38 (3.6)	0.75 (4.8)	−4.27 (4.6)	0.23 (3.3)	1.80	0.64	2.50
Denmark	−1.50 (0.6)	0.77 (4.3)	−1.19 (1.7)	−0.06 (0.8)	2.21	0.52	2.21
France	−16.33 (2.0)	0.75 (5.6)	−5.16 (2.4)	0.53 (2.7)	1.43	0.65	1.46
Germany	−2.04 (0.7)	1.20 (5.2)	−1.66 (2.5)	−0.17 (2.0)	2.20	0.60	1.74
Ireland	−10.36 (1.6)	1.20 (8.0)	−5.38 (2.3)	0.21 (2.1)	2.46	0.77	1.95
Italy	−8.21 (1.0)	1.06 (6.3)	−4.69 (1.6)	0.10 (1.0)	3.28	0.68	2.05
Netherlands	−9.20 (2.0)	0.91 (4.8)	−3.26 (2.8)	0.07 (0.6)	2.77	0.58	1.42
UK	−4.71 (0.6)	1.01 (6.0)	−2.03 (0.9)	0.10 (0.6)	2.65	0.68	2.01
Finland	−11.76 (2.7)	0.72 (4.4)	−3.82 (3.1)	0.22 (2.4)	2.18	0.54	1.30
Norway	−0.94 (0.1)	0.71 (4.4)	−0.79 (0.3)	−0.06 (0.7)	2.49	0.49	1.55
Sweden	−20.21 (1.6)	0.91 (4.1)	−5.74 (1.8)	−0.14 (1.3)	3.39	0.51	2.39
Austria	−18.24 (2.1)	0.90 (4.7)	−5.63 (2.6)	−0.19 (2.2)	2.34	0.55	2.28
Spain	−1.67 (0.1)	0.79 (3.4)	−1.83 (0.5)	0.18 (0.4)	5.32	0.36	2.27
Switzerland	−2.23 (2.0)	1.04 (7.1)	−0.61 (4.4)	−0.05 (1.4)	1.13	0.75	1.65
Australia	−5.21 (1.2)	0.88 (6.0)	−1.78 (1.5)	0.12 (1.4)	2.18	0.72	2.02
New Zealand	−6.27 (1.5)	0.50 (2.6)	−1.18 (1.7)	0.12 (1.0)	2.54	0.30	1.77
Japan	−41.05 (4.2)	0.94 (6.1)	−11.06 (4.5)	0.04 (0.5)	2.60	0.69	1.27
Canada	−7.91 (2.6)	0.42 (4.2)	−3.22 (3.0)	0.05 (1.3)	1.06	0.62	1.51
US	−2.69 (1.1)	0.35 (2.4)	−1.10 (1.3)	0.02 (0.6)	0.93	0.32	2.54
EC average	−7.97 (1.5)	0.96 (5.6)	−3.45 (2.4)	0.13 (0.9)	2.35	0.64	1.92
OECD average	−9.57 (1.6)	0.83 (5.0)	−3.39 (2.3)	0.07 (0.5)	2.37	0.58	1.89

Notes: t-statistics are in parentheses. The coefficient on $\dot{w}_{-1}$ is 1 minus the coefficient on $\dot{p}$. The equation was estimated in the form $\dot{w} - \dot{w}_{-1} = a_1 + a_2(\dot{p} - \dot{w}_{-1}) + a_3 \log U + a_4 t$. Hence R^2 measures the proportion of $\mathrm{Var}(\dot{w} - \dot{w}_{-1})$ explained. t = date minus 1970.

TABLE 3.2
Price Equation 1957–1980

Country	$\dot{w}$	$\dot{U}$	Constant/100	(SE)100	DW
Belgium	−0.19 (1.0)	−3.34 (4.3)	0.08 (0.2)	1.90	2.04
Denmark	0.64 (4.3)	−1.59 (3.0)	−0.95 (2.2)	2.10	1.59
France	0.57 (2.9)	−2.85 (2.1)	1.49 (2.9)	2.05	1.05
Germany	0.37 (3.5)	−0.13 (0.2)	−0.15 (0.5)	1.53	1.35
Ireland	0.54 (4.4)	−0.35 (0.6)	0.45 (0.8)	2.77	1.05
Italy	0.50 (3.3)	−2.52 (2.6)	−0.09 (0.1)	3.84	1.02
Netherlands	0.47 (2.4)	−0.83 (0.5)	−0.11 (0.2)	3.04	1.50
UK	0.55 (6.2)	0.28 (0.5)	−0.18 (0.5)	1.77	1.66
Finland	0.74 (4.7)	1.48 (3.1)	0.28 (0.7)	1.95	0.77
Norway	0.58 (3.4)	0.53 (0.4)	0.68 (1.3)	2.64	0.95
Sweden	0.45 (4.2)	0.46 (0.4)	−0.54 (1.2)	2.18	1.34
Austria	0.46 (3.3)	−1.62 (1.0)	−0.26 (0.6)	2.09	1.11
Spain	0.46 (3.3)	0.88 (0.8)	−0.47 (0.5)	4.07	1.37
Switzerland	0.29 (1.7)	−1.63 (0.6)	0.27 (1.1)	1.21	1.99
Australia	0.54 (6.3)	−2.58 (5.1)	1.33 (4.3)	1.39	1.80
New Zealand	0.50 (2.8)	−0.37 (0.2)	0.26 (0.5)	2.34	1.19
Japan	0.41 (2.0)	−11.29 (2.7)	1.34 (1.8)	3.57	1.06
Canada	1.04 (5.1)	−0.29 (0.8)	−1.09 (3.4)	1.50	0.98
US	0.66 (2.5)	0.10 (0.4)	0.13 (0.5)	1.24	0.88
EC average	0.43 (3.3)	−1.42 (1.6)	0.07 (0.5)	2.38	1.41
OECD average	0.50 (3.4)	−1.35 (1.0)	0.13 (0.3)	2.27	1.30

Note: The coefficient on $\dot{w}_{-1}$ is 1 minus the coefficient of $\dot{w}$. The equation was estimated in the form $\dot{p} - \frac{1}{2}s(\dot{m} + \dot{m}_{-1}) +$
$\dot{x} - \dot{w}_{-1} = b_1 + b_2(\dot{w} - \dot{w}_{-1}) + b_3\dot{U}$. t-statistics are in parentheses.

TABLE 3.3

Prediction Errors in Wage and Price Equations
(Eight EC Countries, weighted by GDP) 1957-1982

Year	Wage Inflation (1)	Prediction error in Table 3.1 (2)	Price inflation (3)	Prediction error in Table 3.2 (4)
1957	7.09	0.47	3.46	−0.89
1958	6.52	−0.50	4.44	2.58
1959	4.29	−0.79	2.06	1.84
1960	7.84	1.93	1.82	−0.11
1961	8.02	0.51	2.93	−0.99
1962	9.11	0.51	3.76	0.32
1963	7.58	−0.99	4.06	0.14
1964	8.47	−0.71	3.61	0.13
1965	8.26	−0.54	3.52	0.76
1966	6.64	−2.06	3.65	1.00
1967	5.04	−1.65	2.62	1.62
1968	6.84	−0.44	3.21	1.91
1969	8.90	−0.12	4.23	0.92
1970	13.06	3.61	4.53	−2.26
1971	11.70	1.33	6.05	−2.01
1972	10.31	0.13	6.00	0.42
1973	13.38	0.75	7.91	−0.32
1974	15.72	−0.42	12.09	−2.64
1975	16.22	1.07	11.82	−1.88
1976	11.53	−1.08	9.59	−0.86
1977	11.45	−0.35	8.96	−0.17
1978	9.88	0.63	6.68	−1.06
1979	10.77	−0.40	8.35	1.04
1980	12.19	−0.87	10.47	0.49
1981	11.23	−0.89	10.16	0.86
1982	10.66	0.28	9.43	1.31

Notes: The equations are estimated to 1980. Column (2) shows $\dot{w} - \hat{\dot{w}}$ and column (4) shows $\dot{p} - \hat{\dot{p}}$.

the rate of change of wage inflation and of the contribution of the different explanatory variables in predicting it. Column (1) shows the actual change in wage inflation. Columns (2) to (6) show the contribution to this coming from each of the relevant variables. For ease of understanding, each contribution has been measured as a difference from 1973. The last column shows the unexplained residual error.[8] (The structure of the table corresponds to equation (3) in footnote 3.)

This framework enables us to think about the sources of the growth of unemployment, since any growth in inflationary pressure must either lead to a growth in inflation or a growth in unemployment. Let us take the influences in turn. Column (2) shows the inflation effects of changes in relative import prices. As it happens, these effects were roughly constant in our reference year of 1973 (taking the year as a whole). Thus changes in relative import prices were tending to reduce inflation by around two points a year up to 1973 and have tended to increase it on average by about one point a year since then.[9] This is a worsening of around three points a year. Column (3) shows the effects of productivity growth. The fall in productivity growth has produced a worsening in inflationary pressure of the same order (around four points a year comparing pre- and post-1973). However, nearly as important as the effects of these two has been the effect of 'time' in the wage equation, which has raised inflationary pressure steadily by around $5\frac{1}{2}$ points since 1957, and $2\frac{1}{2}$ points since 1970.

Thus the growth of the NAIRU since the early 1970s can be attributed to additional inflationary pressure arising in roughly equal measure from higher relative import prices, lower productivity growth, and 'time'. As regards the first two of these, the problem is that wage-setters have not been willing to accept the lower feasible growth rate of real wages without the bludgeon of unemployment to force them to do so.[10] For this reason higher productivity growth would be good for employment.

But what are we to make of the pure time trend in the inflation equation? It simply proxies for other trended variables which we have not so far discussed. These must be variables that affect the match between the pattern of labour demand and supply, or variables reflecting long-term changes in labour militancy, or variables affecting the willingness of people to supply labour. Let us consider these in turn. First, does increasing mismatch have any role to play? It could explain a rise in unemployment for any given level of vacancies. We have not been able to investigate this except for Britain, where one can consider two tests. The first, and most direct, test is to take data on unemployment and vacancies subdivided by region, industry, or occupation. One can then construct three indices of mismatching for each year. Our colleague Stephen Nickell (1982) has done this, and none of the three indices (for regional, industrial, or occupational mismatch) shows any sign of rising over the 1970s.[11] Another test is to go back to the possible sources of increasing mismatch—of which the most plausible is an alleged increase in the rate of structural change in the pattern of demand, due perhaps to the oil shock. It is of course not easy to measure changes in the structure of demand for labour, but the changes in the induced structure of employment are easy to measure. If we calculate an index of the year-to-year changes in the structure of employment, there is absolutely no sign that this goes up in the 1970s.[12] If there had been increased change in the structure of demand, we would expect it to be reflected in increased changes in the structure of employment (unless it were offset by increasing rigidity

TABLE 3.4

Accounting for Changes in the Rate of Wage Inflation (Eight EC Countries, weighted by GDP) 1957-1982
(For 'contributions' 1973 = 0)

Percentage

| Year | Change in wage inflation | Contribution of | | | | | |
| | | Relative import price growth | Productivity growth | Unemployment | Time | Change in unemployment | Error |
	(1)	(2)	(3)	(4)	(5)	(6)	(7)
1957	-0.89	-0.37	-1.24	1.59	-3.51	1.93	-0.98
1958	-0.56	-2.25	-1.54	0.89	-3.29	0.73	3.21
1959	-2.23	-2.87	-1.54	0.76	-3.07	0.84	1.96
1960	3.55	-0.72	-1.46	2.34	-2.85	1.72	2.85
1961	0.18	-1.12	-1.41	3.59	-2.63	0.99	-0.91
1962	1.09	-1.97	-1.40	3.48	-2.41	0.49	1.22
1963	-1.53	-1.37	-1.31	3.10	-2.19	0.42	-1.85
1964	0.89	-0.87	-1.49	4.00	-1.97	-0.01	-0.44
1965	-0.21	-0.98	-1.67	3.33	-1.75	-1.30	0.48
1966	-1.61	-1.06	-1.53	3.00	-1.53	-0.44	-1.72
1967	-1.60	-1.19	-1.37	0.82	-1.31	-0.13	-0.09

Year	(1)	(2)	(3)	(4)	(5)	(6)	(7)
1968	1.80	-0.87	-1.17	0.62	-1.09	-0.52	3.16
1969	2.06	-0.55	-1.04	1.20	-0.88	0.00	1.64
1970	4.15	-0.48	-0.85	1.35	-0.66	0.19	2.93
1971	-1.36	-0.92	-0.67	0.60	-0.44	-0.21	-1.39
1972	-1.38	-2.01	-0.67	-0.28	-0.22	-0.95	1.07
1973	3.06	0.00	0.00	0.00	0.00	0.00	1.38
1974	2.34	5.47	1.50	-0.70	0.22	0.29	-6.13
1975	0.51	2.43	2.34	-2.88	0.44	-1.99	-1.50
1976	-4.69	-1.50	2.69	-3.66	0.66	-0.93	-3.63
1977	-0.08	-0.01	3.75	-3.97	0.88	-0.72	-0.97
1978	-1.56	-1.76	3.75	-4.15	1.09	-0.53	-0.93
1979	0.88	-1.09	3.75	-4.33	1.31	-0.99	1.26
1980	1.43	0.83	3.75	-4.72	1.53	-0.29	-0.64
1981	-0.97	1.60	3.75	-6.21	1.75	-2.16	-0.66
1982	-0.57	0.31	3.75	-7.24	1.97	-2.05	1.72

Notes: If $\ddot{w}$ is regressed on forecast $\ddot{w}$, the t-statistic is 2.9. In 1973, the actual values of each component in the equation

$$\ddot{w} = a_1 s(\tfrac{1}{2}\dot{m} + \tfrac{1}{2}\dot{m}_{-1}) + a_2 \dot{x} + a_3 \log U + a_4 t + a_5 \dot{U} + a_6 + e$$

were

$$3.06 = 0.12 - 6.85 + 21.58 + 0.66 + 0.00 - 13.83 + 1.38.$$

Thus in any other year

Col. (1) = 3.06 − 1.38 + Cols. (2) + (3) + (4) + (5) + (6) + (7).

in the supply of labour). So we conclude that in Britain at least there is little evidence that unemployment has risen due to increasing mismatch arising from an increased pace of structural change.

Next, has inflationary pressure increased due to increased militancy? If it had, one would expect that wage pressure would have increased at any given tightness of the market. The difficulty is to find an appropriate measure of tightness. Unemployment will not do, since it could perfectly well have risen because the labour force had become less willing to work. By contrast, vacancies should measure the tightness of the market as perceived by employers.[13] Vacancies registered with employment exchanges are not the same as total vacancies, but we have used them as they are the only available statistics. Table 3.5 shows the same wage equations as Table 3.1 but for 1962–80 and with log vacancies replacing log unemployment.[14] In all cases a higher level of vacancies raises wage inflation. But in only Belgium, Australia, and New Zealand is the time trend of wage inflation (for given price inflation, lagged wage inflation, and vacancies) positive, with t-values of only 1.0, 1.2, and 0.9. In most other countries the time trend, though negative, was insignificant. So there seems to be no clear evidence of increased militancy. It is of course possible that total vacancies have risen less than registered vacancies, in which case the time trend would have been more positive if total vacancies had been included. But it seems unlikely that a significant time trend would have appeared, except perhaps in Belgium and Australasia.[15]

If militancy has not generally increased, this leaves us with the third possibility—that increased wage pressure at given unemployment is due to fewer of the unemployed being willing to take what work is available. To think about this, consider the relationship between unemployment and vacancies (U/V curve). Increased militancy would imply a shift along the U/V curve rather than a shift of the curve.[16] Yet in most countries the curve has shifted out by massive amounts— on average by a factor of three over 20 years (see Fig. 3.1). Only a very small fraction of this can be due to changes in the propensity to register vacancies or unemployment. So something else is going on. If the natural rate of vacancies has not risen in most countries, the natural rate of unemployment (relating to steady inflation at a given rate of growth of feasible real wages) must have done so. This must imply a reduction in the fraction of the unemployed who are willing to take the vacancies that are available.

Before we speculate about the reasons for this, it is interesting to decompose statistically the shifts that have occurred in the measured U/V curve. For this purpose we estimated simultaneously the U/V relationship with its time trend, and the wage equations with first U and then V as arguments. These equations involve a system of cross-equation restrictions.[17]

TABLE 3.5

Wage Equation (using Vacancies) 1962–1980

Country	Constant/100	$\dot{p}$	$(\log V)/100$	$t/100$	(SE)100	R^2	DW
Belgium	−3.85 (1.9)	0.63 (3.9)	3.39 (4.5)	0.08 (1.0)	1.54	0.78	2.22
Germany	−17.58 (1.9)	0.85 (3.5)	3.45 (2.4)	−0.03 (0.2)	1.88	0.59	1.86
Netherlands	−11.43 (1.0)	0.77 (3.4)	3.32 (1.3)	−0.07 (0.4)	2.21	0.55	1.59
UK	−7.06 (0.5)	0.99 (5.0)	1.86 (0.7)	−0.03 (0.3)	2.85	0.69	1.86
Sweden	−9.30 (0.6)	1.13 (4.2)	3.52 (0.8)	−0.45 (2.6)	3.45	0.61	2.51
Austria	−14.63 (1.8)	0.83 (4.0)	5.11 (2.3)	−0.07 (0.6)	2.55	0.58	2.59
Australia	−10.36 (1.7)	0.87 (5.2)	3.28 (2.0)	0.13 (1.2)	2.31	0.75	2.37
New Zealand	−3.22 (1.1)	0.48 (2.4)	3.21 (1.5)	0.20 (0.9)	2.45	0.35	1.54
Japan	−80.86 (7.8)	0.91 (8.8)	14.37 (8.3)	−0.26 (3.7)	1.65	0.89	2.24

Notes: See Table 3.1.

Fig. 3.1: Unemployment and vacancies in Germany, UK, Netherlands, and Belgium: 1962–82 (Unweighted averages)

From them we can compute in Table 3.6 the annual increase in the natural rate of unemployment (g_U), and the natural rate of vacancies (g_V) (for a given growth rate of real wages), as well as the shift of the U/V curve, as measured by the annual growth of unemployment for given vacancies $(g_{U|V})$. The latter has to equal $g_U + \alpha g_V$ where α is the (absolute) elasticity of unemployment with respect to vacancies along the U/V curve.[18] As Table 3.6 shows, the main reason for the outward shift of the U/V curves in EC countries and in Japan has been the rise in the natural rate of unemployment.[19]

The question then arises as to why the labour force should have become less available for work. One important factor may be changes in the real value of social security benefits and in real incomes, taken together with a less stringent application of the work test to claimants for benefit.[20] But a glance at the history of unemployment does raise the thought that past unemployment may itself reduce the effective supply of labour. With this in mind, we tried estimating the wage equation with past unemployment as an exploratory variable.[21] This performed about as well as time in explaining wage inflation. When time was introduced as well as lagged unemployment, the t-statistics on both were roughly equal (1.2 and 0.8 respectively).

Thus we remain agnostic about whether one can argue that higher unemployment of itself undermines the work ethic and thus raises the

TABLE 3.6
*Growth of Natural Rate of Unemployment and Vacancies
and U/V Shift 1962–1980*

Percentage p.a.

	g_U (1)	g_V (2)	a (3)	$g_U + \alpha g_V$ (4)
Belgium	6.56 (6.6)	−2.15 (1.3)	0.59 (8.1)	5.30 (6.9)
Germany	2.95 (0.7)	1.15 (0.4)	1.41 (24.2)	4.56 (10.2)
Netherlands	5.23 (1.1)	1.41 (0.3)	1.17 (16.3)	6.89 (14.7)
UK	7.35 (2.5)	1.15 (0.3)	0.85 (10.4)	8.32 (20.1)
Sweden	−17.75 (0.7)	20.21 (0.7)	0.97 (8.1)	1.93 (4.4)
Austria	−2.17 (2.0)	1.24 (0.9)	0.77 (14.0)	−1.22 (4.6)
Australia	9.32 (3.8)	−4.19 (1.8)	1.06 (12.5)	4.89 (8.2)
New Zealand	7.84 (0.9)	−6.12 (2.1)	2.92 (8.7)	−10.02 (2.9)
Japan	2.62 (10.1)	1.85 (4.3)	0.61 (12.0)	3.74 (18.3)

Note: *t*-statistics in parentheses.

NAIRU. But whatever the reason for the upward time trend in the NAIRU, the Phillips curve stands up as a sufficiently robust relationship to provide the centre-piece for determining the medium-term level of unemployment. Only a policy that can shift the Phillips curve can do any good; we suggest one in Section III.

First, however, we need to analyse the proximate determinants of employment. If workers fight falls in the feasible rate of growth of real wages at full employment, then according to neo-classical theory the real wage will tend to a level too high for full employment, and unemployment will result.

II. Can We have More Jobs without a Fall in Real Wages?

But is the assumption that real wages are the proximate determinants of labour demand consistent with the evidence?[22] If product markets are competitive and firms are on their labour-demand curves, employment should be explained by the real wage (relative to product prices), real prices of materials, the capital stock, and the state of technology. This was Keynes's view in the *General Theory*, though he later panicked in the face of evidence that the real wage was not always contra-cyclical. To explain this phenomenon, Barro and Grossman (1971) suggested that at times there might be excess supply in the product market, so that firms employed fewer workers than one would predict from the level of real wages. This would break the negative relationship between real wages and employment.

However, Sargent (1978) attempted to rehabilitate neo-classical theory by noting that if there were costs of adjusting employment, the number of jobs would not be adapted simply to the *current* real wage. Rather it would adjust slowly towards a level that was influenced by future expected real wages, which might themselves reflect the past history of real wages. Sargent was able to explain employment in US manufacturing in terms of lagged real wages (measured relative to the Consumer Price Index). But as Geary and Kennan (1982) pointed out, the proper measure of the real wage is the wage relative to the producer's output price. Using this, they showed that for most of the countries studied there was no clear relation between employment and past (or future) real wages. Thus it seemed that one should either abandon the notion of a competitive labour-demand curve altogether, or accept the idea of two different regimes, on and off the competitive labour-demand function.

However Geary and Kennan took no account of the prices of materials, nor of physical capital. In Symons (1982), one of us investigated for British manufacturing a labour-demand function that allowed for these other variables. Somewhat to our surprise, the real wage was significant the first time the equation was run, and subsequent attempts to undermine this result have in general been unsuccessful.[23] Parallel work by Nickell and Andrews (1983) for aggregate employment in Britain also came up with significant wage effects— an elasticity of abour one-half ($t = 3$), compared with a figure of about two obtained by Symons for manufacturing.[24]

Given the importance of the issue and the small-sample problems associated with any individual study, we decided to look at more countries (France, Germany, Japan, Canada, and the USA), in order to see whether there was general support for the neo-classical model. We did not therefore attempt to find the 'best' equation for each country. Rather our approach was initially to avoid specification search, and adopt for all countries a common specification based largely on our prior beliefs. We could then see how well this worked in general in the five countries. In each case we estimated for manufacturing industry a quarterly employment function in which the log of employment is regressed on the log of the real product wage (current value and four lags), the log of real prices of materials (current value and four lags), time, time^2, and time^3, and two lags of the dependent variable. The time terms are included in order to allow for capital accumulation and technical progress. The regressions were done for 1955(Q1) to 1980(4), and also (for comparison) for the pre-OPEC period (to 1973(1)). The data are described in the Data Appendix (Part 2).

Table 3.7 shows the results of estimation by ordinary least squares.

The British results (Symons 1982) are also included, although these relate to slightly different periods and a more elaborate model. There is of course a problem with ordinary-least-squares estimates. They may be subject to simultaneity bias, since a positive error in the demand function may increase both employment and the real wage in the current period via the labour-supply schedule. Thus the effect of the current real wage on employment may be estimated as positive, when in fact it is negative. To attempt to correct for this we re-estimated all the equations using instrumental variables.[25] The results are shown in Table 3.8.

The real-wage elasticity is on average around 0.7 using OLS and 1.4 using instrumental variables.[26] (It is also 1.5 using OLS over the pre-OPEC period.)[27] Using instrumental variables all countries have negative wage effects, as do all countries except the US for ordinary least squares. To test the significance of the wage effects we computed F-tests for the effect of leaving out all the wage variables.[28] These were significant at the 95 per cent level in well over half the countries.[29] Though the significance levels were below this elsewhere, the overall impression, given the absence of specification search, is that real wages do matter; and the chance of obtaining the results we have, if real wages actually did not matter, is negligible. Interestingly the average lag on the wage effects was quite long in all countries—of the order of two years. This confirms the validity of the Sargent approach.

Turning to the effect of the real price of materials, we found similar average elasticities to those for real wages, and similar significance levels. There is of course no reason in pure theory why a rise in real materials prices should lower employment, but it is not surprising that if fewer materials are used (because their real price has risen) the marginal product of a given amount of labour is in fact reduced.

Why have other researchers (and especially Geary and Kennan) not found results like ours for the real-wage effect? The basic reason is that they have not simultaneously included real input prices. If we repeat the estimation of Table 3.7 omitting real input prices we find that the real-wage effect becomes less negative in every country (see Table 3.9).[30]

But even if wages matter in general, does it follow that private employment cannot rise without a fall in the real product wage? In particular is there not some evidence in favour of the Barro–Grossman view that when aggregate demand is low enough employment may be below the level predicted by the real wage, and hence capable of being increased without a fall in the real wage. To examine this, a first approach is to see whether we improve our explanation of employment by including aggregate-demand shift variables in the employment function.[31]

TABLE 3.7

Labour-demand Functions in Manufacturing (Ordinary Least Squares) 1955(1)–1980(4)[a]

	Germany	France	Japan	Canada	US	Britain	Average
Elasticities							
Wage	−0.3	−0.2	−0.5	−2.0	0.4	−1.8	−0.7
Price of materials	−1.3	−0.5	−1.0	−1.3	−0.4	−0.4	−0.8
F-test[b] on elasticities							
Wage	2.9	1.3	7.5	3.1	0.4	3.2	—
Price of materials	5.3	1.2	2.0	1.8	1.8	7.5	—
F-test[b] on demand variables							
(a) Government spending	1.0[c]	5.4	0.5[c]	0.5	1.3	0.3	—
(b) Average tax rate	0.8[c]	0.8[c]	1.2[c]	1.5	4.6[c]	0.9	—
(c) Real M1	0.4[c]	4.7[c]	2.3[c]	1.5	3.7	1.5	—
(d) World trade	1.1	4.4	1.8	4.9[c]	2.4[c]	0.9	—
(a) + (b) + (c) + (d)	1.2[d]	2.0[d]	1.2[d]	1.5[d]	1.7[d]	0.8	—

Mean lags						
Wage	13	1	7	7	5[e]	10	7
Price of materials	7	7	11	6	3[e]	f	7
Pre-OPEC elasticities						
Wage	−0.7	−0.1	−3.6	−1.7	−0.8	−2.3	−1.5
Price of materials	−1.0	−0.1	−7.4	−0.9	1.7	−0.6	−1.4
F-test[b] on stability	0.4	0.1	0.5	2.0	0.1	5.5	—

[a] Britain is 1960(1)–1977(2).
[b] Critical F-values (95 per cent level) are: For elasticities, 2.3 (Britain 3.2). For demand variables taken singly, 2.3–2.5; taken together, 1.8–1.9. For stability, 1.6 (Britain 2.1).
[c] Estimated coefficients inconsistent with aggregate-demand effects, i.e. cumulative effect not significantly positive in first three quarters.
[d] Effects of demand variables as in c.
[e] Taken from IV (instrumental variable) estimates.
[f] Impact and long-run effects have opposite signs so mean lag has little meaning.

TABLE 3.8

Labour-demand Functions in Manufacturing
(Instrumental Variables) 1955(1)–1980(4)

	Germany	France	Japan	Canada	US	Average
Elasticities						
Wage	−0.4	−0.3	−2.4	−2.6	−1.3	−1.4
Price of materials	−1.2	−0.0	−2.6	−1.8	−4.6	−2.0
F-*tests*[a]						
Wage	2.3	1.4	7.7	3.5	0.7	−
Price of materials	5.3	1.7	1.8	2.3	1.3	−

[a] Critical F-value (95 per cent level) = 2.3.

An innovation in aggregate demand will increase employment when firms are off their labour-demand curves and leave it unchanged otherwise. If firms are typically off their demand curves, then a distributed lag of demand variables should enter the employment functions, generating a positive response initially at least. In Table 3.7 we show the effect of including government expenditure on goods and services, the average tax rate, the volume of world trade, and real money balances (M1).[32] Taking each of these separately, and also jointly, we have 5×6 cases. Often the effects have the wrong sign and only in France (for government expenditure and world trade) is there a significant positive effect. Meanwhile the significance of real wages and real input prices does not change. So we conclude that we *have* estimated a structural demand for labour equation which is independent of the structural demand for output equation. When the demand for output increases, employment increases through increases in prices relative to wages.

III. Tax-based Incomes Policies

If the fundamental economic problem is the high NAIRU, one has to think of ways of reducing it. Many elements are required in this strategy. We need demand-side policies, like employment subsidies, to raise demand in the slacker labour markets. We need supply-side policies, on training and labour mobility, to increase supply to the tighter labour markets. We also need measures to discourage voluntary unemployment, especially better income support for poor working families and stricter enforcement of the work test for unemployment benefit. But above all we need an incomes policy which will offset any tendency of unions to produce an excessive NAIRU.

Traditional incomes policies in many countries have the disadvantage of being *dirigiste* and of relying on central determination of

TABLE 3.9
Reduced Real-wage Elasticity when Real Materials Price is Omitted
(Ordinary Least Squares) 1955(1)–1980(4)

	Real-wage elasticity						
	Germany	France	Japan	Canada	US	Britain	Average
Without input prices	0.7	−0.1	0.0	−0.7	0.5	0.1	0.1
With input prices	−0.3	−0.2	−0.5	−2.0	0.4	−1.8	−0.7

pay relativities. A more decentralized type of policy relying on tax incentives is more attractive, at least for those predisposed towards the use of markets. Such a tax-based incomes policy has been much discussed in the United States (Wallich and Weintraub 1971).[33] It has been the policy of the British Liberal Party since the early 1970s and has recently been endorsed by the British Social Democratic Party.[34] Consider the following version of the proposal. Each year the government would declare a norm for the rate of growth of hourly earnings. If an employer increased his average hourly earnings by more than this, all his excess payments would be subject to a tax. The tax would have nothing to do with the pay of any individual— only with the average hourly earnings at the level of the firm. In addition we want the policy to be revenue-neutral. We do not want any increase in the net tax burden on the company sector as a whole, since this might lead to an increased mark-up of prices over costs. There would therefore be a reduction in the general rate of employers' social security taxes designed to give away as much as the expected total proceeds of the 'inflation tax'. But an individual firm's reduction in social security tax would of course be proportional to its total wage-bill, while its inflation tax would be proportional to its *excess* wage growth. The disincentive to excess wage growth would thus be severe.

The intention of the tax is to modify the Phillips curve by reducing the constant term in the wage equation. One can explain how this comes about, first on informal grounds, and then using a formal model.

Informally, it seems reasonable to suppose that in a climate of given expectations and unemployment, both firms and workers would have incentives to settle for less than without the tax. Consider firms first. Under the tax any firm that gives a £1 wage increase will lose not only the pound, but also £1 times the tax rate. If the tax rate were 100 per cent, it would lose £2; if the tax rate were infinite, it would lose everything. This provides employers with a stronger incentive to resist wage claims. This is so even though the employer with an average wage increase receives as much rebate as he pays tax. For the rebate is unaffected by his current wage increase, while the tax depends crucially upon it. If the firm can now save £2 by paying £1 less, it will be more likely than before to pay £1 less. Of course, if all firms conspired to give the same increase, then there would be no way in which they could affect their net tax liability by paying less. But so long as industry is not fully organized on a collective basis, firms will respond to a wage-inflation tax just as drivers respond to a tax on speeding—even though drivers, if they colluded, would notice that higher fines would be offset by lower taxes.

The scheme will also discourage workers from pushing wage claims so far. For the scheme reduces the employer's demand for labour at high wages (since he pays a net tax per worker) and increases the employer's demand for labour at low wages (since he receives a net subsidy per worker). The union realizes this and concludes that an additional wage claim will now have more of an effect on unemployment than it would otherwise have. It therefore chooses a lower wage claim.

To examine both these effects more rigorously, we have to specify some formal model of the economy and then work it through. We shall concentrate on the long-run level of employment. There are essentially three possible models of this, each of which has elements of truth in it, and in each of which we shall find that the inflation tax does reduce unemployment.

The first model is one in which workers are organized into unions but employers are fragmented (Jackman and Layard 1982a). The unions are thus the prime movers in wage determination and do the best they can for their members, after taking into account the employment effects of their actions. Each representative union faces a competitive demand curve for labour in its sector, illustrated as DD in Fig. 3.2. Subject to this constraint, it maximizes the wage bill in its industry *plus* the income that members who cannot get work in this industry can expect to get elsewhere. This latter, of course, depends on the general national level of unemployment, which is why (in this model) unemployment has such a dampening effect on wage settlements. Point A shows the union's choice of wage and employment in the absence of an inflation tax. If we assume that *ex post* workers have to get paid the same wages as they think prevail elsewhere, then unemployment equals $\theta/(\eta - 1 + \theta)$, where η is the elasticity of demand and θ the fraction of workers in an industry hired from outside. Thus the unemployment rate is higher, the lower the elasticity of demand and the greater the consequent monopoly power of the unions.[35]

So how can one reduce the level of unemployment? Obviously, by making the effective-demand curve faced by unions more elastic. This is exactly what the inflation tax does. If a firm gives more than the average wage increase, the firm is subject to a net tax per worker, while if it gives less than the average wage increase it is subject to a net subsidy. This reduces the demand for labour at high wages and raises it at low wages. Thus, a tax-based incomes policy (TIP) works, appropriately enough, by tipping the demand curve—to the dotted line $D'D'$ shown in Fig. 3.2. Unemployment is now given by $\theta/\{\eta(1 + \delta t) - 1 + \theta\}$ where t is the rate of inflation tax and δ is the union's real rate of discount. So unemployment has fallen and employment risen. This is illustrated at point B. The basic point of this model is that an inflation tax works by confronting the unions with worse

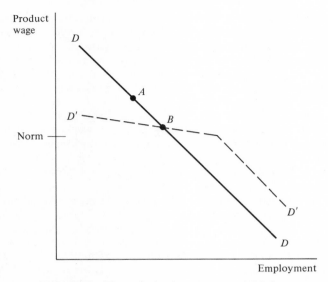

Fig. 3.2: The labour market in a representative industry

consequences if they raise wages. It thus reduces their monopoly power, but does this by a tax rather than by the thorny route of labour legislation.

A second model of the world is one where wages are set by bargaining between firms and unions, and a third is the purely competitive model of the labour market. Both these cases have been examined by Christopher Pissarides (1982, 1983) in the context of a labour market where unemployment and vacancies co-exist due to frictions in the labour market and a product market which is competitive. In both cases Pissarides found that a wage tax would increase the level of employment.[36]

In all these three models the mechanism through which employment is being raised is the reduction in the equilibrium real wage. This raises two questions. First, is it valid to distinguish as we did in Sections I and II between the real wage issue and the issue of the NAIRU? The answer is that in the long run there is no distinction, and the NAIRU and the real wage are simultaneously determined. But many of those who simply argue in terms of the real wage imply that, if real wages could be magically lowered, all would be well. They fail to note that real wages can only be temporarily reduced below their long-run level. Unless the NAIRU is lowered, a one-shot reduction in the real wage will not help for long because forces will rapidly come into play that will raise the real wage to its former level.

A second question is whether it is politically feasible to reduce the NAIRU, if it means lowering the real product wage (for a given capital stock). This may not be as difficult as might appear. First we need to distinguish between the gross wage relative to the price of output and the net wage relative to the price of consumption. If the level of output is higher, the tax base is higher, and therefore, with government expenditure constant, tax rates can be lowered. This will alleviate the fall in real take-home pay, and might even prevent it altogether.[37] Second, the preceding analysis assumes the capital stock fixed. But a higher level of activity will lead to more investment and a higher capital stock. So the level of product wage associated with any given level of employment will itself be higher.

A whole host of administrative issues arise in relation to an inflation tax, but it turns out that, in the British context at least, reasonably inexpensive solutions exist (Jackman and Layard 1982b). There is also the question of the treatment of the public sector. It would not make sense to apply the tax in the non-trading public sector. But the public sector would benefit from the tax in two ways. First, in so far as public-sector wages follow private-sector wages, anything which affects private-sector wages helps in the public sector. Second, lower private-sector wages reduce the rate of increase in the cost of living and this will also help in the public sector.

One obvious issue is how to introduce an inflation tax of this kind. In the year after the announcement of the tax, firms may not have adequate records of earnings and hours for the previous year. But if the tax were announced in advance, there would be a danger of firms conceding big wage increases before the tax came in, so as to reduce their tax liability in the following year. This suggests that the government might have to announce simultaneously the introduction of a 'conventional' one-year incomes policy, plus the fact that it would be followed in the second year and thereafter by a tax. Thus, when the tax eventually came in every firm would have a data base for the previous year. Conventional incomes policies differ between countries and might vary from a freeze to a fixed percentage increase. Whatever the form of the 'conventional' policy it would be bound to be fairly rigid. When it was followed by a tax, people would welcome the greater flexibility this permitted, while respecting the tax as an extension of a more familiar type of incomes restraint.

Clearly any form of intervention has its costs. One would like a tax on all wage growth to reduce all wage growth in all sectors by the same proportion, and thus be non-distortionary. Since the marginal tax rate is the same in all sectors, could one hope for this? The problem is that the *average* tax burden will be higher in the sectors where wages grow fastest. It is therefore possible that these sectors would be more restrained in their wage behaviour than other sectors. This could be unfortunate if the sectors where wages would otherwise grow fastest would be those with the greatest need to attract labour or to offer productivity bonuses for better working practices. If so there would be real costs.

Another type of cost might arise from the fact that a tax on average wages is an implicit subsidy to unskilled labour, since hiring unskilled people reduces average wages. It is also a tax on skilled labour. For given supplies of skilled and unskilled people this is a good thing, since excess supply of the unskilled is so much higher than of the skilled. But it might in the longer run discourage the acquisition of skill. None of these costs are negligible, but they would certainly be outweighed by the benefits of a higher level of employment. Unless someone can think of a less costly way of reducing the NAIRU they should seriously consider this one.

Data Appendix

Part 1

The data sources up to and including 1980 are as follows.

Symbols

MEI	OECD *Main Economic Indicators*
OECD *NA*	OECD *National Accounts*
OECD *LFS*	OECD *Labour Force Statistics*

1. *Wage inflation*

Definition: Average hourly earnings in manufacturing (most countries).
Source: Most countries: *MEI* various. France, Italy, and Netherlands: ILO Yearbooks chained. UK: British Labour Statistics Historical Abstract, Economic Trends Annual Supplement, and ILO Yearbooks.

2. *Price inflation*

Definition: Ratio of consumer expenditure to constant-price consumer expenditure (1975 prices).
Source: OECD *NA*.

3. *Unemployment rate*

Definition: Unemployed as percentage of employed and unemployed (unemployed based on country definitions, and employed includes self-employed).
Source: OECD *LFS* (most countries).

4. *Trend productivity growth*

Definition: See text.
Source: Employment—OECD *LFS* (most countries). GDP—OECD *NA*.

5. *Import prices relative to consumption deflator, multiplied by share of imports in GDP*

Definition: Import price is value of imports divided by volume of imports at 1975 prices.
Source: OECD *NA*.

6. *Vacancies (thousands)*

Definition: Registrations at employment exchanges.
Source: *MEI*.

For 1981 and 1982 the series have been updated by setting 1981 equal to 1980 times the 'relevant' growth rate (1981 over 1980) and setting 1982 equal to 1981 times the relevant growth rate (1982 Q2 over 1981 Q2). The 'relevant' growth rate is that of the variable itself except for

2. *Price inflation.* The consumer price index was used. Source: *MEI*.
3. *Unemployment rate.* The unemployment rate (adjusted) was used. Source: *MEI*.
5. *Import prices.* Source: IMF, *International Financial Statistics*.

D. GRUBB, R. LAYARD, AND J. SYMONS

Part 2

Symbols
MEI   OECD *Main Economic Indicators*
OECD *NA* OECD *National Accounts, 1962-1979*, vol. 2
CSR   *Canadian Statistical Review*
RSDBJ Research and Statistics Department, Bank of Japan
ILO *MBS* ILO *Monthly Bulletin of Statistics*
UN *MBS* UN *Monthly Bulletin of Statistics*
FMBS   *Bulletin Mensuel de Statistique*
USBLS US Bureau of Labour Statistics

	Germany	France	Japan	Canada	US
Hourly earnings	UN *MBS*	Wage rates, *MEI*	*MEI*	*MEI*	*MEI*
Number of workers	*MEI*	*MEI*	*MEI*	*MEI*	*MEI*
Materials prices	UN *MBS*	*MEI*	RSDBJ	*CSR*	USBLS
Output prices[a]	*MEI*	*FMBS*	RSDBJ	*CSR*	USBLS
Weekly hours	*MEI*	—	ILO *MBS*	*MEI*	*MEI*
Social security taxes	OECD *NA*	OECD *NA*	OECD *NA*	OECD *NA*	OECD *NA*
Unemployment rate	*MEI*	*MEI*	*MEI*	*MEI*	*MEI*
Government expenditure	*MEI* and OECD *NA*	OECD *NA*	OECD *NA*	OECD *NA*	OECD *NA*
Average tax rate[b]	OECD *NA*	OECD *NA*	OECD *NA*	OECD *NA*	OECD *NA*
World trade, world exported-material prices, world export prices, country price of exported manufactures	UN *MBS*	UN *MBS*	UN *MBS*	UN *MBS*	UN *MBS*

[a] Wholesale prices of domestically produced manufactures (domestic scales).
[b] Share of taxes in GDP at market prices.

The data were assembled by Tayo Casas-Bedos. The hourly earnings variable (E) is modified in two ways. First it is adjusted for the average rate of employers' social security contributions; and then in order to allow for the overtime premium, it is transformed into W according to the formula

$$W = EH^{-0.25}$$

where H is hours worked per week. The justification is as follows:

$$E = W\left(1 + \theta\,\frac{H - \bar{H}}{H}\right)$$

where $\bar{H}$ is normal hours and θ is the overtime premium. Then

$$\dot{e} = \dot{w} + \theta\,\frac{\bar{H}}{H}\,\dot{h}$$

where the lower case variables represent logs. Then as an approximation we take

$$\dot{e} = \dot{w} + 0.25\,\dot{h},$$

which is integrated to the required form. This adjustment was not necessary in the case of France, where the *MEI* series is net of overtime payments.

Notes and Sources

* Section I is by Grubb and Layard, Section II by Layard and Symons, and Section III by Layard. We are extremely grateful to Richard Jackman, with whom we have been working on these problems for the last two years. This paper draws heavily on ideas in Grubb, Jackman, and Layard (1982 and 1983) and Jackman and Layard (1982a). We are grateful to the Social Science Research Council and the Esmee Fairbairn Trust for financial support.

[1] For fuller discussions of this approach see Grubb *et al.* (1982 and 1983).

[2] This implies a relation between unemployment and the real product wage (adjusted for productivity and relative import prices), of the kind discussed in Section II of the chapter.

[3] Let $\dot{w}$ be the hourly wage inflation ($\log W - \log W_{-1}$), $\dot{p}$ product-price inflation, U the unemployment rate, t time, $\dot{m}$ the proportional change in the ratio of import prices to product prices, s the share of imports in GDP, and x trend output per man-hour. Then we estimate

(1) $\dot{w} = \alpha\dot{p} + (1-\alpha)\dot{w}_{-1} - \beta\ln U + \delta t + \text{const.}$

(2) $\dot{p} = s(\tfrac{1}{2}\dot{m} + \tfrac{1}{2}\dot{m}_{-1}) - \dot{x} + \theta\dot{w} + (1-\theta)\dot{w}_{-1} - \gamma\dot{U} + \text{const.}$

Hence

(3) $\dot{w} = \dfrac{\alpha}{1-\alpha\theta}\,\{s(\tfrac{1}{2}\dot{m} + \tfrac{1}{2}\dot{m}_{-1}) - \dot{x} - \gamma\dot{U}\} + \dfrac{1}{1-\alpha\theta}\,(-\beta\ln U + \delta t) + \text{const.}$

Note that $\alpha/(1-\alpha\theta)$ is the reciprocal of the sum of the average lags in the wage and price equations (Grubb *et al.* (1983)). Note also that (2) assumes, in its static form, that the production function is of the form $Y = f\{aF(L, K), M\}$ where F is Cobb–Douglas and L, K. M are labour, capital, and materials.

[4] The estimates are OLS. In Grubb *et al.* (1983) we used 2SLS, with very similar results. The data are described in the Data Appendix (Part 1).

[5] In terms of goodness of fit over the period 1957–80 there was nothing to choose between log U and U. $1/U$ did much worse.

[6]

$$\text{If } \ddot{w} = -\gamma \log U, -\frac{\mathrm{d}\ddot{w}}{\mathrm{d}U} = \frac{\gamma}{U} \text{ and } \frac{\mathrm{d}}{\mathrm{d}U}\left(-\frac{\mathrm{d}\ddot{w}}{\mathrm{d}U}\right) = \frac{-\gamma}{U^2} < 0.$$

[7] Trend productivity is treated as a function of time consisting of linear segments (one per business cycle). It is found by estimating on annual data for the years 1951–80 the function

$$l = \beta l_{-1} + (1 - \beta)y - f(t)$$

where l is log employment, y is log GDP and $f(t)$ is the log productivity term. The cycles differed between countries, but were measured from peak to peak. Since 1973–4 two segments were included: 1973–4 to 1976, and 1976 to 1980. The first segment was included to allow for any possible change of level in 1973–4 to 1976. For 1981 and 1982 we assumed in Tables 3.2–4 that productivity growth was as in 1976–80.

In Grubb *et al.* (1982) we discuss at some length how far change in trend productivity growth can be considered exogenous and conclude that it can to a considerable degree.

[8] The residual errors are bound to be fairly large since they equal the weighted errors of both the wage and price equations divided by the estimated sum of the average lags, which is itself subject to estimation error. The residual error is

$$\frac{\alpha}{1 - \alpha\theta}\left(\frac{\epsilon_1}{\alpha} + \epsilon_2\right).$$

[9] The effects in columns (2) and (3) may seem surprisingly large. But, as explained in footnote 3, the effect of a one-period rise of λ in the rate of growth of relative import prices (or fall in productivity growth) upon the rate of change of wage inflation is λ divided by the sum of the average lags in the wage and price equations. To understand the reason for this, suppose

$$\dot{w} = \alpha\dot{p} + (1 - \alpha)\dot{w}_{-i} \text{ and } \dot{p} = \dot{w} + s\dot{m}. \text{ Then } \dot{w} - \dot{w}_{-i} = \frac{\alpha}{1 - \alpha} s\dot{m}.$$

Hence the *annual* change in wage inflation when $\dot{m}$ changes will be smaller the larger i.

[10] There may have been *some* adaptation, see Grubb *et al.* (1982).

[11] The index used was

$$\sum_i \left(\frac{U_i V_i}{UV}\right)^{\frac{1}{2}}$$

where U_i and $\check{V}_i$ are unemployment and vacancies in the ith category and U and V are the total.

[12] The index is

$$\sum_{i=1}^{26} \left|\Delta \frac{E_i}{E}\right|$$

where E_i is employment in the ith sector (Standard Industrial Classification) and

E is total employment. For the years 1964–83 the annual figures are (in percentages): 2.4, 1.6, 1.8, 2.8, 1.7, 2.3, 2.8, 2.5, 3.4, 2.6, 2.0, 3.0, 2.4, 1.2, 0.8, 2.8, 2.5, 4.3, 2.4, 2.3.

[13] For a fuller discussion of the interpretation of vacancies see Jackman, Layard, and Pissarides (1983).

[14] We have included all countries for which the OECD provides statistics on registered vacancies, except for those four countries (Finland, France, Norway, and Switzerland) where a_3 had a t-statistic greater than three in the equation

$$\ln V = a_0 + a_1 \ln U + a_2 t + a_3 t^2.$$

In such countries we felt that the series were too unreliable.

[15] To see this, note that in Table 3.6 we should need to produce a significant negative growth rate for the natural rate of vacancies, for example to reduce the figure of +1.15 per cent for Germany (with its standard error of about 4 per cent) to say −8 per cent (for a 95 per cent significance level). A 9 per cent growth in the registration rate seems implausible.

[16] Using a simple demand (D) and supply (S) diagram, with employment (E) less than either S or D, we can trace $V (= D - E)$ and $U (= S - E)$ as a function of the real wage. Changes in the real wage then trace out the U/V curve:

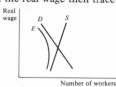

[17] (1) Wage equation with U

$$\dot{w} = \alpha \dot{p} + (1 - \alpha)\dot{w}_{-1} - \beta_U \log U + \delta_U t + \text{const.}$$

(2) Wage equation with V

$$\dot{w} = \alpha \dot{p} + (1 - \alpha)\dot{w}_{-1} + \beta_V \log V + \delta_V t + \text{const.}$$

Hence:
(3) U/V curve

$$\log U = -\frac{\beta_V}{\beta_U} \log V + \left(\frac{\delta_U - \delta_V}{\beta_U}\right) t + \text{const.}$$

Note that a rise in δ_U means a higher natural rate of U; and a rise in δ_V means a lower natural rate of V. If militancy increased one would expect δ_V and δ_U to rise by the same amount, so that the U/V curve did not move.

In simultaneous estimation, parameter values were chosen to minimize an appropriately weighted average of the residual sum of squares of four equations —(1), (2), (3), and (3) written with $\log V$ on the left-hand side and $\log U$ on the right.

[18] Using the notation of footnote 17, $g_U = \delta_U/\beta_U$, $g_V = -\delta_V/\beta_V$, and $\alpha = \beta_V/\beta_U$. $g_{U|V} = (\delta_U - \delta_V)/\beta_U = g_U + \alpha g_V$. Geometrically, the annual shifts are $g_{U|V} = AC = AB + BC = g_U + \alpha BD = g_U + \alpha g_V$. Note that g_U and g_V reflect only the effect of t and not of changes in $\dot{x}$ or $\dot{m}$.

[19] Outside the EC the Swedish estimates have low t-values. In Austria the natural rate of unemployment seems to have fallen, as does the natural rate of vacancies in Australia and New Zealand. The U/V shift may also be due in part to employment protection legislation.

[20] Nickell (1979); Layard (1982), p. 43.

[21] The variable representing past unemployment was

$$\sum_{i=1}^{11} (12 - i) U_{-i}/66.$$

[22] For a fuller version of this section see Symons and Layard (1983).

[23] However, although the model fitted well up to 1977, it did not perform well thereafter unless real interest rates were introduced (as influences on the cost of work in progress) and *ad hoc* allowances were made for the effects of incomes policies on expected wages.

[24] See below. A study of UK road haulage by Hopcroft and Symons (1983) also found a real-wage elasticity of one-half ($t = 4.8$). For UK manufacturing 1956–78, Bruno and Sachs (1982) found a real-wage elasticity of 0.3 ($t = 2.0$).

[25] The instruments are the unemployment rate (four lags), the nominal price level (four lags), and the world price of materials relative to the world price of manufactured exports (current value and four lags). The first two are Phillips curve variables to deal with endogenous real wages and the last is to deal with endogeneity in the prices of materials.

[26] There is a problem with interpreting our long-run coefficients as the long-run elasticity of demand for labour with respect to expected wages, if firms respond to expected wages over some horizon. If, for example,

$$l_t = \lambda l_{t-1} - \alpha \left(\sum_{i=0}^{\infty} \delta^i E_t w_{t+1} \right) \quad (\delta < 1)$$

and the real wage w_t is generated by an AR1 so that

$$E_t w_{t+i} = \rho^i(w_t - w^*) + w^* \quad (\rho < 1)$$

where w^* is the unobserved long-run wage, then the true and the measured elasticities are in the ratio $(1 - \rho\delta)/(1 - \delta)$. Two factors are mitigating: the bias is positive (so that elasticities are even larger than measured); and vanishes if $\rho = 1$ (or, in general, if w_t has a unit root). In fact one cannot usually reject the unit-root hypothesis.

[27] However, a Chow test of parameter stability comparing the two periods is failed only by Britain (at the 95 per cent level).

[28] The tests are somewhat undemanding owing to the high autocorrelation in the lagged terms, which thus over-consume degrees of freedom. Fewer terms would be more significant, but less 'true'.

[29] In Germany, the (negative) wage elasticities are much higher if negotiated wage rates are used in place of hourly earnings. Using OLS, the elasticity is 0.8. Using this variable the impact effect is negative, whereas using hourly earnings it is positive.

[30] This is based on the OLS estimates, where a similar effect is found also in the pre-OPEC data (except for the US, whose effect should almost certainly be estimated by instrumental variables, since the impact effect of wages is estimated by OLS as positive). The change in estimated wage effects when material prices are omitted is even more pronounced using instrumental variables.

[31] A more sophisticated approach would be to allow for regimes where demand shift variables determined employment and regimes where real wages did so.

[32] (i) There is a problem with the last, because the *ex ante* real interest rate *should* appear in the neo-classical labour-demand function since it affects the real cost of work in progress. But we did not have the data to include it.

(ii) We have also tested *world* manufacturing prices relative to domestic manufacturing prices (including as well relative export prices). This is a demand variable if it is interpreted as measuring substitution of foreign exports for own exports in world markets. Only Canada had significant results with plausible dynamics. In other cases either the impact effect was wrongly signed for three quarters (in a cumulative sense) or the total effect was insignificant.

[33] See also *Brookings Papers on Economic Activity*, No. 2, 1978, which was exclusively devoted to this.

[34] Liberal/SDP Alliance Commission on Employment and Industrial Recovery (1982) and Social Democratic Party (1982). See also the 1983 election manifesto of the Liberal/SDP Alliance. In France a form of tax-based prices and incomes policy was in force for eight months in 1975 but was dropped due to the excessive complexity of the scheme.

[35] If unemployment would be lower if union power were reduced, this does not imply that the rise in unemployment in the 1970s was due to increased union power (see Section I). As Jackman and Layard (1982a) argue, it could occur with constant union power, linked to misperception about feasible real-wage growth.

[36] He also found the same for a world where unions fixed wages.

[37] To find out whether net real wages would rise we need to know the sign of

$$d\{W(1-t)\} = dW \left(1 - t - W \frac{dt}{dW} \right)$$

where t is the tax rate and W the gross wage rate. Assuming no change in the budget deficit the government budget constraint is

$$tWE - (1 - E)B = \text{constant}$$

where E is employment and B unemployment benefit. Hence

$$(t + B/W) \frac{dE}{dW} \cdot \frac{W}{E} + t + \frac{dt}{dW} W = 0.$$

Hence when wages fall, net wages rise if

$$-\frac{dE}{dW} \cdot \frac{W}{E} > \frac{1}{t + B/W}.$$

Of course if the budget deficit were allowed to rise a less stringent condition would apply.

References

Barro, R. and Grossman, H. (1971), 'A General Disequilibrium Model of Income and Employment', *American Economic Review* LXI.1, 82–93.

Bruno, M. and Sachs, J. (1982), 'Input Price Shocks and the Slowdown in Economic Growth: The Case of UK Manufacturing', *Review of Economic Studies* XLIX.159, 679–705.

Geary, P. T. and Kennan, J. (1982), 'The Employment–Real Wage Relationship: an International Study', *Journal of Political Economy* 90.4, Aug., 854–72.

88   D. GRUBB, R. LAYARD, AND J. SYMONS

Grubb, D., Jackman, R., and Layard, R. (1982), 'Causes of the Current Stag-
flation', *Review of Economic Studies* XLIC.159, 707–30.
Grubb, D., Jackman, R., and Layard, R. (1983), 'Wage Rigidity and Unemploy-
ment in OECD Countries', *European Economic Review* 21.1/2, 11–39.
Hopcroft, M. and Symons, J. (1983), 'A Demand for Labour Schedule in the
Road Haulage Industry', Centre for Labour Economics, London School
of Economics, Discussion Paper No. 169.
Jackman, R. and Layard, R. (1982a), 'Trade Unions, the NAIRU, and a Wage-
Inflation Tax', *Economica* 49, Aug., 232–9.
Jackman, R. and Layard, R. (1982b), 'An Inflation Tax', *Fiscal Studies* 3.1,
47–59.
Jackman, R., Layard, R., and Pissarides, C. (1983), 'On Vacancies', Centre for
Labour Economics, London School of Economics, Discussion Paper
No. 165.
Layard, R. (1982), *More Jobs, Less Inflation*, Grant McIntyre.
Liberal/SDP Alliance Commission on Employment and Industrial Recovery
(1982), *Back to Work* (Interim Report), Poland Street Publications,
9 Poland Street, London W1, Aug.
Nickell, S. (1979), 'The Effect of Unemployment and Related Benefits on the
Duration of Unemployment', *Economic Journal* 89.353, Mar., 34–50.
Nickell, S. (1982), 'The Determinants of Equilibrium Unemployment in Britain',
Economic Journal 92.367, Sept., 555–76.
Nickell, S. and Andrews, M. (1983), 'Unions, Real Wages and Employment in
Britain, 1951–79', *Oxford Economic Papers*, 35.4, Nov., 509–30.
Pissarides, C. (1982), 'The Effect of a Wage Tax on Equilibrium Unemployment',
Centre for Labour Economics, London School of Economics, Discussion
Paper No. 118.
Pissarides, C. (1983), 'Tax-based incomes policies and the long-run inflation-
unemployment trade-off', Centre for Labour Economics, London School
of Economics, Discussion Paper No. 146.
Sargent, T. J. (1978), 'Estimates of Dynamic Labor Demand Schedules under
Rational Expectations', *Journal of Political Economy* 86.6, Dec., 1009–45.
Social Democratic Party (1982), *Economic Policy*, Policy Document No. 1.
SDP, 4 Cowley Street, London SW1.
Symons, J. (1982), 'Relative Prices and the Demand for Labour in British Manu-
facturing', Centre for Labour Economics, London School of Economics,
Discussion Paper No. 137.
Symons, J. and Layard, R. (1983), 'Neo-classical Demand for Labour Functions
for Six Major Economies', Centre for Labour Economics, London School
of Economics, Discussion Paper No. 166.
Wallich, H. C. and Weintraub, S. (1971), 'A Tax-Based Incomes Policy', *Journal
of Economic Issues* 5, 1–19.

4
Stabilization Policy and Wage Formation in Economies with Strong Trade Unions

LARS CALMFORS

Strong trade unions and highly centralized wage bargaining are characteristic features of several of the smaller European economies. The aim of
this chapter is to discuss the relation between stabilization policy and
wage formation in these economies. The *first* section sketches an empirical background. The *second* section develops a theoretical framework.

I. An Empirical Background

The main problem for all OECD countries during the last decade has
been the new types of shocks. Whereas the 1950s and 1960s were
characterized by temporary demand disturbances, the 1970s have
been dominated by permanent supply shocks: domestic wage disturbances, and two oil-price shocks, slower productivity growth, and new
competitors in the world market.

The temporary demand disturbances of the 1950s and 1960s could
be met by counter-cyclical monetary and fiscal policies. The new types
of shocks have required slower real-wage growth. But a rapid real-wage
adjustment did not come about after the first oil shock in 1973-4.
The resulting divergence between 'warranted' and actual real wages
is usually seen as a major cause of the international stagnation (cf.,
for example, Bruno 1981 or Sachs 1979, 1982).

The small European economies

As a starting-point I shall take the experiences of seven smaller European economies: Sweden, Finland, Norway, Denmark, Belgium, the
Netherlands, and Austria. According to the classification by Blyth
(1979) in Fig. 4.1, these countries all have a high degree of unionization and centralization of wage bargaining.[1]

Table 4.1 shows how the consumer real wage (the wage income of
employees deflated by the consumer price index) and the product

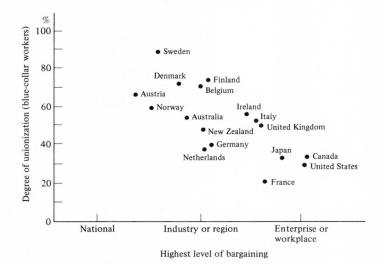

Fig. 4.1: Unionization and centralization of wage bargaining
Source: Blyth (1979).

real wage in manufacturing (the wage cost to employers deflated by
the valued added price) have developed in the seven economies. It
gives a picture of very modest adjustments in consumer real-wage
growth in 1974-6 (in Sweden and Norway the consumer real wage
even increased more rapidly than in 1964-73). It is not until the
1977-82 period that a significant decline took place. There was more
of an adjustment in the product real wage in manufacturing in 1974-6,
but here too, the major adjustment came later. In these respects there
is a clear difference from the larger OECD countries, where the deceleration in real-wage growth came earlier.

One major policy problem in all the seven small economies has
thus been to accomplish a real-wage adjustment that permits a return
to both full employment and external balance. According to the
conventional wisdom, such an adjustment can be made in three different ways: (1) through a *devaluation policy* that increases the rate
of price inflation above the rate of wage inflation; (2) through *restrictive demand policies* that lower the rate of wage inflation below the
rate of price inflation; or (3) through some kind of *incomes policy* that
lowers wage inflation without demand deflation.

The seven countries differ widely in their choice of methods. The
different strategies used are compared below with the help of Figs. 4.2
A–G. The *first* panel in each diagram shows the development of the
consumer real wage and decomposes it into changes in price and wage

inflation.[2] The *second* panel shows gross profit shares, relative unit labour costs, and the effective exchange rate. The *third* panel shows open unemployment, net financial savings of the government sector, and the current account.

Individual country experiences[3]

Despite the differences in policy strategies the similarities in overall macroeconomic development between the countries are surprisingly great. The standard development is a peak in both annual money-wage and annual real-wage increases around 1974-5, whereas relative unit labour costs peak and the profit share in manufacturing falls dramatically in 1975-7. In the last years of the seventies this development is reversed and an adjustment of real-wage growth, relative costs, and profit shares starts. Despite this, open unemployment has been rising especially towards the end of the period and both the current account and the public sector usually show large deficits.

There are *three* characteristic features of the *Swedish* choice of adjustment strategy. *First*, direct government intervention in wage formation has been almost totally absent (the exceptions are an attempt in 1980 at buying wage moderation in exchange for tax reductions that failed and some 'jawboning' in 1982-3.[4] *Second*, open unemployment has been kept very low by international standards but at a high price in terms of current-account and government budget performance. *Third*, there has been an excessive reliance on exchange-rate policy as the method of accomplishing a real-wage adjustment: major discretionary devaluations against a currency basket were undertaken in 1977, 1981, and 1982. The result has been reductions in real wages in all years from 1977 onwards except in 1979, a reduction in relative unit labour costs, and an increase again in the profit share in manufacturing. But the price has been a continued rapid inflation (in fact inflation reached an overall peak for the period shown as late as 1980).

Like Sweden, *Finland* opted for a devaluation policy in 1977-8. But in contrast to Sweden these policies were combined with very restrictive demand policies that caused unemployment to rise significantly. The government has also taken a more direct part in wage formation and voluntary agreements between the government and the labour-market parties have been made. These 'social contracts' have included tax reliefs, increases in welfare payments, and price controls. These policies were very successful in 1977-9; real-wage growth and relative unit labour costs were lowered and the profit share in manufacturing increased. This resulted in a period of rapid export-led growth and a better current-account and government budget development than in Sweden. But despite a certain reduction, open unemployment has remained at a considerably higher level than in

TABLE 4.1
Real-wage Developments
(Average annual percentage changes)

	Consumer real wage[a]			Product real wage[b]		
	1964–73	1974–6	1977–82	1964–73	1974–6	1977–81
Sweden	3.7	4.1	−2.0	7.6	3.5	1.7
Norway	3.6	7.3	−1.0	5.5	4.9	0.6
Finland	5.0	2.9	0.5	6.5	4.1	3.7
Denmark	5.0	4.7	−1.1	7.4	7.0	2.6
Belgium	6.2	5.8	1.6	8.7	10.4	5.4
Netherlands	5.4[c]	4.2	0.5	n.a.	5.6	4.8
Austria	5.1	4.3	1.4	7.8[c]	6.5	3.4
Average for small countries	4.9	4.8	0	7.2[d]	6.0	3.2
Average for seven large OECD countries[e]	4.2[f]	2.9 (2.9)[f]	0.9 (0.8)[f]	6.7	4.8	3.9
Average for four large European OECD countries[g]	5.1	3.4	1.6	6.6	5.0	4.3

^a Real-wage income in terms of consumer price index for workers in manufacturing.
^b Total wage cost for all employees in manufacturing in terms of implicit value-added deflator in purchasers' value adjusted for indirect taxes less subsidies. For Finland, Norway, and Austria, the product real wage is for workers in manufacturing only.
^c 1965–73.
^d Excluding the Netherlands.
^e Italy, Germany, France, Britain, Japan, Canada, and the US.
^f Excluding Japan.
^g Italy, Germany, France, and Britain.

Sources: Bureau of Labor Statistics, US Department of Labor. Swedish Employers' Confederation, 'Wages and total labor costs for workers, International Surveys 1963–1980'. OECD, *National Accounts of OECD countries*. IMF, *International Financial Statistics*. OECD, *Economic Outlook*, July 1983.

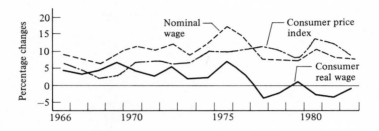

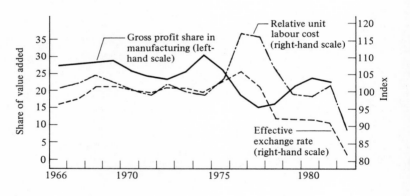

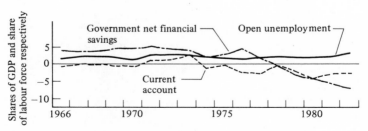

Fig. 4.2A: Sweden

For sources on Figs. 4.2A–G see page 101

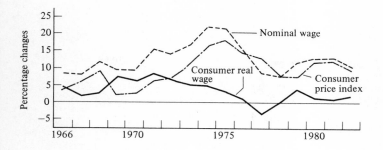

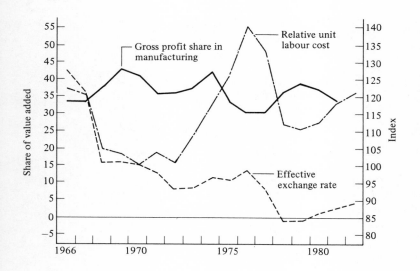

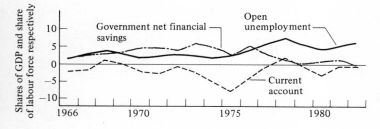

Fig. 4.2B: Finland

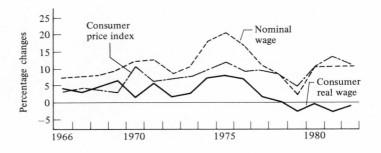

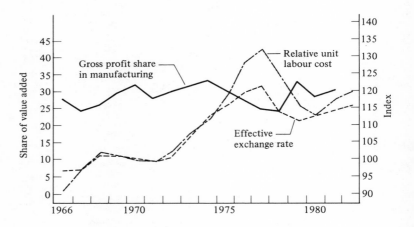

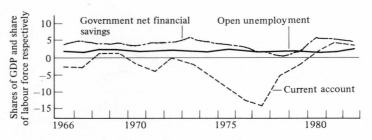

Fig. 4.2C: Norway

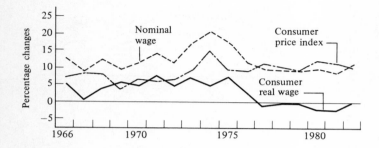

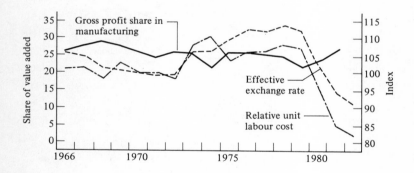

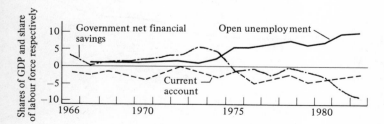

Fig. 4.2D: Denmark

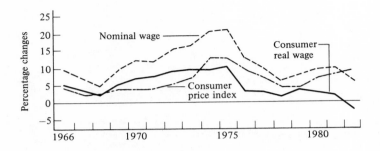

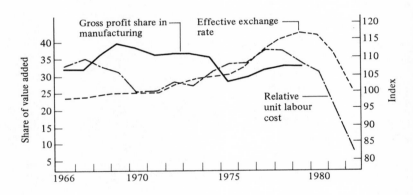

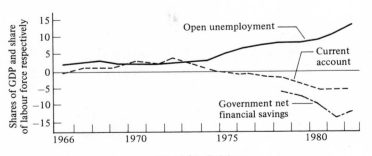

Fig. 4.2E: Belgium

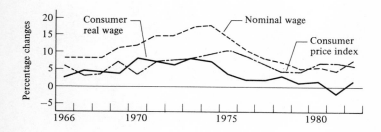

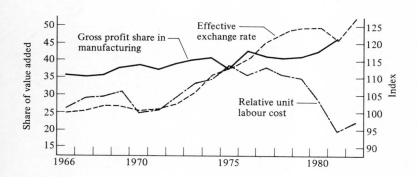

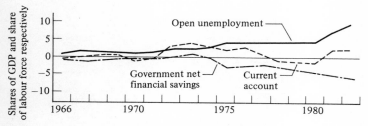

Fig. 4.2F: The Netherlands

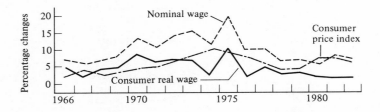

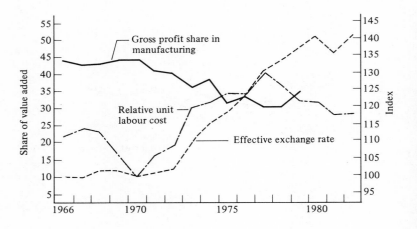

Fig. 4.2G: Austria

Sweden. An increased rate of wage inflation in 1979–81 contributed to higher real-wage growth again, with the result that relative unit labour costs increased and the profit share fell again. This development illustrates the difficulties of achieving a *permanent* adjustment of real wages and relative costs. Higher capacity utilization can rapidly cause wage inflation again. This explains why new devaluations were made in 1982.

Norway chose a devaluation strategy similar to the Swedish one in 1977–8 (although the devaluations were smaller). Norway also resembles Sweden in its choice of demand policies that have kept open unemployment low. But deficit problems have been avoided because of the oil revenues that have accrued mainly to the government. Another difference is the Norwegian incomes policy tradition: since the early sixties there has existed 'a formal means of bringing together government and representatives of the central bodies of trade unions and employers, together with farmers and fishermen, to discuss the economic forecast and its analysis before the bargaining commenced'.[5] In the second half of the seventies these informal incomes policies were complemented with 'social contracts' in which the government attempted to buy wage moderation in exchange for continued employment policies and tax concessions. (The 1977 Tripartite Agreement even included a government commitment to adjust taxes to achieve a guaranteed growth of real disposable income.) A formal wage and price freeze was also in effect in 1978–9. Together these measures have succeeded in achieving real-wage reductions from 1978 onwards. This development has a counterpart in reduced relative unit labour costs and an increased profit share in manufacturing. In 1981–2 wage inflation has, however, again eroded the relative cost position. This has been counteracted through two smaller devaluations in 1982.

Denmark differs from the other Nordic countries to the extent that a hard-currency option was tried for a longer time (by pegging to the D-Mark). Although severe deficit problems have emerged, open unemployment has at the same time been permitted to rise drastically.

Sources for Figs. 4.2A–G. Nominal wage and consumer price index: Various issues of Swedish Employers' Confederation, 'Wages and Total Labour Costs for Workers: International Survey'; IMF, *International Financial Statistics*; and OECD, *Economic Outlook*, July 1983. Gross profit share in manufacturing: OECD, *Economic Outlook*, Historical Statistics 1960–81, Paris, 1983, for all countries except Austria and Belgium, where calculations from the Swedish Employers' Confederation have been used. Effective exchange rates and relative unit labour costs have been supplied by Sixten Korkman and Masamichi Khono at the OECD secretariat. MERM weights have been used (cf. Rhomberg 1976). Unemployment, current account, and government net financial savings: OECD, *Economic Outlook*, Dec. 1982 and July 1983; OECD, *National Accounts 1964–81*, vol. II, Paris, 1983.

But this policy was not successful in improving the relative cost position and raising the profit share of manufacturing. It was not until the hard-currency policy was abandoned and a major depreciation of the effective exchange rate took place in 1979 that the relative cost and profit situation improved. The most surprising feature of the Danish development is probably that the high unemployment has not resulted in significantly lower wage increases than in the other Nordic countries even though the government has intervened directly in wage formation. One possible explanation is the system of wage indexation, which has guaranteed automatic compensation for consumer-price increases. Government intervention has also been quite modest: laws regulating wages for 1977–8 and 1979–80 mainly represented a way out when employers and trade unions could not agree, although certain marginal changes in the indexation system were also made. Stronger incomes policy measures were not undertaken until 1982 when there was a one-year wage freeze and a suspension of indexation for three years.

The *Belgian* experience has many similarities with the Danish one. A hard-currency policy has been followed. Open unemployment has risen dramatically. Still, money-wage increases have remained on a Nordic level. The hard-currency policy has, however, held down price inflation. The outcome has been a much smaller decrease in real-wage growth than in the Nordic countries—in fact a real-wage reduction did not occur until 1982. Yet there has been an improvement in the relative cost position partly helped by an effective depreciation in 1981 (reflecting the rise of the dollar). As the increase in unemployment and the deficit problems suggest, the real-wage adjustment has been far too small. This explains why a devaluation was undertaken in 1982. Incomes policy measures have also been taken: a two-year real-wage freeze was introduced in 1981 and in 1982 limitations on wage indexation were introduced.

The Netherlands and *Austria* have both stuck to a hard-currency option by pegging to the D-Mark during the whole period after the first oil crisis (the effective depreciation in 1981 again reflects the rise of the dollar). Both provide examples of how adjustments of real wages and relative costs can be made by reducing wage inflation instead of raising price inflation. In fact, money-wage increases have been lowered even below the rates of the early seventies. The fall in the rate of real-wage growth has been largest in the Netherlands—the Austrian real-wage development in 1977–81 closely resembles the Belgian one (the same holds for relative costs). In the Netherlands, there has been a rise in open unemployment, whereas only a modest increase has taken place in Austria. In both countries, incomes policies have formed part of the adjustment process. In the Netherlands, a continuous incomes policy has been operated. There is no corresponding list of incomes policy measures in the other countries. It includes legislative action, voluntary and compulsory guide-lines (the latter being backed by threats of legislation), tax reliefs in order to buy wage moderation, and expansive fiscal policy measures conditional on wage restraint. In Austria, incomes policies have worked more informally through the traditional co-operation between the government, employers, and trade unions within the 'social partnership' that has been formalized within the tripartite Joint Commission for Prices and Wages.[6]

Factors behind the choice of strategy

The most striking conclusion from the empirical review is probably the difficulty of arriving at clear-cut conclusions about suitable adjustment strategies. None of the countries is close to anything that can be labelled macroeconomic equilibrium.

The social-contract strategy of Austria has perhaps been the most successful one, since it has helped to bring about a certain real-wage adjustment without heavy unemployment or rapid inflation. But the adjustment has been comparatively small and serious deficit problems remain here, too. Sweden is an example of an opposite strategy: through rapid inflation a very significant real-wage adjustment has been achieved at the same time as open unemployment has been held down, but the deficit problems are even more pronounced.

The effects of unemployment on wage formation seem diverse. In Belgium and Denmark, high rates of unemployment by themselves proved rather unsuccessful in accomplishing a real-wage adjustment and finally resort had to be made to devaluations. In the Netherlands, the effects have been more significant. Norway and Finland on the other hand are cases where low or reduced rates of unemployment may have broken the trend towards increased international competitiveness.

What is most surprising is perhaps that similar countries have chosen so widely differing adjustment strategies. This may reflect both different political *priorities* between the various macroeconomic goals and different perceptions about the *causes* of the real-wage problem. I shall concentrate on this last aspect.

Like Sachs (1982) it may then be helpful to distinguish between the following three real-wage concepts: (1) the actual real wage; (2) the real wage 'desired' by wage-setters (i.e. the outcome that the bargaining parties aimed at); and (3) the real wage that gives full employment. Using these concepts one can distinguish between *two* causes of excessive real wages.

The *first* possibility is that the actual real wage is higher than both the desired and the full-employment real wage. This may occur because of downward inflexibility of money wages. Wage-setters may during recent years have gradually come to realize the need for a real-wage adjustment but can have failed to accomplish this because of the combination of a lower 'floor' for money-wage increases and 'too low' price inflation.[7] If this is the case, the obvious solution is to resort to devaluation.

The *second* and difficult case is when both the actual and desired real wage exceed the full-employment real wage. Then a devaluation policy can at best work temporarily: price inflation will soon trigger off new wage increases. Instead policies must aim at changing the desired real wage.

It is always impossible to judge with certainty *ex ante* the particular situation in which a given country finds itself. And it is still too early to draw conclusions *ex post*: the long-run outcomes of various policies are still unclear.

What I shall do is to focus on the *second* case, which is *analytically* the most interesting one. As my starting-point I shall take the widely held opinion that the active employment policies during the post-war period have been a major factor behind a too rapid real-wage growth.[8] It is particularly natural to stress this link in an analysis of the smaller European OECD economies where the pursuit of full-employment targets has been especially strong.

With this view, the real-wage problem is thus seen as a more fundamental long-run problem than just a short-run failure to adjust to the supply shocks of the seventies. For example Sachs (1979) discusses this hypothesis as an explanation of the post-war trend towards lower profit shares in manufacturing in the European OECD countries (cf. also Söderström and Viotti 1979 and Lindbeck 1983).

The idea is to set up a model that catches the specific labour-market characteristics of the smaller OECD countries. The analysis will be speculative in the sense that it merely *suggests* possible explanations: empirical work is needed to test whether there are systematic differences in wage behaviour between countries with different institutional set-ups in the labour market.

II. A Theoretical Framework

The main idea is to model stabilization policy and wage formation as a *game* between the government and wage-earner organizations. A very simple framework will be used.[9] But in the end some of the major simplifications are modified.

I shall make the heroic assumption that only *one* trade union organizes *all* labour and that this trade union *unilaterally* determines the wage rate. Employers are assumed to accept the wage rate set by the trade union and make individual output and employment decisions on the basis of it.[10] These simplifications can be seen as a schematic picture of an economy where the majority of wage-earners are organized in a small number of wage-earner organizations, and where the factors determining the wage demands of trade unions also exert a major influence on the final outcome of wage negotiations between unions and employer organizations.

How will such a trade union act? Assume that it cares about the real wage and about the level of employment. When it sets the wage rate, it thus trades off the positive effects of a higher real wage against increased unemployment.[11]

The decision problem of the trade union is depicted in Fig. 4.3A. The goals of the trade union are illustrated by a series of indifference curves which each show combinations of real wage and employment that it regards as giving the same welfare. The further north-east an indifference curve lies, the higher is the welfare experienced by the trade union. The negatively sloped line shows the relation between the demand for labour and the real wage.[12]

The trade union now chooses a combination of real wage and employment that gives it the highest welfare. It thus chooses the point where the employment line is tangent to an indifference curve (point A with the real wage w_0 and the employment level E_0 in Fig. 4.3A).[13]

It is quite likely that a trade union acting in this way sets a wage that results in lower employment than the government finds acceptable. But to focus on the effects of government policies I shall assume that the government accepts the employment level E_0 as its employment target.

Temporary shocks and stabilization policy

One can imagine various types of disturbances in the model. The trade union may, for example, overestimate international price increases—as probably was the case in Sweden in the wage agreement for 1975-6—and therefore choose such a high nominal wage rate that the result becomes a higher real wage and therefore a lower level of employment than desired.[14] In Fig. 4.3A the real wage becomes w_1 instead of w_0, and employment E_1 instead of E_0.

One can also think of other types of disturbances (for example an increase in the relative price of oil or a productivity decline) that lower the demand for labour at a *given* real wage. In Fig. 4.4A the demand schedule for labour is shifted to the left from I to II. If the disturbance is not anticipated and the real wage has therefore been set in advance to w_0, the consequence is a fall in employment from E_0 to E_2.

In both cases the government can stabilize employment by increasing

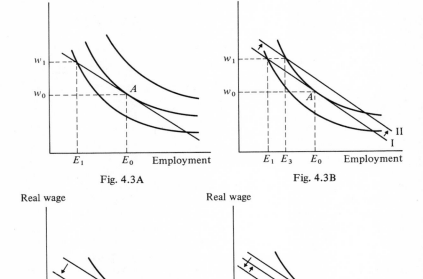

Fig. 4.3A   Fig. 4.3B

Fig. 4.4A   Fig. 4.4B

government expenditure. To simplify, I shall assume that these expenditure increases take the form of directly employing labour in the public sector at the same wage as in the private sector (which is assumed to consist of only one production sector).[15] In Figs. 4.3B and 4.4B the demand schedule is shifted to the right again, with the consequence that the fall in employment is counteracted (employment falls only to E_3).

One can now sketch an 'ideal' interaction between the government and the trade union. When there are *temporary* disturbances, the government stabilizes employment through active stabilization policies. In exchange, the trade union sets a real wage that under normal circumstances results in high employment. In the terminology of the Scandinavian model of wage formation, wages follow a stable 'main course', whereas temporary disturbances are met by temporary government policy measures. This would seem to correspond to a common picture of the division of labour between labour-market organizations and governments in the Scandinavian countries in the 1950s and 1960s.[16]

Accommodation of permanent shocks

The employment policies above are purely stabilizing: they reduce employment variations in the case of temporary shocks but do not affect the equilibrium of the economy in the absence of shocks. But the situation changes when disturbances are *permanent*.

Take the case of a permanent fall in the demand for labour caused by, for example, a permanent relative price increase for oil. If there is a parallel shift to the left of the demand schedule as in Fig. 4.5, the result will be a fall in both the real wage and employment once

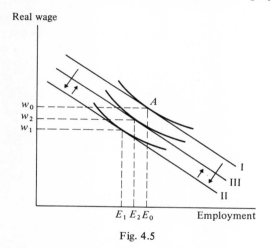

Fig. 4.5

the trade union perceives this shift.[17] But if the demand schedule is shifted to the right again through fiscal policies, the fall in employment becomes smaller but so does the real-wage adjustment. This picture would seem to catch important aspects of what happened in those OECD countries that tried to 'bridge' the recession after the first oil crisis.

So far the assumption of *centralized* wage-setting has played no major role. The conclusion that an offsetting demand policy reduces the real-wage adjustment follows from any reasonable model of wage formation regardless of the degree of centralization. But below I shall focus on an effect of general demand policies that is specific to centralized wage setting.[18]

Suppose that government employment policies are *unconditional* in the sense that employment goals are pursued independently of the origins of shocks, i.e. also in the case of wage disturbances. This is my reading of policies in the smaller European economies during the sixties and early seventies.

Such a situation is depicted in Fig. 4.6. Line I shows the labour-demand schedule in the absence of exogenous shocks at a given level of public employment. If the trade union believes in this labour demand schedule, it will choose the real wage w_0. If the real wage is increased to w_1, employment is expected to fall to E_1. This would cause expected welfare to decrease for the trade union. But now assume that it expects government to increase employment in the public sector in the event of such a real-wage increase, so that total employment only falls to E_4 ($E_4 - E_1$ extra workers become employed in the public sector). For the same reason the trade union expects an increase in the real wage to w_2 to lead only to a fall in total employment to E_2. If these expected policy reactions are taken into account, the perceived labour-demand schedule becomes less elastic (line II).[19]

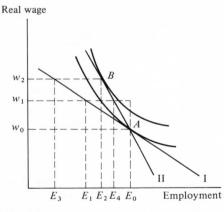

Fig. 4.6

If the trade union expects such policy reactions from the government, it is likely to change its own behaviour. This is most easily illustrated if we assume away all intertemporal considerations by the trade union. Then point A no longer gives the highest welfare. If the real-wage rate is increased to w_1, employment falls only to E_4, whereas the indifference curve shows that the trade union is willing to accept a fall to E_2. The trade union can thus make a welfare gain by increasing the real wage above w_0. As the diagram has been drawn, the highest welfare level is now attained at the real wage w_2 and employment E_2 at point B.[20]

The accommodation policy thus affects the equilibrium of the economy in the absence of exogenous shocks. It causes the trade union to choose a higher real wage with the paradoxical result that employment falls. The explanation is simple: accommodation policies lower the price of an increased real wage in terms of unemployment and therefore create an incentive for the trade union to choose a higher real wage and lower employment.[21] At the same time employment policies cause an expansion of the public sector (public-sector employment is increased by $E_2 - E_3$). In combination with increased costs for unemployment benefits and lower tax incomes (employment falls by $E_0 - E_2$), this causes a government budget deficit (if the budget was balanced at A). In an open economy this will have its counterpart in a current-account deficit.

In my example, intertemporal considerations were neglected. In a more complex analysis they could be introduced. A superrational trade union would make a full-fledged intertemporal optimization and weigh the benefits from increased government expenditure against possible future welfare losses (future government expenditure may have to be cut down or future taxes increased). If the size of the public sector is regarded as too small by the trade union, it will still make a net welfare gain from an expansion of the public sector and it will thus pay to let a wage increase trigger it off.[22]

The fact that the trade-union movements in the countries studied have usually been lobbying for an expansion of the public sector—in fact they have in the past been among the strongest pressure groups —gives strong support to the view that trade unions indeed did regard the public sector as too small.[23] One could enumerate several possible reasons for this: (1) trade unions are mostly continuously socialist-dominated whereas the political power (at least potentially) changes between socialist and bourgeois parties; (2) governments (especially bourgeois ones) may see themselves also as representatives of 'capitalists', who may receive small benefits from increased government expenditure but have to bear a large share of future tax costs; (3) the future costs of budget deficits may be underestimated or not understood by trade-union decision-makers (especially if budget deficits are misinterpreted as being only cyclical); (4) trade-union decision-making may simply fail to take long-run effects into account.[24]

III. Methods of Real-wage Adjustment

The starting-point for the subsequent analysis is that employment policies in economies with centralized wage-setting have indeed contributed to stagflation and government budget deficits. I shall discuss
four possible strategies to cope with this situation: (1) a non-
accommodation policy; (2) continued accommodation but with less
ambitious employment targets; (3) a tax-based incomes policy (TIP);
and (4) a social contract.[25] To simplify I shall continue to neglect
intertemporal considerations and use Fig. 4.6, assuming that the economy has ended up at point B. The government is assumed to aim at
reaching point A.[26]

A non-accommodation policy

A first possible strategy for the government is to choose a non-
accommodation policy, i.e. to abstain from policy measures in
order to reduce unemployment caused by an excessive real wage.
If the government announces that it will follow such a policy, incentives for a real-wage adjustment are created.

In Fig. 4.6, the government can announce that it will no longer
use fiscal policy in order to keep up employment when the real wage
exceeds w_0. The labour-demand schedule is then pivoted back from
II to I. Then the real wage w_0 again gives the highest welfare for the
trade union. If this real wage is chosen, employment increases again.

The problem with this policy is *credibility*. If the trade union
believes that the government will not dare to pursue an announced
non-accommodation policy and that the policy declarations are only
an attempt to 'talk down' the real wage, it may stick to the real wage
w_2. The government is then faced with a difficult dilemma. If it chooses
the non-accommodation policy, employment falls to E_3. If it continues
to accommodate then no incentives for a return to macroeconomic
balance are created.

If the economy gets caught in such a credibility trap, it may be tempt-
ing to try to avoid it through a devaluation. By increasing the price
level, the real wage may be reduced to w_0 again (if there is some short-run
stickiness of the money wage).[27] But such a policy can only be a
temporary solution. As long as the government does not show that it is
prepared to accept unemployment when the real wage is too high, the
trade union is likely to continue to strive for the real wage w_2; it may
believe that this real wage will be accommodated through fiscal policies
if only it succeeds in achieving it. If the government and the trade
union in this way try to achieve inconsistent real-wage goals, a vicious
wage–exchange rate spiral may emerge.[28] The Finnish devaluation cycle
analysed by, for example, Korkman (1978) may be an example of that.

If a credibility problem arises, it seems impossible to avoid a period of temporary unemployment in order to convince the trade union that the government means serious business.

An accommodation policy with a lower employment target

A second possibility is to continue accommodation policies but to lower the employment target around which the employment stabilization takes place (this is *one* possible interpretation of, for example, Belgian and Danish policies, where higher unemployment has been accepted at the same time as employment programmes have been launched in order to prevent further unemployment increases). Such a policy shifts the employment curve II parallel to the left in Fig. 4.7.[29]

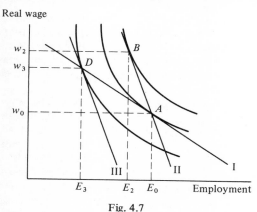

Fig. 4.7

It creates an incentive for the trade union to reduce the real wage, but employment will then also fall. If the employment target is reduced by so much that the size of the public sector is restored to the original level that prevailed at A, the new equilibrium is at D.[30] But if the government budget was balanced at A, this point still involves a government budget deficit; since employment is lower than at A, tax incomes are smaller and the cost of unemployment benefits larger. To restore budget balance, the employment line must be shifted even further to the left. This further reduces the equilibrium level of employment.

In principle this policy of continued accommodation around a lower employment target meets the same credibility problem as the non-accommodation policy above. If the trade union does not believe a policy announcement that the employment target has been lowered, it may continue to set the real wage w_2.

If one compares the equilibrium outcomes of the non-accommodation policy and the accommodation policy with a lower employment target, the latter is clearly inferior for both the government and the trade union: employment is lower at D than at A and the trade union finds itself on a lower indifference curve.

Tax-based incomes policies (TIP)

A third possibility is to use taxes to create incentives for a real-wage adjustment. So-called tax-based incomes policies (TIP) are often presented as a Keynesian alternative to a non-accommodation policy.[31] The idea is to use tax increases instead of unemployment as the deterrent against too high wages.

Most TIP proposals, however, presuppose *decentralized* wage-setting. This is, for example, the case in Layard (1982) where a TIP is analysed with a model similar to mine. His proposal is to impose a tax on *individual firms* on that part of the wage bill that corresponds to wage increases above a certain norm. The effect is to flatten the individual firms' labour-demand schedules and thereby create incentives for trade unions bargaining with individual firms to choose lower real wages.

As in most TIP proposals Layard combines the wage tax with a general tax rebate that is distributed among firms in proportion to their total wage-bill. The tax rebate is chosen so that the overall fiscal effect on labour demand becomes zero (the average employer's cost per worker does not change). As a consequence, the TIP will create no aggregate unemployment if the average real wage exceeds the norm. The trick with a TIP of this type is thus that incentives for wage restraint are created on the *microeconomic* level without giving rise to unwanted *macroeconomic* effects if the policy fails. The reason why the system presupposes decentralized wage-setting is that then the tax paid by a certain firm is influenced by the wage setting of the *individual* trade union (that organizes the labour force of the firm), whereas the tax rebate paid out to the union is determined by the aggregate wage development, which the individual firm can affect only marginally. This also explains why the scheme cannot work in a *centralized* system. In the same way as the trade union in my model anticipates employment policies, it will realize that a Layard tax-cum-rebate keeps employers' cost per worker unchanged. My trade union's behaviour will therefore not change.

If a TIP on firms is to work in my model, the tax-rebate part has to be dropped. But then the TIP loses all its advantages and amounts to the same thing as a non-accommodation policy. There is simply no way of affecting wages in my model through a TIP on firms without also affecting aggregate labour demand.

A TIP in a centralized system instead has to be directed towards personal income taxes of the members of trade unions. This is also the form in which proposals for tax-based incomes policies in these economies are usually cast (cf. Hansen 1958 for the first proposal). But it is also an advantage of a centralized system that such a tax policy is possible; in a decentralized system such a policy would presuppose that special tax arrangements were made for the members of each individual union.

In my model, personal income taxes could be made to depend on the real wage in such a way that the maximum after-tax real wage is attained at the real wage desired by the government w_0. When the real wage exceeds w_0, the tax could be increased in such a way that the after-tax real wage is decreased as shown in Fig. 4.8. In that case

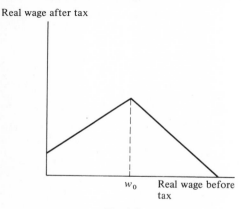

Fig. 4.8

the trade union attains the highest welfare by choosing w_0 also in the case when the government pursues the type of employment policy discussed above.

But such a TIP suffers from a similar credibility problem as the non-accommodation policy. If the trade union does not believe that the government dares to pursue the TIP that has been announced, no real-wage adjustment will take place. Then the threat of a tax increase must be triggered off. But with a TIP, unlike with a non-accommodation policy, the government can continue to stabilize employment so that unemployment can be held down.

A social contract

A fourth possibility is that the government and the trade union try to reach a social contract, i.e. a mutual agreement where the government buys wage restraint from the trade union in exchange for employment policy measures. Such a social contract would seem to catch important features of both the Austrian and Norwegian systems.

It is easily verified that there exist possible social contracts that are superior to the non-co-operative equilibrium at B. Instead of reducing public employment again if the real wage is lowered below w_2, the government could, for example, offer to keep public employment unchanged in exchange for a real-wage reduction to w_4 in Fig. 4.9 (the employment line IV is drawn given the same level of public employment as in B). Both the trade union and the government would benefit from such a bargain. The trade union attains a higher welfare level in E than in B.[32] The government attains higher employment and the budget deficit is reduced (the rise in employment means higher tax incomes and lower unemployment-benefit costs, the lower wage lowers total wage costs in the public sector).

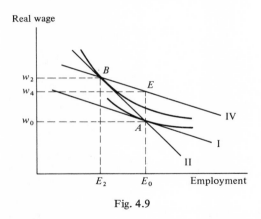

Fig. 4.9

Other social contracts that are superior to the equilibrium with accommodation policies also exist. Although the government employment target may be reached through such social contracts, they do, however, all share the defect that budget balance is not restored.[33]

Conclusions from the model

The conclusions are clear-cut:

(1) A social contract is better than unconditional employment policies but will not restore full macroeconomic equilibrium. Although high employment may be restored, the government budget deficit is likely to remain.

(2) Continued accommodation policies around a lower employment

target are inferior to a non-accommodation policy. Although the government budget deficit may be eliminated, high employment will not be restored.

(3) A return to full macroeconomic equilibrium requires either a shift to a non-accommodation policy or to a tax-based incomes policy directed against wage-earners.

In my model a non-accommodation policy and a TIP directed against wage-earners produce the same result in the long run. The difference lies in the transitional problems if the policies do not 'bite' in the short run: unemployment in the case of non-accommodation, lower after-tax real wages for employed workers in the case of a TIP. In my simplified framework, the choice between the two methods depends upon whether one wants to let the burden of adjustment fall on a minority, the unemployed, or on the majority, employed wage-earners.

IV. A Modified Analysis

So far the conclusions have been drawn from a very simple model. In a more complete analysis more factors must be considered. Below I shall also take into account: (1) that there is a mutual *interdependence* between the *political* and the *economic* system; (2) that in reality there exist *several trade unions* in the economies with centralized wage-setting; and (3) that there is likely to exist a limit to how low nominal wage increases can be.

The interdependence between the economic and political systems

Different views on economic policy in a democracy can reinforce the credibility problems. If there is a political opposition opposing the policies pursued by the government, they immediately become less credible. One could even think of cases when trade unions at times of high unemployment deliberately choose high real wages in order to contribute to a failure of government policies.[34] The idea would be to force through a shift to more expansionary policies either because the government in power itself feels compelled to change its policies in order not to lose the next election *or* because it actually loses the next election. In order to decrease this risk, it is important to have a consensus on the basic rules of the game for stabilization policies between the political parties that could conceivably come into power.

It is also important to find a 'narrow path' between too strong and too weak effects when a non-accommodation policy or a TIP is introduced. If the effects are too small, it is not clear that a policy change really has taken place, and the incentives for trade unions to change their behaviour may be too weak. If the effects become too strong, the risk is that these effects are seen mainly as the consequence of unfair policies on the part of the government and not as the consequence of the behaviour of trade unions. The main result is then likely to be political demands for a change in government policy rather than demands from wage-earners that their organizations should aim at lower wage increases.

The competition between trade unions

Another factor to take into account is the *competition* between *different* wage-earner organizations. Even if different wage-earner organizations sometimes act in collaboration, the tensions between them dominate on other occasions. Wage differentials between groups often seem to play as important a role as the real wage and employment in determining the behaviour of trade unions.[35]

Concern about wage differentials may create problems for a TIP. The reason is the practical impossibility of directing tax changes so that they only affect the members of certain trade unions. Therefore it is easy to conceive of situations akin to the prisoner's dilemma where no organization dares to accept a real-wage decrease, even though everybody knows that the consequence will be a general tax increase: out of fear that others will get higher wages, no union dares to be the first to accept lower real wages. Its members risk getting a lowered relative wage at the same time as they may have to bear part of the tax increases that are triggered off by the behaviour of the other organizations.

The competition between trade unions in a semi-centralized system may thus lock the economy into stagflation with a TIP directed against wage-earners. To avoid this it would seem necessary to combine the TIP with a more traditional incomes policy. If some kind of concerted action can be achieved through active government intervention in the wage formation process, a TIP of this type can be used as an incentive for *all* trade unions to accept lower real wages. But the problem remains that it will pay for the individual trade union to break out of such an agreement.

Wage rivalry is likely to be a much smaller problem for a non-accommodation policy: any group that does not adjust its wage to prevailing demand conditions will suffer a loss of employment. But it is important that no group is exempt from the policy. It is not likely to produce desired results if employees in the government sector have their own organization(s) and if employment there is insensitive to wages (which has been the case in, for example, the Scandinavian countries). Then there is a serious risk that wages are pushed up in the government sector and that this spreads to the private sector: trade unions there may be willing to sacrifice employment in order to protect their relative wages. To avoid this it seems necessary to introduce the same link between wages and employment in the public sector as in the rest of the economy.

A floor for nominal wage increases

A last complication is that there may be a floor for nominal wage increases. There is always a need for changes in relative wages. If these are to be accomplished without nominal wage *decreases* for certain groups, a certain positive level of nominal wage increases is required. In Sweden, for instance, this lower limit was probably raised during the seventies as a consequence of the increased frequency of special arrangements for various groups. This increases the demand for a certain minimum level for average nominal wage increases if *all* groups are still to have general wage increases.

Such a lower floor for nominal wage increases means that a real-wage adjustment can be a long process. Denmark and Belgium in the late seventies and early eighties may be such examples. If one is to avoid such a situation and speed up the adjustment process, devaluations of the types finally undertaken in these countries (and in Finland 1976-7) may be a necessary *complement* to other measures. But they have the drawback that they may reinforce the inertia of nominal wages, since they weaken the incentives to accept low increases.

V. Conclusions

How do the above modifications change the conclusions? The case for a TIP directed at wage-earners is obviously seriously weakened. Such a TIP would seem to have to be combined with more traditional incomes policies. But this presupposes that the government can force all trade unions to co-operate. If this is not the case, there is, of course, still the possibility of using a TIP on firms to influence wage changes in excess of the central agreements—wage drift—which is more in line with the original proposals. But if centralized wage-setting remains unaffected, the efficiency of the policy is seriously weakened. Wage increases negotiated at a central level will only be affected to the extent that these depend upon attempts to 'compensate' for relative wage changes due to wage drift.

As regards the overall policy conclusions from my analysis, one should be careful. I have set up a very simple model to analyse *one* possible hypothesis about the link between employment policies and stagflation. The main message is probably that *if* my hypothesis is true, no easy solution may exist: in fact there seems to be no alternative to a transitional period of high unemployment.

Notes and Sources

* I am grateful to Eva Uddén-Jondal for help with the empirical material and to Sholeh Blom, Birgitta Eliason, and Anita Oxenham for typing.

[1] The figure shows the highest level of wage bargaining. Wage contracts on this level are translated into lower-level contracts through more decentralized bargaining (cf. also Bratt 1981 or Faxén 1982). The Netherlands may appear to be out of place but its well-developed incomes policy tradition and high frequency of government intervention still give bargaining a centralized character.

[2] The expression real wage will subsequently be used to denote the consumer real wage.

[3] The brief accounts below build on various issues of OECD country surveys, Blyth (1979), Bratt (1981) and Faxén (1982).

[4] With these exceptions, direct government intervention has been confined to the role that the public sector plays as a major employer, but in that capacity the effect on several occasions seems to have been to add to wage pressures (this was especially the case in 1980).

[5] Blyth (1979).

[6] Formally, the commission has the right only to regulate prices but not wages (although it can affect the timing of wage negotiations). Nevertheless, it is usually regarded as a semi-governmental institution exerting a moderating influence on wage increases. Cf. the OECD country surveys of Austria, Blyth (1979) or Faxén (1982).

[7] Cf. also p. 117 below.

[8] The McCracken report, *Towards Full Employment and Price Stability* (1977), expresses it in the following way: 'During the course of the great postwar expansion those responsible for price setting and wage bargaining in many countries became so convinced that governments could, and would, maintain high levels of demand and employment that they increasingly behaved as if there was no way in which they could price themselves out of markets or out of jobs.'

[9] The model is presented in greater detail in Calmfors (1982) and Calmfors and Horn (1983a, b). Cf. also Driffill (1983) for a similar analysis.

[10] Alternatively I could have assumed that a certain fraction of the labour force is unorganized but that their wages are set at the same level as those of the trade-union members. This is a common principle in wage contracts in the Nordic countries.

[11] This is the usual assumption in the literature on the behaviour of trade unions. It can be derived from normal assumptions on the preferences of individual members. Cf. Calfors (1982), McDonald and Solow (1981), or Oswald (1982).

[12] I assume that the capital stock is given in the short run, so that labour demand in any given sector depends on the product real wage (the ratio between the money wage and the output price). The trade union cares about the real wage in terms of the consumer price index. In a model with only *one* private sector, these two definitions coincide, but in, for example, a standard two-sector model with traded and non-traded goods, the analysis becomes more complicated. But as long as government policy parameters are constant, there is still a one-to-one correspondence between the consumer real wage and labour demand. Cf. Helpman (1977), Rødseth (1979), or Calmfors (1982).

[13] The assumptions that the trade union sets the wage and employers determine employment has been criticized on the ground that it does not produce a Pareto-efficient bargain (cf. McDonald and Solow 1981): by negotiating an agreement on both the wage and employment, both workers and employers could attain a higher welfare level. The reason for not choosing that type of framework is—apart from the analytical complexities—that centralized bargaining in the countries discussed does not take place in this way. It is only wage rates that are determined centrally; central employers' federations do not have the right to bargain about employment. The reason for this is probably to be found in the difficulties of breaking down centrally negotiated employment changes to the level of individual firms.

[14] Cf., for example, the various issues of *The Swedish Economy*.

[15] The same shift of the labour-demand schedule could be accomplished through direct subsidization of the whole (or parts of) the private sector or through reduced payroll taxes. In an open-economy two-sector model it could also be achieved through increased government spending on non-traded goods provided that non-traded goods are more labour-intensive than traded goods *or* that the supply of non-traded goods is perfectly elastic (cf. Helpman 1977, Rødseth 1979, or Calmfors 1982).

[16] Cf., for example, Aukrust (1977), Edgren, Faxén, and Odhner (1973), Calmfors (1977), or Lindbeck (1979).

[17] Cf., for example, Calmfors (1982), Calmfors and Horn (1983a), or Oswald (1982). The effect is analogous to an income effect of a shift of the budget line in the theory of demand.

[18] The effect analysed below can arise under *decentralized* wage setting only if demand policies are *selective* and directed at specific industries. The model can be reinterpreted to cover this case.

[19] If we denote the real wage w, employment in the absence of stabilization policies N, the government employment target $\bar{E}$, and the number of workers that are employed in the public sector for employment-policy reasons G, the government employment policy rule is:

(i) $$G = \gamma\{\bar{E} - N(w)\} \qquad 0 < \gamma < 1.$$

Actual employment E when government employment policies are taken into account therefore becomes:

(ii) $$E = N(w) + G = \gamma\bar{E} + (1 - \gamma)\,N(w).$$

[20] We neglect the utility derived from increased *output* in the public sector. This effect can easily be included and indeed strengthens the conclusion above. Cf. Calmfors and Horn (1983a, b).

[21] The effect is analogous to a substitution effect in the theory of demand.

[22] Cf. Calmfors and Horn (1983a, b) for a detailed analysis.

[23] An account of the Swedish debate is given in Lindbeck (1974).

[24] The list is, of course, speculative. A full analysis requires a complete model of democratic decision-making in both trade unions and the political system.

[25] A fifth method is to let the government take over the responsibility for wage setting through permanent legislation. I do not consider this, since the model is not suitable for analysing the possibilities of such a policy.

[26] I thus restrict the analysis to the equilibrium of the economy in the absence of shocks. This means that I cannot, as Driffill (1983), analyse the optimal degree of stabilization in a situation when the government is unable to distinguish whether unemployment is caused by wage disturbances or exogenous shocks.

[27] A devaluation policy thus accommodates the money wage chosen by the trade union, at the same time as it reduces the *real* wage.

[28] From the simple model above it is impossible to determine the outcome of such a strategy for the long-run average real wage. This requires a richer model that takes account of inflation as an argument in explicit utility functions for both the government and the trade union. My guess is that governments care more about inflation than trade unions, and that the government therefore is likely to give in first.

[29] According to equation (ii) in footnote 19, the change in employment for a given wage rate is $dE = \gamma d\bar{E}$.

[30] This is the case analysed by Driffill (1983).

[31] The original proposal was made by Wallich and Weintraub (1971). Cf. also, for example, Seidmann (1978).

[32] To simplify, the diagram has been drawn on the assumption that changes in public employment do not result in output changes in the public sector that affect the perceived welfare of the trade union. Taking such effects into account does not change the conclusion that a social contract that is superior to B exists, as shown by Calmfors and Horn (1983b).

[33] Cf. Calmfors and Horn (1983b). The reason is that all such co-operative equilibria involve higher public employment and a higher real wage than at A (the indifference curve passing through B in Fig. 4.9 cuts the E_0-line above that point).

[34] This situation is more likely to occur with socialist-dominated trade unions and a bourgeois government.

[35] Cf., for example, Oswald (1979) or Gylfason and Lindbeck (1982).

References

Aukrust, O. (1977), 'Inflation in the Open Economy: A Norwegian Model', in L. Krause and W. S. Salant (eds.), *Worldwide Inflation—Theory and Recent Experience*, The Brookings Institution, Washington, DC.

Blyth, C. A. (1979), 'The Interaction between Collective Bargaining and Government Policies in Selected Member Countries', *Collective Bargaining and Government Policies*, OECD.

Bratt, C. (1981), *Arbetsmarknaden i 16 länder*, SAF, Stockholm.

Bruno, M. (1981), 'Raw Materials, Profits and the Productivity Slowdown', Working Paper No. 660, National Bureau of Economic Research, Cambridge, Mass.

Calmfors, L. (1977), 'Inflation in Sweden', in L. Krause and W. S. Salant (eds.), *Worldwide Inflation—Theory and Recent Experience*, The Brookings Institution, Washington, DC.

Calmfors, L. (1982), 'Employment Policies, Wage Formation and Trade Union Behavior in a Small Open Economy', *Scandinavian Journal of Economics*, No. 2.

Calmfors, L. and Horn, H. (1983a), 'Employment Policies and Centralized Wage Setting', Institute for International Economic Studies, Stockholm University, Seminar Paper No. 238.

Calmfors, L. and Horn, H. (1983b), 'Employment Policies, Trade Unions and the Adjustment of Real Wages', Institute for International Economic Studies, Stockholm University, mimeo.

Driffill, E. J. (1983), 'Can Stabilization Policy Increase the Equilibrium Unemployment Rate?', University of Southampton, Discussion Paper in Economics and Econometrics, No. 8312.

Edgren, G., Faxén, K.-O., and Odhner, C.-E. (1973), *Wage Formation and the Economy*, Allen and Unwin, London.

Faxén, K.-O. (1982), 'Incomes Policy and Centralized Wage Formation', SAF, Stockholm, mimeo.

Gylfason, T. and Lindbeck, A. (1982), 'Wage Rigidity and Wage Rivalry: An Oligopolistic Approach', Institute for International Economic Studies, Seminar Paper No. 225.

Hansen, B. (1958), *Economic Theory of Fiscal Policy*, Uppsala.

Helpman, E. (1977), 'Non-traded Goods and Macroeconomic Policy under a Fixed Exchange Rate', *Quarterly Journal of Economics*, Aug.

Korkman, S. (1978), 'The Devaluation Cycle', *Oxford Economic Papers*.

Layard, R. (1982), 'Is Incomes Policy the Answer to Unemployment?', *Economica*, Aug.

Lindbeck, A. (1974), *Swedish Economic Policy*, The MacMillan Press, London and Basingstoke.

Lindbeck, A. (1979), 'Imported and Structural Inflation and Aggregate Demand: The Scandinavian Model Reconstructed', in A. Lindbeck (ed.), *Inflation and Employment in Open Economies*, North-Holland, Amsterdam and New York.

Lindbeck, A. (1983), 'The Recent Slowdown of Productivity Growth', *Economic Journal*, Mar.

McDonald, I. M. and Solow, R. M. (1981), 'Wage Bargaining and Employment', *American Economic Review*, Dec.

OECD country surveys for Austria, Belgium, Denmark, Finland, the Netherlands, Norway, and Sweden. Various issues.

Oswald, A. (1979), 'Wage Determination in an Economy with Many Trade Unions', *Oxford Economic Papers*, No. 3.

Oswald, A. (1982), 'The Microeconomic Theory of the Trade Union', *Economic Journal*, Sept.

Rhomberg, R. R. (1976), 'A Multilateral Exchange Rate Model', *IMF Staff Papers*, Mar.

Rødseth, A. (1979), Macroeconomic Policy in a Small Open Economy', *Scandinavian Journal of Economics*, No. 1.

Sachs, J. (1979), 'Wages, Profits and Macroeconomic Adjustment: A Comparative Study', *Brookings Papers on Economic Activity*, No. 2.

Sachs, J. (1982), 'Stabilization Policies in the World Economy: Scope and Skepticism', *American Economic Review*, Mar.

Seidmann, L. S. (1978), 'Tax-based Incomes Policy', *Brookings Papers on Economic Activity*, No. 2.

Söderström, H. T. and Viotti, S. (1979), 'Money Wage Disturbances and the Endogeneity of the Public Sector in an Open Economy', in A. Lindbeck (ed.), *Inflation and Employment in Open Economies*, North-Holland, Amsterdam and New York.

The Swedish Economy, various issues, Ministry of Economic Affairs and the National Institute of Economic Research, Stockholm.

Towards Full Employment and Price Stability. A Report to the OECD by a Group of Independent Experts (The McCracken report) (1977), OECD.

Wallich, H. C. and Weintraub, S. (1971), 'A Tax-based Incomes Policy', *Journal of Economic Issues*, No. 5.

5

Current Control Problems with Public Expenditure in Five European Countries

VICTOR HALBERSTADT, KEES GOUDSWAARD, and BART LE BLANC

I. Introduction

Current discussions about budget-control policies touch upon the core of public finance. Some of the basic issues at present under debate have a long historical record. For example, about one hundred years ago, there began a debate about a basic issue in the theory and practice of public finance concerning both the optimal distribution of resources between the public and the private sector and optimal methods of taxation (Musgrave and Peacock 1958). With only a brief interval encompassing the period of the two world wars, this discussion has continued. It is, however, not so clear how relevant this has been for the practice of public finance.

Over the past two decades, the character of this debate has undergone considerable change. Practitioners and theorists of economic policy, in particular those concerned with public finance, have felt compelled to look anew at the economics and politics of taxing and spending (for example Bator 1960, Sharkansky 1969, Wildavsky 1980).

Partly in accordance with earlier theory (Musgrave 1959), but in fact because of politically voiced doubts about the size and efficiency of the public sector, fiscal means and political ends are again being scrutinized. This process has been strongly reinforced by both the poor economic performance of many economies since the 1970s and by the *badly controlled and seemingly uncontrollable growth of the public sector*. Of paramount importance in the present discussion seems the often-expressed assumption that the magnitude of *public-sector borrowing requirements* are important determinants of this economic slack and serve as effective obstacles on the road to recovery (Lehment 1982).

What does all this imply for industrialized democracies? Both the scope of government and the scale of spending and taxation have led to a fundamental reconsideration of the role of the public sector in many countries (Usher 1981). True enough, if simple budget-control policies are to be implemented theoretical problems hardly predominate. Rather, it seems that obstacles to budget control are due to either institutional constraints (bureaucracy, legal provisions, etc.) or the resistance of particular veto groups to making the required changes. Decisions governing the growth of the public sector were generally taken when considerable economic growth prevailed and still looked promising. Now that growth prospects are different, difficult issues arise in all countries concerning the control of and cuts in public spending. In this paper we will discuss these issues by giving an overview of public-sector performance and policies in five EC countries, Belgium, Denmark, Ireland, Italy, and the Netherlands, where public-sector growth and especially budget deficits have been, to put it mildly, very pronounced in recent years.

In the context of this paper a new and very important conceptual problem concerning budget-control policies requires attention. In the days before the welfare state the government budget covered almost all governmental finance. This is no longer so. In most industrialized democracies a fairly substantial and increasing part of the public sector is now in fact handled *outside* what has been regarded as the proper public budget. For example, most income transfer programmes in the Netherlands are administered by public, *non-government*, agencies; their revenues and outlays are not included in government budget accounts except for government contributions. The same applies to off-budget expenditure such as tax expenditure, direct and guaranteed loans, and the expenditure of public enterprises. This transformation of the public sector has occurred in all industrialized countries. It goes without saying that this has considerable consequences for control and for policy-making (for example Schick 1981). The concepts of the public-sector budget and the government budget therefore differ, the former encompassing the latter. This conceptual problem originates in basic legislative decisions taken in the years when not only social insurance programmes but also tax preferences and loans to various groups (enterprises, home owners, etc.), were introduced. As a consequence the terminology and the policies involved in budget-cutting exercises require a new approach which has only recently become commonly accepted.[1]

The chapter is organized as follows. In Section II, we deal with the macroeconomic and public-sector performance of the five countries mentioned, over the period 1961–82. Section III briefly describes recent public-sector policies in these countries. The final two sections are of a more general nature and do not deal with the five countries as such. In Section IV, some major current issues concerning public expenditure control are surveyed. Finally, in Section V, we look at some recent developments in the control of budgetary policy.

II. Empirical Background on Macroeconomic and Public-sector Performance: The Cases of Belgium, Denmark, Ireland, Italy, and the Netherlands

In this section we will present an empirical background on public-sector performance in five European countries. These countries are to be considered suitable for analysis because of the highly unfavourable development of their public finances. Public-sector performance, however, must be viewed against the background of macroeconomic performance. Therefore we begin with some summary remarks on a few key economic figures.

As in almost all industrialized countries, economic performance in Belgium, Denmark, Ireland, Italy, and the Netherlands has been disappointing during the seventies and eighties. Economic performance in the five countries discussed can briefly be summarized as follows (Table 5.1):

(1) The *rate of growth* in GDP fell in all five countries during the 1970s and has further stagnated from 1980 to 1982, except, perhaps, in Ireland.

(2) The *volume growth of fixed investments* declined in all of the countries during the period considered. Capital formation collapsed, especially after the two oil shocks. Moreover, after the second oil shock there have so far been no signs of any recovery.

(3) The deterioration of *world trade* is reflected in a decreasing volume growth of exports and imports in all five countries. These countries varied, however, as regards their current balance. Denmark and Ireland experienced rather large deficits on the current account of their balance of payments during the entire period considered. The Irish deficit reached a very high 13.2 per cent of GDP in 1981. In Belgium, substantial balance-of-payments problems arose in the late 1970s. In the Netherlands, the current balance turned into a surplus which is rather high.[2]

(4) All countries showed an increasing *inflation* during most of the 1970s but the rise in consumer prices was sharper in Ireland (20.4 per cent in 1981) and Italy than in Belgium and (especially) the Netherlands, where inflation is relatively low. Denmark takes an intermediate position.

(5) Unit *labour costs* rose very sharply in the period considered but the growth slowed down after 1976 in Belgium and the Netherlands. A large part of this growth was caused by increased *non-wage labour costs*, especially employers' statutory contributions to social security programmes.

(6) Finally, the *unemployment* rate of the five countries increased from an unweighted average of 2.8 per cent of the total labour force

in the 1960s to more than 10 per cent in 1982. The unemployment level was relatively high in Belgium and Ireland, but the growth in unemployment was the most pronounced in the Netherlands.

Public-sector growth in all five countries discussed has been very striking, even accepting that available data do not always permit entirely valid international comparisons. The GDP share of *general government expenditure* in 1981 varied from 51.0 per cent in Italy to 59.5 per cent in Denmark and in the Netherlands (Table 5.2). The average share in 1981 amounted to 57.3 per cent against 34.1 per cent in the 1960s in these five countries. This represents a growth of more than 23 percentage points. Growth in public expenditure has even accelerated in the early eighties. *Current receipts* also grew rapidly in all countries but at a slower pace than expenditure, a fact which is reflected in growing deficits. *Net borrowing of general government* exceeded 10 per cent of GDP in 1981 in Belgium, Ireland, and Italy. The average deficit in the five countries increased from −1.1 per cent in 1970 to −10.5 per cent in 1981, an extremely high percentage. There were no signs of a decline in the borrowing requirements in 1982 and 1983.

Table 5.3 shows that not only total expenditure, but also almost all the *individual elements of expenditure* grew more rapidly than GDP. The large *current transfers* block expanded substantially in all countries in the period 1960-80 and amounted in 1980, on average, to 22.7 per cent of GDP in the countries under review. In the Netherlands, transfer expenditures grew more than $1\frac{1}{2}$ times faster than GDP and amounted to a very high 32 per cent of GDP in 1980, of which almost 28 per cent is made up of transfers to housholds. The rapid expansion of the social security system in the Netherlands is, for example, strikingly illustrated by the case of disability programmes (Halberstadt, Haveman, Wolfe, and Goudswaard 1981). The number of disability benefit recipients (including sickness) increased from 410,000 to 906,000 between 1968 and 1978.[3] The expenditure on disability programmes in this period grew from 3.9 per cent of GDP to 7.7 per cent, a truly impressive growth, which is, of course, partly caused by economic development, but certainly also by deliberate policy measures.

Public consumption grew somewhat less than transfers, except in Ireland. The average elasticity of public consumption with respect to GDP in the period 1960–80 was 1.23. However, the principal part of public consumption—the compensation of employees—also expanded substantially. In Denmark, public consumption is larger than in the other countries due to the fact that many services are provided by the government directly. Other current expenditures,

TABLE 5.1

Selected Indicators of Economic Performance in Five EC Countries 1961–1982

	Average 1961–70	1971	1972	1973	1974	1975	1976	1977	1978	1979	1980	1981	1982[a]
1. Growth of real GDP at market prices													
Belgium	5.0	3.9	5.3	6.2	4.5	-1.9	5.3	1.0	3.2	2.3	2.5	-1.7	-0.5
Denmark	4.6	2.4	5.4	3.8	-0.7	-1.0	6.9	1.9	1.3	3.0	-0.2	-0.2	2.0
Ireland	4.3	3.4	6.4	4.6	4.2	2.0	2.1	6.9	6.7	2.4	1.9	1.1	2.0
Italy	5.7	1.6	3.2	7.0	4.1	-3.6	5.9	1.9	2.7	4.9	4.0	-0.2	0.8
Netherlands	5.2	4.3	3.4	5.7	3.5	-1.0	5.3	2.4	2.7	1.8	0.6	-1.1	0.0
2. Gross fixed-capital formation (annual volume growth)													
Belgium	5.9	-1.5	3.3	6.8	7.0	-1.6	3.2	-0.4	2.1	-0.7	5.6	-8.5	-3.4
Denmark	7.5	1.6	10.0	7.1	-11.3	-12.6	19.8	-2.7	1.1	-3.0	-13.7	-16.3	3.5
Ireland	9.9	8.9	7.8	16.2	-11.6	-4.3	10.0	5.6	17.8	16.4	-7.7	5.0	1.7
Italy	5.3	-3.2	0.9	7.7	3.3	-12.7	2.3	-0.4	-0.1	4.5	-0.2	-0.2	0.2
Netherlands	7.2	3.4	-2.8	4.5	-3.8	-4.9	-2.8	11.7	3.9	0.0	-2.7	-11.3	-2.0
3. Current balance (percentage of GDP)													
Belgium[b]	0.9	2.2	3.9	2.8	1.5	0.5	0.2	-0.7	-0.7	-1.8	-5.2	-5.4	-0.4
Denmark	-2.2	-2.4	-0.3	-1.7	-3.0	-1.5	-4.7	-3.8	-2.7	-4.6	-3.4	-3.2	-4.1
Ireland	-2.3	-3.8	-2.2	-3.1	-9.5	-0.2	-3.5	-2.9	-2.4	-10.1	-8.4	-13.2	-9.0
Italy	1.8	1.8	1.6	-1.7	-4.6	-0.2	-1.5	1.2	2.4	1.6	-2.5	-2.3	-1.3
Netherlands	0.0	-0.3	3.0	4.0	3.2	2.5	3.2	0.8	-0.9	-1.4	-1.4	2.3	4.0

4. Consumer prices (percentage change)

Belgium	3.0	4.3	5.5	7.0	12.7	12.8	9.2	7.1	4.5	4.5	6.6	9.1	9.0
Denmark	5.9	5.8	6.6	9.3	15.3	9.6	9.0	11.1	10.0	9.6	12.3	10.7	9.9
Ireland	4.8	8.9	8.7	11.4	17.0	20.9	18.0	13.6	7.6	13.3	18.2	20.4	18.5
Italy	3.9	4.8	5.7	10.8	19.1	17.0	16.8	18.4	12.1	14.8	13.0	19.0	16.6
Netherlands	4.0	7.5	7.8	8.0	9.6	10.2	8.8	6.4	4.1	4.2	6.5	6.5	6.3

5. Unit labour costs in industry

Belgium	5.2[c]					17.2	8.8	8.0	4.3	4.5	6.1	7.9	5.0
Denmark	7.7[c]					13.7	6.3	8.7	7.5	7.0	6.3	8.3	8.8
Ireland	7.4[c]					24.9	16.8	7.7	10.2	17.4	18.9	16.8	12.5
Italy	6.5[c]					25.7	15.1	9.9	13.3	13.4	18.4	22.7	15.3
Netherlands	7.3[c]					13.7	5.1	5.9	5.1	5.5	5.4	3.1	3.7

6. Unemployment (percentage of labour force)

Belgium	2.1	2.2	2.8	2.9	3.2	5.3	6.8	7.8	8.4	8.7	9.3	11.7	13.9
Denmark	1.2	1.2	1.2	0.7	2.0	4.6	4.7	5.8	6.5	5.3	6.9	8.1	9.1
Ireland	4.6	5.2	6.0	5.6	6.0	8.5	9.4	9.2	8.4	7.4	8.3	10.3	12.1
Italy	5.1	5.1	5.2	4.9	4.8	5.3	5.6	6.4	7.1	7.5	7.6	8.9	9.9
Netherlands	0.9	1.3	2.3	2.3	2.8	4.0	4.3	4.1	4.1	4.1	5.0	7.5	10.4

[a] Estimates.
[b] 1961–79, Belgium and Luxemburg.
[c] 1961–74, total economy.
Sources: OECD (1982b); Commission of the European Communities (1981, 1982, 1983).

TABLE 5.2

Public-sector Finance in Five EC Countries 1961–1982

	Average 1961–70	1971	1972	1973	1974	1975	1976	1977	1978	1979	1980	1981	1982[a]
1. Expenditure of general government (percentage of GDP)													
Belgium	33.2	38.1	39.1	39.4	39.7	44.7	45.3	47.0	48.4	51.6	54.2	59.3	59.7
Denmark	33.0	44.5	43.7	42.7	48.5	49.5	47.7	49.3	52.0	54.3	58.4	59.5	60.6
Ireland	32.4	40.5	39.0	39.2	43.7	47.8	47.5	46.4	46.5	50.5	53.8	57.4	59.3
Italy	32.4	35.8	37.6	36.5	36.2	44.9	42.3	43.3	46.7	45.6	45.9	51.0	52.6
Netherlands	39.6	46.6	47.2	47.8	49.6	54.6	54.5	54.6	55.8	58.1	58.0	59.5	59.8
2. Current receipts of general government (percentage of GDP)[b]													
Belgium	31.9	35.9	35.8	36.6	37.9	40.7	40.5	42.0	43.0	44.7	44.8	45.9	46.9
Denmark	33.7	48.1	48.3	48.6	50.3	47.5	46.9	47.6	49.7	51.2	52.5	52.4	51.1
Ireland	29.7	36.7	35.4	35.1	36.1	36.2	39.4	38.9	36.0	38.7	41.0	42.0	44.6
Italy	30.0	31.3	31.1	30.6	30.8	31.6	33.3	34.3	36.2	36.2	37.8	39.9	41.0
Netherlands	38.7	46.1	47.2	48.9	49.5	51.9	52.2	53.0	53.7	56.1	54.6	55.0	54.1
3. Net borrowing of general government (percentage of GDP)													
Belgium	−1.3	−2.1	−3.3	−2.7	−1.8	−4.1	−4.8	−4.9	−5.5	−6.9	−9.4	−13.4	−12.8
Denmark	0.6	3.6	4.6	5.9	1.8	−2.0	−0.8	−1.7	−2.2	−3.1	−5.9	−7.1	−9.5
Ireland	−2.8	−3.8	−3.5	−4.1	−7.5	−11.6	−8.1	−7.6	−10.4	−11.9	−12.8	−15.4	−14.7
Italy	−2.1	−4.6	−6.5	−5.8	−5.4	−13.3	−9.0	−9.0	−10.5	−9.4	−8.4	−11.9	−11.6
Netherlands	−0.9	−0.5	−0.0	1.1	−0.1	−2.7	−2.4	−1.5	−2.1	−2.0	−3.4	−4.5	−5.7

[a] Preliminary figures.
[b] Including social security contributions.
Sources: Commission of the European Communities (1981, 1982); recent figures from the European Commission.

TABLE 5.3

Composition of Public Expenditure in 1980, Percentages of GDP (80), and the Elasticity of Each Item with respect to GDP (e) 1960–1980

		Belgium	Denmark	Ireland	Italy	Netherlands
1. Current transfers	80	24.2	20.7	17.2	19.4	32.0
	e	1.38	1.47	1.25	1.16	1.52
of which: Subsidies	80	2.8	3.2	3.8	3.0	2.3
	e	1.13	2.19	1.06	1.33	1.31
Transfers to households	80	21.10	16.2	13.2	16.0	27.7
	e	1.36	1.38	1.32	1.11	1.52
Other transfers	80	0.4	1.3	0.2	0.4	1.9
	e	2.0	1.78	1.75	1.25	2.12
2. Public consumption	80	18.4	26.5	22.9	16.1	18.5
	e	1.22	1.35	1.31	1.12	1.16
of which: Compensation of employees	80	13.6	18.7	14.7	12.2	13.2
	e	1.24	1.43	1.36	1.13	1.21
3. Other current uses[a]	80	6.0	5.3	7.5	6.4	3.4
	e	1.43	1.76	1.25	1.57	1.12
4. Gross capital formation	80	4.2	3.0	6.2	3.1	3.2
	e	1.33	0.96	1.33	0.93	0.91
5. Net capital transfers	80	0.5	0.7	1.3	0.9	2.1
6. Total expenditure	80	53.4	56.2	55.1	46.0	59.3
	e	1.31	1.38	1.31	1.15	1.30

[a] Mainly interest payments.
Source: Commission of the European Communities (1981).

which category mainly consists of interest payments on government debt, showed the largest growth (an average GDP elasticity of 1.43 from 1960 to 1980).

The only expenditure item which showed a declining GDP share, but then only in Denmark, Italy, and the Netherlands, was *gross capital formation*, an expenditure category for which budget control has been the most effective. The relatively declining importance of public investment reinforces the weakening of the economic structure. The GDP share of gross capital formation was substantially higher in Ireland than in the other countries, reflecting the high priority assigned there to the infrastructure.

The negative effects of these developments are clear and well known. Costs of productive use of labour and capital are increased. Shifted tax burdens and employer contributions to social insurance programmes lead to higher (non-wage) labour costs. Private investment is to a certain extent crowded out because of high government borrowing requirements. Productive public expenditure is crowded out because of high outlays on income transfers and interest payments.

The crumbling financial basis of the public sector is painfully and clearly illustrated by the changing composition of the *total number of income recipients*. Table 5.4 provides the data. The number of benefit recipients as a percentage of the income recipients in the market sector more than *doubled* in Italy and the Netherlands between 1963 and 1980. In Belgium, this ratio grew by more than 20 percentage points from 1973 to 1980. The number of benefit recipients as a percentage of total employment about doubled from 1963 to 1980 in Belgium, Denmark, Italy, and the Netherlands. Ireland has shown a growth of 150 per cent in this ratio.

The number of income recipients in the public sector, both employed persons and benefit recipients, amounted to respectively 56 per cent and 61 per cent of the number of income recipients in the market sector in 1963 in the Netherlands and Italy, and to 88 per cent in 1973 in Belgium. This ratio, the *dependency burden,* increased to respectively 108, 118, and 123 per cent in the Netherlands, Belgium, and Italy in 1980. In Ireland, the dependency burden increased from 101 per cent in 1977 to 109 per cent in 1982. This entails an ever-growing burden on disposable incomes in the market sector.

III. Public-sector Policies

In Section II, we indicated that the development of public expenditure and borrowing requirements seems to have been uncontrolled in the five countries studied. Therefore, it is interesting to take a brief look at fiscal and budgetary policies in these countries. In this section we present

TABLE 5.4
Number of Income Recipients 1963–1982

	1963	1970	1973	1975	1977	1980	1982
1. Benefit recipients as percentage of the income recipients in the market sector							
Belgium	–	–	–	72	–	85	–
Ireland	–	–	63	–	68	67	72
Italy	49	–	92	–	100	103	–
Netherlands	39	–	58	–	75	80	89
2. Benefit recipients as percentage of total employment							
Belgium	37[a]	45	50	57	–	64	–
Denmark	28[a]	41	–	55	–	64	–
Ireland	29	34	–	–	–	44[b]	–
Italy	43	–	78	–	83	85	–
Netherlands	33	–	47	–	58	62	68
3. Income recipients in the public sector as percentage of the income recipients in the market sector							
Belgium	–	–	88	99	–	118	–
Ireland	–	–	–	–	101	101	109
Italy	61	–	110	–	119	123	–
Netherlands	56	–	81	–	103	108	121

a 1965.
b 1979.

Sources: OECD; National Bank of Belgium; Denmark Statistics.; Report of the Department of Social Welfare, Dublin, Ireland, various issues; Central Statistical Office, Italy; Social and Economic Council, the Netherlands.

a short overview of these policies, with special emphasis on the Netherlands.

Belgium

The Belgian economy shows fundamental budgetary and, partly related, economic imbalances. The large government deficits over many years caused a government debt of 77 per cent of GNP in 1980 and thus large debt charges (OECD 1982c, p. 26). Interest payments increased annually by more than 1 per cent of GNP in the early eighties and amounted already to 7.9 per cent of GNP in 1981 against 3.3 per cent in 1973 (OECD 1982c, p. 22). Also, the savings surplus of the private sector has in recent years become insufficient to finance the deficit, which in turn necessitated borrowing heavily from abroad: in 1981, 47 per cent of the central government borrowing requirement was thus covered. Foreign public debt has grown from almost zero in 1977 to 10.7 per cent of GDP in 1981 (Commission of the European Communities 1982, p. 42).

The control of public finance became a major policy objective only in 1979. 'Non-compulsory expenditure'[4] was targeted to remain the same in real terms in order to reduce the central government borrowing requirement by 1 per cent of GNP per year. However, the central government deficit on current transactions was almost twice as large as forecast in 1980 and even nearly three times as large in 1981 (OECD 1982c, p. 29). Also public consumption showed a volume growth of 1 per cent on average in 1980–1.

In response to the imbalances in the Belgian economy, a new government launched an economic recovery programme at the beginning of 1982. This programme included an $8\frac{1}{2}$ per cent devaluation of the franc within the EMS, the control of prices and incomes,[5] and retrenchments of public expenditure in order to restructure industry and restore competitiveness and profitability. Some transfer outlays, public consumption, and also capital outlays were to decrease. The retrenchments in capital expenditure were even larger in 1983. The government announced that nominal expenditures were targeted to rise by 7.5 per cent in 1983, which implied a real decline. Because of the rapid expansion of expenditure relating to unemployment and public debt, capital outlays are planned to undergo a real decline of almost 20 per cent. In the medium term, the government objective is to reduce the borrowing requirement by one-half, which implies a yearly reduction of about $1\frac{3}{4}$ per cent of GNP until 1985.

Finally, a special problem with respect to the reduction of the deficit concerns off-budget expenditures such as loan guarantees and credits to industry. In particular, commitments made earlier to the steel industry are now leading to substantially higher cash outlays.

Denmark

Denmark faces similar problems to Belgium. The balance of payments showed a deficit during the entire period reviewed. The expansion of the public sector was very rapid during the 1970s. After the first oil crisis, the budget balance turned from a surplus to a deficit. These deficits were partly financed with foreign loans, and, as a consequence, a large foreign debt was created of 25 per cent of GDP in 1980, against $10\frac{3}{4}$ per cent in 1973 (OECD 1982a, p. 18).

In the mid-1970s, the incompatibility of rapid public-sector growth and balanced external and internal economic development was acknowledged, which led to several attempts to reduce the rate of growth of public expenditure. However, because of automatic stabilizers, the generous social security system, increased interest payments, and also increased outlays on employment programmes in the public sector, expenditure growth did not slow down.

Since 1980, fiscal policy was intended to be quite restrictive, as indicated by increased tax rates in 1980 and 1981 and also by cuts in planned expenditures. For 1981 a cut in public expenditure plans of kr. 8bn. (more than 2 per cent of GDP) was announced, including the effect of a 2 per cent ceiling on real local government spending (OECD 1982a, p. 53). Next, a ceiling was set on non-cyclical spending (Commission of the European Communities 1982, p. 50).

For 1983 rather large cuts of 3.75 per cent of GNP were planned, especially with respect to incomes in the public sector. Civil service salaries and transfer incomes, which were growing by 12 and 18 per cent respectively in 1982, were targeted to rise by only 4 per cent in 1983. However, a concrete proposal to lower unemployment benefits from 90 to 80 per cent of previous wages was rejected by parliament at the end of 1982.

Ireland

Economic and fiscal policy in Ireland has over the years been directed at rapid industrialization and a diversification of the economic structure. To achieve this, it was (and is) necessary to attract foreign direct investment and to undertake large public capital programmes. The government deficits were reasonably low until the first oil crisis and due predominantly to these capital expenditures. However, as in the other countries reviewed here, the deficit began to grow substantially after 1973, partly due to discretionary government action, partly due to automatic stabilizers.

The stance of fiscal policy became more restrictive, especially since 1981. In July 1981, the new government introduced a corrective package including increases in taxation (focusing on VAT), increases of some public charges, and cuts in public expenditure. These expenditure cuts included a slower growth in capital outlays, but were partly offset by increases in social security payments.

This policy stance was reinforced in 1982 in order to reduce external and internal deficits. The Irish government is specifically trying to slow down wage increases of public employees. Much of the planned reduction of the deficit, however, has in practice to be realized by a further substantial increase of the tax burden (OECD 1982d), since equivalent cuts in public expenditure are not politically acceptable.

In the National Economic Plan 1983-1987,[6] the following goal was stated: 'to reduce Exchequer borrowing progressively to levels compatible with the long-term ability of the economy to borrow and repay' (*The Way Forward* 1982, p. 14). This reduction is to be effected 'essentially by eliminating the current budget deficit by 1986 through a combination of measures including eliminating wasteful and unjustifiable public expenditures, reducing the numbers employed in the public service and moderating the public pay bill, making working methods in the public services more efficient and charging those who can afford to pay for certain services'. In addition, the following policy measures deserve mentioning in this context:

— a system of monitoring the performance of commercial semi-State bodies, which constitute the wider public sector, is being introduced to ensure that they operate efficiently and remunerate the substantial amount of Exchequer capital invested in them;
— staff mobility to areas of greatest need will be implemented after consultation with staff interests especially through the identification of existing activities that can no longer be justified in present conditons;
— the aim will be that any new services can only be provided if an existing one is discontinued. (*The Way Forward* 1982, pp. 110–11.)

However, whether the measures announced are sufficient to attain an effective control of public expenditure may be questioned.

Italy

During the 1970s economic and fiscal policy in Italy was mainly directed at short-term demand management. Public-sector expenditure and borrowing requirements grew rapidly, just as in the other countries studied. This growth was partly due to institutional factors and the lack of control processes—for example, large responsibilities of local authorities with regard to expenditure and borrowing.

Therefore, some reforms of budgetary procedures were carried through in the course of the 1970s (OECD 1980, pp. 30-1). Firstly, in addition to the budget on a commitment basis a budget in cash terms was presented in 1979, together with a finance bill, in which budget policy and overall economic policy were discussed. Secondly, the deficit and the financing of the deficit were presented in terms of the entire public sector, instead of central government alone. Thirdly, in 1979 a three-year budget on a commitment basis for the period 1980-2 was presented.

Three-year economic plans were designed for the period 1979-81 and 1981-3. The main emphasis of the 1981-3 programme was on the improvement of productivity, mainly through public investment, which was planned to grow from $5\frac{1}{2}$ per cent of GDP in 1981 to $7\frac{1}{2}$ per cent in 1983 (OECD 1981, p. 27).

In the second half of 1980, some restrictive budgetary measures were taken, including higher VAT rates and excise duties and higher advance payments of income tax (Commission of the European Communities 1981, p. 100). In 1981 the government announced yearly reductions in current expenditure equivalent to 1 per cent of GDP over the period 1981-3, partly in order to raise capital expenditure, as mentioned above.

However, most of the planned investments were not implemented, partly because of administrative difficulties. Also, few concrete measures have been taken to cut current expenditure. In fact, a significant deterioration of the public finances took place in 1981 with a growth of the general government borrowing requirement to almost 12 per cent of GDP. This was partly due to the recession, but also to deferred effects of increases in civil service salaries and several transfer payments. Minimum pensions increased over the eighteen-month period ending in July 1981 by 50 per cent (OECD 1981, p. 33). Next, interest payments increased substantially by 40 per cent in 1981, reaching $7\frac{1}{2}$ per cent of GDP.

The public-sector deficit was targeted to be reduced by about 3 per cent of GDP in 1982, but the possibility of realizing this aim did not seem to be high. Therefore, the Italian government introduced in July 1982 a package of measures to increase tax receipts by 2 per cent of GDP. Of course, these measures to raise the tax burden signify that public expenditures are by no means controlled yet.

The Netherlands[7]

Economic performance in the Netherlands deteriorated at the end of the 1970s and the beginning of the 1980s more sharply than in many other countries, at least with respect to unemployment and economic growth. The policy stance, which was expansionary after the first oil shock, became restrictive after 1977, keeping inflation low, but not preventing a further large growth of the public sector, clearly illustrated by income transfer expenditures and the number of benefit recipients. This rapid expenditure growth brought with it a growing deficit. This is remarkable in the Dutch case, because of the increasing importance of natural gas revenues as a source of government finance: total gas revenues (non-tax revenues plus profit taxes) amounted to 5.5 per cent of GNP in 1981 against, for example, 2.5 per cent in 1975, and only 0.5 per cent in 1970. The underlying problem of public-sector imbalance was thus disguised, the disease remained hidden.

If we look at Dutch public-sector policy in some more detail a startling picture emerges. From the early 1960s to the late 1970s Dutch fiscal policy was dominated by the so-called structural (that is irrespective of short-term fluctuations) budget policy or *trend-based budget policy*. Discretionary fiscal policy as applied until 1961 implied in practice a continuing upward pressure on outlays, both in a recession and in a boom period. In the early 1960s, Jelle Zijlstra, then Minister of Finance and *auctor intellectualis* of the trend-based budget policy expressed it as follows:

One cannot expect our parliamentarians to have studied the textbooks on business cycles and to have captured their content . . . In other words: modern anticyclical policy also has an educational side to it . . . For that purpose simple rules are required.[8] (Zijlstra 1962, p. 34.)

In the philosophy of trend-based budget policy the government deficit is attuned to the medium-term development of the economy using as a bench-mark—if possible—a year in which the economy is supposedly 'in equilibrium'. Implied in this approach is that the structural budget deficit should equal the structural savings surplus of the private sector,[9] minus capital exports intentionally reserved for aid to developing countries. This instrument of budgetary policy was expected to lay a sound foundation for balanced economic growth (Burger 1975, p. 219).

The structural budget margin is calculated on the basis of the structural deficit, the tax revenues resulting from expected medium-term real growth, and a progression factor (tax yield elasticity), plus non-tax receipts. This margin indicates the amount annually available for an increase of expenditure and/or autonomous reduction of taxes. The choice between these two possibilities is, of course, a political one.

The trend-based budget policy served as a useful tool for economic policy for several years and provided a framework for decision-making. However, the importance of this relatively simple concept declined quickly in the course of the 1970s. Apart from introducing subtle so-called technical changes into this concept, which made it more complex almost annually and therefore less useful for its original purpose, it could not prevent both outlays and tax burdens from rising rapidly.

The budget margin was generally fully used for increasing government expenditure. Moreover, various programmes to stimulate the economy were launched in the 1970s which were financed on top of the calculated budget margin. Despite the intended temporary character of these programmes, expenditures were in fact continuously increased.

With respect to government expenditure, *multi-year budgeting estimates* have been made annually since the beginning of the 1970s. Four-year 'rolling' estimates were calculated in order that (a) the consequences of decisions involving relatively low expenditures in the first year(s) could in principle be shown early and clearly, and (b) the consequences of unchanged policies with regard to expenditures and revenues could be outlined as early as possible. However, in practice the system increased the downward inflexibility of government expenditure.

In 1976 a rather fundamental reorientation of fiscal policy was announced. The unfavourable trend of investment and employment was partly attributable to increasing labour costs, which therefore had to be mitigated. To protect free disposable incomes and to prevent further shifting processes leading to higher (non-wage) labour costs, the growth rate of taxes and social security contributions was to be reduced. For these reasons the so-called 'One Percent Policy' was introduced in 1976. This policy norm implied that over the medium term the growth of the *total tax burden*[10] had to be restricted to one percentage point annually in terms of GNP. The total tax burden had risen on average by 1.5 percentage points annually over the previous ten years and was with unchanged policies (in retrospect rather optimistically) expected to increase by 1.6 percentage points per year over a four-year period. Consequently, the first major cuts in public expenditure gradually leading to a fl. 8.8bn. lower level in 1980 (2.8 per cent of GNP in 1980) were planned.

The policy of restraining public-sector growth was reassessed in 1978, with the launching of the *Blueprint 81* (*Bestek '81*) programme. With worsening economic performance and expectations of further deterioration, a stabilization of the total tax burden was aimed for, together with public expenditure cuts reaching fl. 10bn. after three years.

Within the framework of these two trend-related budget policies, a generally accepted goal was set for the structural budget deficit (general government excluding social insurance financing) in the second half of the 1970s. However, due to the failure to realize net cuts in total expenditures and the fact that economic growth fell short of expectations, the actual budget deficit increased rapidly at the end of the 1970s. This high deficit led to the abandonment of the trend-based budget policy in 1979 and to growing pressure on the national capital market because of the high borrowing requirements; also interest payments increased rapidly. The targeted actual deficit was amply exceeded each year in the recent past. This, together with government revenues far below forecasts, gave rise to several proposals for expenditure cuts, following each other ever more rapidly since 1980, but all characterized by lax enforcement.

Finally, policies related to *social insurance* deserve special mention because of the very large and rapidly growing share of these outlays in national income. Programming and budgeting of income transfer expenditure has hardly taken place in the past; and if it has, it has been very inadequate. Only in the late seventies have the disadvantages of the uninhibited programme growth, with its ever-increasing burden on both the private and the public sector, become generally understood. Since 1976, a number of proposals to slow down this growth have been launched. Within the framework of the 'One Percent Policy' and *Blueprint 81*, for example, total structural expenditure cuts of respectively about fl. 5bn. and about fl. 4.5bn. were targeted (Le Blanc 1982, pp. 29–30). These proposals, mainly in the fields of child allowances, health care, and indexing mechanisms, implied to a large degree benefit reductions and only to a small extent a reduction in the number of benefit recipients. However, these expenditure cuts were only partially realized, or in some cases not at all, because of public and parliamentary opposition. Until now, though announced by successive governments since 1976, no major changes in the basic structure of the social insurance system have been carried through. Nor can their implementation be expected in the next few years.

The end of the 1970s therefore provided a weakened structure of the Dutch public sector, which led to various new policy initiatives in 1981 and 1982.

For 1983, adjustments (expenditure cuts and increases in tax burdens) of fl. 15bn. were planned (4 per cent of GNP in 1983). For the period 1984-6 yearly additional retrenchments of fl. 7bn. are targeted, especially in the field of incomes in the public sector, in order to lower borrowing requirements. However, few of these cuts are indicated in sufficiently precise terms and, as a consequence, many cuts are, as before, at risk. Also the forecast for world trade in the medium term (an annual growth rate of 3 per cent) seems overly optimistic. This in turn could imply lower than expected real growth of GNP with all its consequent problems. Dutch public finances, therefore, stand a good chance of remaining uncontrolled.

IV. Major Issues in Public Expenditure Control

The discussion in Section III makes it clear that public expenditures are not under effective control, as illustrated by the explosive growth in many spending programmes. It is, one is bound to observe, so much easier to announce cuts in public spending than to implement them. But *why* this is the case is easier stated than proved, which must be explained by the lack of in-depth studies on why retrenchment policies so far almost always seem to fail, especially, but not only, if one takes the public expenditure/GNP ratio as the measure of success.

True enough, pre-Second-World-War history provides some cases of successful lowering of public expenditure in real terms. Germany in the early 1920s (Netzband and Widmaier 1964), and the Netherlands ten years later (Commissie Welter 1932) are good examples. But that is long ago and it seems difficult to repeat such exercises successfully today. It is certainly remarkable that the notion that public expenditures are out of control is now so strongly felt everywhere. Both critics and supporters of increased public expenditures share this *feeling*, while very few government administrators suggest that they really have a grip on programmes. *Evidence* of poor control of public expenditures is easy to find. The budget, Schick (1981, p. 1) observes, no longer controls: '*force majeure* rules public finance'. This, of course, implies that the various budgets of the public sector are less and less useful for effective economic policy. Also, financial-control capacity, while this was so central at the time of the introduction and development of public budgets, had dwindled.

Of course, the rapid and continuous increase in the share of public expenditure in GDP in the past two decades has been accompanied by a variety of proposals for restoring fiscal discipline. Performance Budgeting, Planning–Programming–Budgeting Systems, Management by Objectives, Zero-base budgeting, Sunset Legislation, all had and/or have promising characteristics. But none of these approaches to budgeting have so far been effective (Harkin 1982). This must be regretted, since it is important to link resource commitment to intended results. Whatever the explanation for the failure of these various approaches to containment of the public sector, the issue remains and becomes much more complicated when the size of the pie shrinks. As observed by Vaubel (1981, p. 1), the question is no longer 'how can the political process be reformed so as to generate decisions in favour of expenditure cuts?' but 'how can public expenditure best be cut when the government in power is committed to cuts?'.

The question thus phrased immediately brings out that attitudes towards total spending seem at best ambivalent and at worst confused because the real problem involves not *narrow* special interests but *broad* special interests, which can be illustrated, for example, by the employment effects of defence spending and the large number of beneficiaries involved in most income transfer programmes (Penner 1982). This probably explains why better budget control is not easy to achieve but rather is an arduous step-by-step process requiring much effort. As Penner (1982, p. 31) rightly concludes: 'It will not be obtained by simple-minded blunderbuss techniques. Devices such as the constitutional amendments are only likely to complicate the decision making with no real results. The one rule with certain validity is to beware of politicians bearing simple solutions.'

One simple solution is to limit spending by *limiting tax receipts.* The way out here, of course, is via public-sector deficits as an easy source for increased spending, which creates enormous policy risks. Also, to make structural cuts in taxes *before* cutting expenditures seems a strategy full of frightening uncertainties.

Another simple solution is *across-the-board* cuts in spending. Governments with clear priorities will probably not choose this method and both political and academic opinions point out its inefficiencies. None the less, even though the possibilities for applications of across-the-board cutting are limited, it is not necessarily undesirable as such. Even if only part of the budget were to be reduced this way it might still be helpful when there are no alternatives readily available, although the risks of misallocations are not inconsiderable.

Gradual and sustained rather than abrupt implementation of a reduction in the level of public expenditures then? This option allows for careful consideration of the optimal size and composition of public expenditure cuts, facilitates the adjustment of expectations, and may help to avoid too large a reduction in effective demand. Surely a reasonable option, were it not for the fact that a gradual decrease in public spending will perhaps be undone before (or for fear of) elections.

Finally, the 'Big Bang' alternative, of which little has been said or proved in literature. One can, it seems, easily conclude that industrialized democracies do not at present seem to lend themselves to such treatment.

Without easy solutions available governments are thus forced to focus on such *small bangs* as, for example, freezes in hiring, freezes of civil service salaries, and cuts in transfer programmes. The only realistic way seems to be a return to financial controls and a move towards long-term cutback planning. However, Levine *et al.* (1980) find in their study of various US local governments that this approach stands little chance of success unless one accepts that a phase of *denial and delay*, followed by a phase of *stretching,* precedes fundamental reform of expenditure programmes. That then leaves time to deal with what must probably be considered the major problem in reducing public spending: the growing inflexibility of programmes.

Evidence for the US and the Netherlands in Tables 5.5 and 5.6 suggests that the technical flexibility of public expenditure in the short run is really very small. But both in the short and the long run *social, bureaucratic, and political flexibilities* seem specially relevant.[11] Recent experiences in many Western European countries provide ample proof that these are very important, if not the most important, issues in budget control and budget cutting.

Of course, bureaucratic, social, and political resistance is inter-related with the growing complexity in political decision-making. This complexity is in turn linked to the conscious achievement of social objectives. These express themselves in rigid public finances through the accumulation of programmes, institutions, procedures, and rules which are (or seem) partly irreversible. The result is wide-spread inflexibility, for which different analyses have been provided (for example Robinson and Ysander 1981, Wildavsky 1980), but no solutions as yet. This inflexibility is understandable since social and political resistance to downward changes in public-sector activity touch the fundamental principles of the welfare state: redistribution of income and opportunities through a large variety of programmes in money and in kind. In this respect, the five countries discussed earlier in this paper are not so different from other industrialized democracies. On the contrary, redistributive objectives may be more sought after, especially in Denmark and the Netherlands than in some other countries. But the retrenchment programmes must ultimately lead to improved allocation, efficiency, and productivity, taking full account not only of income distribution but also of employment effects.

In this context, it is important to note that there is also broad agreement on restructuring the budget, i.e. assigning higher priority to productive public expenditure.

V. Concluding Remarks

Recent studies in a number of countries and by the European Communities, the IMF, and the OECD provide a still rather chaotic, but important catalogue of new tools for control of public expenditure. These studies suggest that, apart from action in the fields of, for example, indexation mechanisms, cash management, and non-wage labour costs, two areas for action can be distinguished. The *first* area is concerned with adjustment in decision-making processes and the related setting of priorities. The *second* area concentrates on various possible improvements in financial control (for example Tarschys 1982 and Vaubel 1981). In these concluding remarks the findings of these studies will not be summarized. What matters more is how

TABLE 5.5
Uncontrollable Spending in the US Federal Budget
($ bn.)

	Fiscal year										Estimate	
	1968	1969	1970	1971	1972	1973	1974	1975	1976	TQ[a]	1977	1978
Fixed costs												
Interest	11.1	12.7	14.8	14.8	15.5	17.4	21.5	23.3	26.8	7.0	30.1	33.2
Farm-price support	3.2	4.1	3.8	2.8	4.0	3.6	1.0	0.6	0.6	0.7	1.7	1.0
Other fixed costs	3.0	2.8	3.8	5.2	6.4	6.3	6.8	8.0	8.3	2.6	10.2	10.7
Subtotal	17.3	19.6	22.0	22.8	25.9	27.3	29.3	31.9	36.2	10.3	42.0	44.9
Multi-year contracts and obligations												
Civilians	24.6	25.0	24.5	21.6	19.9	18.3	20.9	23.6	19.1	8.6	23.6	31.4
Defence	17.8	16.9	18.6	18.6	19.4	21.3	22.9	27.1	31.8	11.4	37.5	44.9
Subtotal	42.3	41.9	41.5	40.2	39.2	39.6	43.8	50.7	50.9	20.0	61.1	76.3

Entitlement programmes
Payments to individuals:

Social security	24.8	28.3	31.3	37.2	41.5	50.7	57.6	68.4	76.2	20.7	87.1	95.7
Retirement	4.3	4.8	5.6	6.6	7.7	9.0	10.8	13.3	15.6	4.3	18.0	20.3
Unemployment	2.9	2.9	3.7	6.6	7.5	5.7	6.5	14.0	19.8	4.2	16.4	13.8
Veterans benefits	5.0	5.7	6.6	7.6	8.3	9.3	10.0	12.4	13.9	2.9	13.2	13.1
Medicare and Medicaid	7.2	8.9	9.9	11.2	13.4	14.1	17.2	21.6	26.3	7.0	32.2	37.9
Housing assistance	0.3	0.3	0.5	0.7	1.1	1.6	1.8	2.1	2.5	0.6	2.9	3.8
Public assistance	3.4	3.9	4.7	7.4	8.9	9.1	11.5	16.9	20.2	4.9	21.9	22.9
Revenue sharing	–	–	–	–	–	6.6	6.1	6.1	6.2	1.6	6.8	6.8
Subtotal	47.7	54.9	62.2	77.3	88.4	106.2	121.6	154.8	180.6	46.2	198.7	214.2
Total uncontrollable[b]	107.3	116.4	125.7	140.4	153.5	173.0	194.5	237.5	267.7	76.5	301.7	335.4
Percentage of total outlays uncontrollable	60.0	63.1	54.0	66.4	66.2	70.2	72.5	73.2	73.1	80.7	72.3	73.0

[a] Transitional quarter.
[b] Totals reflect adjustment of offsetting receipts.
Source: LeLoup (1978).

TABLE 5.6
Tentative Approach to Flexibility Trends in Specific Categories in Government Spending in the Netherlands' National Budget 1980

	1980	1981	1982	1983	1984
I Inflexible:					
Legally binding	39	25	13	11	10
II Partially flexible because of:					
Technical complementarity	2	2	3	3	2
Acts/regulations	32	40	48	48	48
Subsidies	8	8	8	8	8
Civil service staff expenditure	11	11	11	11	11
Other	5	8	10	11	12
Subtotal	58	69	80	81	81
III Wholly flexible	3	6	7	8	9
Total	100	100	100	100	100

Source: The Netherlands Budget Memorandum (1981).

the tools are used and the really new tools require further operative experience before they can be properly judged.

Three new developments, however, merit attention here. *Firstly*, the return of interest in *global norms* for multi-annual budgeting, related to budget deficits, total tax burdens, and the growth of public spending. These norms though nominally derived from medium-term 'plans' lack a theoretical basis and are in fact the outcome of a plain political decision process. Today they create the same problems as they did in the good old days when they were first introduced (for example in the Netherlands—see the subsection on the Netherlands in Section III): i.e. the trade-off between simplicity and adequacy. Nevertheless they may help to spread the useful political catalyst that norms, if generally accepted, provide some reasonable support for developing just and effective public-sector policies. An important condition for global norms is an adequate macroeconomic medium-term framework. In the Netherlands the need for multi-annual planning of decision making in budgetary policy was recently stressed again by a civil service Commission on Budgetary Policy (*The Netherlands Budget Memorandum* 1983, Annex 7). According to the first set of recommendations of this Commission, budget(-cutting) policies have to be set up for some years ahead on the basis of *conservative estimates* of macroeconomic and financial developments. These multi-annual programmes are to be regularly evaluated and if necessary adjusted. Moreover, open-ended programmes (especially social insurance) should be included in these (retrenchment) programmes.

A *second* development is the introduction of sectoral and pro-gramme-related targets for public expenditure. These specific norms are available in a considerable variety, as elaborated in the interesting and exhaustive study done by Tarschys (1982, pp. 29–32), for example:

The *Frame*, a finite sum of real resources appropriated for a set of programmes, often a multi-year commitment, as for defence in Sweden;

The *Envelope*, employed in Canada, implies the setting of govern-ment-wide expenditure targets for eleven policy sectors. Major decisions within each sector (Envelope) are delegated to a Cabinet Committee. Each Envelope covers two or more ministries with related policy areas;

Cash limits, well developed in the United Kingdom and essentially a technique of letting inflation do the cutting when a maximum is set for the compensation of price and wage increases;

Credit limits for semi-autonomous bodies, in use in Scandinavian countries;

Sectoral limits for the expansion of public expenditure in a particular area, in use in Denmark and Sweden;

Staff ceilings, sometimes with selective limits to keep the volume of government employment under control, in use in Belgium, the Federal Republic of Germany, and Finland.

These norms do not solve the whole problem of budget control but can, under adequate political and bureaucratic conditions, certainly help in promoting better-balanced decision-making packages. This seems all the more true if they can be combined with incentives for retrenchments, such as material rewards and career-oriented measures.

A *third* development has occurred in the Netherlands, where a wide ranging 'Reconsideration Programme' was set up in 1981 and continued in 1982. Thorough reviews, by civil servants without political instructions, of some general issues and many current expenditure programmes have produced forty-seven reports with a vast variety of possibilities for savings. Excluding health and most income transfers, these reports show how, without political priorities attached, in due time between 1 and 5 per cent of GNP can be cut in the budget of the central government. The studies also provide guide-lines for the introduction of *user-charges* and pay ample attention to *deregulation*. Of course, so far few of the many proposals have been accepted or implemented. The government plans to implement savings of from 0.25 to 1 per cent of GNP on the basis of the Reconsideration Reports, from 1983 to 1986.

Whatever the value and sophistication of these three new developments, there is little doubt that without political support they cannot help much.

A final remark. As people with long years of experience in the public sector sometimes point out, the efficiency and effectiveness of new budgetary tools must not be overrated. What really matters is the courage of politicians. The key question therefore is whether politicians agree on the necessity of fundamental changes in the size and composition of the public sector. Are they able and willing to make difficult choices, also to resist adequately veto groups (for example the elderly), and to risk revenge from their party and the voters, especially when the decisions to be taken may take years to produce fruits?

Notes and Sources

* The views expressed are only attributable to the authors in a personal capacity. The authors are grateful to Professor Francesco Forte (Italy), Mrs Rita Knudsen (Denmark), Mr. R. Beauvois (Belgium), Mr M. Morris (Ireland), Mr. Paolo Roberti (OECD) for supplying data, and to Mr Michael Emerson (EC) and Mr Ken Messere (OECD) for reviewing a draft of this paper. All errors in presentation and interpretation are, of course, our responsibility.

[1] Budget cutting is defined for the purposes of this paper as all measures which contribute to reductions in the estimated amounts (in real terms) of all public expenditure programmes including social insurance, plus corrections on the revenue side as, for example, through the introduction of user-charges.

[2] This is mainly due to lagging natural gas revenues, declining investment-related imports, and successful agricultural exports.

[3] The 1982 estimate is 1,034,000.

[4] Expenditure excluding interest payments and unemployment benefits.

[5] Through a suspension of wage indexation for all above minimum wages.

[6] Presented in October 1982 by a government which fell one month later, but the financial policies were implicitly accepted by its successor.

[7] For a more extensive discussion of the Dutch case see Halberstadt, le Blanc, Goudswaard, and Meys (1982).

[8] 'Man kann den Mitgliedern unserer Parlamente nicht zumuten, dass sie die Handbücher der Konjunkturpolitik gelesen und geistig bewältigt haben . . . Mit anderen Worten: die moderne Konjunkturpolitik hat auch ihre didactische Seite . . . Dazu bedarf es einfacher Regeln.' (Zijlstra 1962, p. 34.) (Translation into English by the authors of this paper.)

[9] Defined as private savings minus that part of private investment which is not financed by government capital transfers.

[10] Taxes plus social insurance contributions plus some non-tax receipts (excluding revenue from natural gas exports) as a percentage of net national income at market prices.

[11] Interest payments on national debt also add considerably to the inflexibility of public budgets. For example, in 1982 interest payments as a percentage of total central government expenditure varied from 8 per cent in the FRG, to 12.6 per cent in Denmark, and 17.3 per cent in Belgium.

References

Bator, Francis M. (1960), *The Question of Government Spending,* New York.

Bestek '81, Hoofdlijnen van het financiële en sociaal-economische beleid voor de middellange termijn (*Blueprint 81,* Outline of medium-term financial and socio-economic policy), Tweede Kamer, 1977–8, 15 081, No. 2.

Buchanan, James M. *et al.* (1978), *The Economics of Politics,* IEA Readings 18, London.

Burger, H. (1975), 'Structural Budget Policy in the Netherlands', *De Economist* 123.3.

Centraal Planbureau (1981, 1982), *Centraal Economisch Plan* (Central Economic Plan), The Hague.

Commissie Welter (1932), *Rapport van de Staatscommissie voor de Verlaging van de Rijksuitgaven* (Report of the Government Commission for Reduction of National Expenditure), The Hague.

Commission of the European Communities (1981), *European Economy,* No. 10, Nov., Brussels.

Commission of the European Communities (1982), *European Economy,* No. 11, Mar., Brussels.

Commission of the European Communities (1983), *Annual Economic Review 1982–83,* Brussels.

De Larosière, J. (1982), Restoring Fiscal Discipline: A Vital Element of a Policy for Economic Recovery, Address to the American Enterprise Institute, Washington DC, 16 Mar. (mimeograph).

Halberstadt, Victor, Haveman, Robert H., Wolfe, Barbara L., and Goudswaard, Kees P. (1983), 'The Economics of Disability Policy in Selected European Community Countries', in F. A. J. van den Bosch and C. Petersen (eds.), *Economische aspecten van arbeidsongeschiktheid; analyse en beleid,* Deventer, 17–66.

Halberstadt, Victor, le Blanc, Bart, Goudswaard, Kees, and Meys, Dick (1982),

148   V. HALBERSTADT, K. GOUDSWAARD, AND B. LE BLANC

'Budget Cutting Policies: Recent Experiences in the Netherlands', paper presented at the 38th Congress of the International Institute of Public Finance at Copenhagen on 'Public Finance and the Quest for Efficiency' 23-6 Aug., Centre for Research in Public Economics, Report 82.20, Leiden/The Hague, June.

Harkin, James M. (1982), 'Effectiveness Budgeting: the limits of Budget Reform', in *Policy Studies Review*, 1.1, Aug.

Heroverweging Collectieve Uitgaven (*Reconsideration of Public Expenditures*) (1981), Tweede Kamer, 1980-1, 16 625, Nos. 1–35, The Hague.

Le Blanc, L. J. C. M. (1982), 'Economie en Sociale Zekerheid, of: hoe Nederland koos, kiest en zal moeten kiezen' (The Economy and Social Security, or: how the Netherlands made, makes, and should make its choices), paper presented at Instituut voor Onderzoek van Overheidsuitgaven (Institute for Research on Public Expenditure) Symposium, May.

Lehment, H. (1982), 'The Macroeconomic Implications of Public Sector Deficits', paper prepared for the Conference of the Centre for European Policy Studies on Western European Priorities, Brussels, 15–17 Dec., published in this volume.

Leloup, L. T. (1978), 'Discretion in National Budgeting: Controlling the Controllables', *Policy Analysis*, No. 4.

Levine, C. H., Rubin, Irene S., and Wolohojian, George G. (1980), 'Fiscal Stress and Local Government Adaptations: Toward a Multi-Stage Theory of Retrenchment', paper presented at the Conference of the Committee on Urban Public Economics, New Orleans, Oct.

Musgrave, Richard A. (1959), *The Theory of Public Finance*, New York.

Musgrave, Richard A. and Peacock, Alan T. (eds.) (1958), *Classics in the Theory of Public Finance*, London/New York.

The Netherlands Budget Memorandum (various years), Ministry of Finance, The Hague.

Netzband, Karl-Bernard and Widmaier, Hans Peter (1964), *Währungs- und Finanzpolitik der Ära Luther, 1923-5*, Basel/Tübingen.

OECD (various years), *Economic Survey, The Netherlands*, Paris.

OECD (1980), *Economic Survey, Italy*, Paris, Mar.

OECD (1981), *Economic Survey, Italy*, Paris, June.

OECD (1982a), *Economic Survey, Denmark*, Paris, Jan.

OECD (1982b), *Economic Outlook*, Paris, July.

OECD (1982c), *Economic Survey, Belgium/Luxembourg*, Paris, Apr.

OECD (1982d), *Economic Survey, Ireland*, Paris, Aug.

Penner, Rudolph G. (1982), 'Fiscal Management', American Enterprise Institute, Washington DC, Summer (mimeograph).

Robinson, A. and Ysander, B. C. (1981), *Flexibility in Budget Policy*, Working Paper No. 50, The Industrial Institute for Economic and Social Research Stockholm.

Schick, Allen (1981), 'Off-Budget Expenditure: An Economic and Political Framework', Working Document (unpublished).

Sharkansky, Ira (1969), *The Politics of Taxing and Spending*, New York.

Sociaal-Economische Raad (1981), *Advies sociaal-economisch beleid op middellange termijn* (Advice on medium-term socio-economic policy), Report 81/07, The Hague, May.

Tarschys, Daniel (1982), 'Curbing Public Expenditures: A Survey of Current Trends', Apr. (unpublished).

Usher, D. (1981), *The Economic Prerequisite to Democracy*, Oxford.

Vaubel, Roland (1981), 'Alternative Methods of Reducing Government Expenditure', Kiel Institute of World Economics, Dec. (mimeograph).

The Way Forward (1982), National Economic Plan 1983-7, Stationery Office, Dublin, Oct.

Wildavsky, A. (1980), *How to limit government spending,* University of California Press, Berkeley.

Zijlstra, J. (1966), 'Möglichkeiten und Grenzen der Konjunkturpolitik', in C. Goedhart (ed.), *Opstellen over Openbare Financiën*, vol. 1, Amsterdam.

6

The Macroeconomic Implications of Public-sector Deficits

Public-sector deficits have increased substantially during the last decade both in Western Europe and in other parts of the world. As can be seen from Fig. 6.1 public-sector deficits of Western European OECD countries measured as percentages of GDP were at a relatively modest level in the 1960s. The period average in the sixties was about 0.3 per cent, with some years (1960–2 and 1969) even showing financial surpluses. In the seventies the period average increased to about 2.3 per cent with a rising trend. In the cyclical peak of 1973 the deficit was already somewhat larger than in the preceding peak years of the sixties. The main increase in the level of public deficits came with the recession of 1974–5 when the ratio of the deficit to GDP reached 4.6 per cent. While the deficits were reduced in 1976–7 to 3 per cent of GDP they increased again

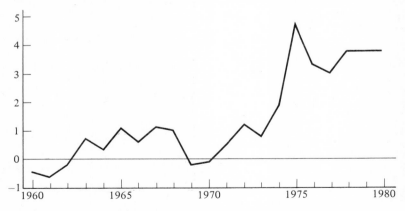

Fig. 6.1: Public-sector deficits of Western European OECD countries as percentage of GDP[a]

[a] Calculated as the difference between total government outlays and current receipts of government; a negative sign indicates a financial surplus.
Source: OECD (1982), Tables R8 and R9.

to 3.8 per cent during the economic upswing at the end of the decade, reflecting a strong pro-cyclical course of fiscal policies in this period. While the rising public-sector deficits have been criticized on various grounds (mainly relating to negative supply effects),[1] they have also been defended by arguing that without the additional deficit-spending there would have been a lower level of aggregate demand and employment.[2]

The focus of this chapter will be on the macroeconomic demand effects of public deficit spending. Section I presents a short survey of the main developments in the theory of fiscal demand management. The survey starts from the original Hicks–Hansen IS–LM model and covers the subsequent extensions of the analysis that have been made through the introduction of open-economy considerations, wealth effects, price–wage repercussions, budget constraints, and expectation effects. Section II reviews the empirical estimates of the demand effects of public deficit spending which have been obtained from various econometric policy simulations for Germany. Section III contains a discussion of certain international policy issues: the conduct of fiscal policy, including the so-called locomotive approach, the recent transatlantic controversy on US fiscal policy and its implications for Western Europe, and finally, the domestic and international implications of strategies that aim at a reduction of public-sector deficits.

I. The Theory of Fiscal Demand Management

Deficit spending in the Hicks–Hansen model

One of the corner-stones of the Keynesian revolution was the analytical demonstration that changes in government spending or taxation which are financed by corresponding changes in the stock of privately held government bonds can affect the level of aggregate demand. In the Hicks–Hansen IS–LM model which soon became a standard framework of analysis, the 'normal' effects of a bond-financed increase in government spending (represented by a rightward shift of the IS curve) are a rise in the rate of interest and an increase in aggregate nominal demand; moreover, since the Hicks–Hansen model includes the assumption of constant nominal wages and a price-elastic supply of goods —reflecting a situation of 'Keynesian unemployment' (Malinvaud 1978)—the increase in aggregate spending leads to an expansion of real output. The positive effect of deficit spending on aggregate demand can be explained by the fact that the increase in the interest rate which results from the additional public borrowing does not only reduce investment demand but also reduces the demand for

money balances. Thus, part of the additional public spending is brought
about by a more intensive use of existing money balances (reflected
in an increase of the velocity of money) rather than a crowding-out
of private investors.[3]

The effect of a bond-financed increase in deficit spending on aggregate demand is influenced by the money-supply strategy of the central
bank. If the central bank aims at a target for a wide monetary aggregate
like M_3 which largely consists of interest-bearing assets, or at a target
for the monetary base where the reserve component includes reserves
on interest-bearing assets, the LM curve will be steeper (and the efficiency of fiscal demand policy be lower) than in the case of a target for
a narrow monetary aggregate like M_1.[4]

Open-economy considerations

The extension of the IS–LM model to the open economy by Fleming
(1962) and Mundell (1968) had major implications for the efficiency
of fiscal demand management. The Fleming–Mundell analysis showed
that international capital mobility reduces the effect of deficit spending
on domestic aggregate demand.[5] In the extreme case of a very small
open economy with perfect capital mobility and flexible exchange
rates it was shown that bond-financed increases in government spending
have virtually no effect on aggregate demand for domestic goods.
There are different ways to explain why international capital mobility
reduces the efficiency of fiscal demand management. An explanation
from the monetary perspective runs as follows: an inflow of capital
reduces the effect of deficit spending on the domestic interest rate;
as a result the velocity of money and, hence, aggregate demand rise
less strongly than in the case of an isolated domestic capital market.
From the goods-market perspective the lower efficiency of fiscal
demand management under international capital mobility is reflected
by the worsening of the trade account which goes along with a capital
inflow. In the case of a very small economy where the additional
government spending is financed exclusively by a capital inflow the
worsening of the trade account equals the increase in public expenditure so that aggregate demand does not respond at all to the fiscal
expansion.

In this context it is worth while to note that international capital
mobility substantially changes the way in which bond-financed government spending 'crowds out' private demand. In the open economy
there are three mechanisms through which crowding-out may be
brought about:

Crowding-out via the domestic interest rate; this mechanism becomes less important under international capital mobility since an

integrated international capital market reduces the effect of deficit spending on the domestic interest rate;

Crowding-out via the foreign interest rate; under conditions of international capital mobility the increase in the interest rate which results from domestic deficit-spending is transmitted to other countries where it leads to a crowding-out of foreign investment and, thereby, a reduction in export demand for domestic investment goods;[6]

Crowding-out via the exchange rate; when capital is mobile internationally a bond-financed increase in government spending may lead to an appreciation of the domestic currency which reduces the demand for domestic tradables; an appreciation is the more likely to occur the closer the degree of substitution between domestic and foreign bonds and the smaller the size of the domestic economy relative to that of the other countries.

Wealth effects

The introduction of wealth effects into the IS–LM analysis showed that deficit spending may not only affect the position of the IS curve but also that of the LM curve (Christ 1968, Silber 1970). If government bonds are considered as private net wealth then an increase in the stock of privately held bonds via public deficit-spending tends to raise the private demand for goods (shifting the IS curve further to the right) but may also increase the demand for money balances (shifting the LM curve to the left).

Whether the efficiency of fiscal demand management is raised or reduced by the existence of wealth effects depends on the relative strength with which the demand for goods and the demand for money react to changes in private wealth. On the basis of a theoretical analysis it may be possible that the leftward shift of the LM curve compensates or even more than compensates the rightward shift of the IS curve so that an increase in bond-financed government spending has no effect or even a negative effect on aggregate demand.[7]

Price–wage repercussions

In the traditional IS–LM analysis a central role was played by the assumption that wages do not react to an increase in aggregate demand.[8] This assumption was challenged by Friedman's (1968) hypothesis of a vertical long-run Phillips curve, which although first discussed in connection with monetary policy also had an important implication for the efficiency of fiscal demand management. The implication is that even if deficit spending has positive effects on aggregate nominal demand, its output and employment effect will only be transitory (see, for example, Dornsbusch and Fischer 1981, pp. 452–4). In the long run, when wages have fully caught up with the increase in aggregate demand, the effect of the fiscal expansion will fall exclusively on prices, raising the price level in proportion to the increase in aggregate nominal demand, while output and employment remain unaffected.

The government budget constraint and its implication for a long-run analysis

The original IS–LM model was constructed for a short-run analysis. The introduction of the government budget constraint (Ott and Ott 1965, Christ 1968) directed the attention towards the longer-run effects of deficit spending. A central question was whether the initial deficit of a bond-financed fiscal expansion would be removed over time by an endogenous increase in tax receipts. The extension of the IS–LM model to a long-run analysis (Blinder and Solow 1973, Tobin and Buiter 1976, Brunner and Meltzer 1976, Dornbusch 1976, Siebke, Knoll, and Schmidtberger 1981) showed that the answer to this question depends on a number of factors, including the properties of the tax system and the effect of changes in wealth on the demand for money. There are circumstances in which bond-financed deficit spending may result in a continuous increase of government deficits if it is not stopped by future discretionary reductions in public spending or increases in tax rates. In such a case a full account of the demand effects of a fiscal expansion makes it necessary to consider also the effects of the future fiscal restriction which is required in order to prevent an explosive increase in budget deficits.

The role of expectations

The impact which expectations have on the success of economic policy actions has received increasing attention in recent years. Several arguments have been advanced in favour of the hypothesis that the efficiency of fiscal demand management may be destroyed or at least reduced by the effect which deficit spending has on the expectations of private-market participants:[9]

Additional government investment, for example in the housing sector, tends to lower the expected rate of return on competing private projects and, hence, tends to reduce private investment demand; this case is referred to in the literature under the name of 'direct' or 'ultrarational' crowding-out (Bailey 1971, David and Scadding 1974).[10]

Private-market participants may expect an increase in future taxes in order to service and repay the additional public debt and react to the expected loss in future disposable income by a reduction in current spending and an increase in saving (Barro 1974); in the IS–LM diagram this 'Ricardian' effect is reflected—like the 'direct' crowding-out effect—by a reduction in the rightward shift of the IS curve.

An increase in public-sector deficits may lead to additional economic uncertainty. If private-market participants react to the additional uncertainty by increasing their demand for liquid assets—including money—then the efficiency of deficit spending's effect on aggregate demand is reduced through a leftward shift of the LM curve; moreover, the increase in uncertainty may also be reflected in a smaller right-ward shift of the IS curve because of a negative impact of uncertainty on private investment demand (Keynes 1936, p. 120, Cebula 1973).

The anticipation of the demand and price effects of fiscal policy reduces the wage and price lag so that the effect of deficit spending on the level of output and employment becomes more short-lived (Giersch 1977, pp. 54–5).

II. Deficit Spending and Aggregate Demand: The Results of Investigations for Germany

Evidence from large macroeconomic models

In recent years there have been various attempts to quantify the effects of government deficit spending on aggregate demand and output through policy simulation in the context of large macroeconometric models for Germany (Krelle, Conrad, Grisse, and Martiensen 1979, Conrad and Kohnert 1980, Westphal 1981, DIW 1981, Pohl 1981, Vesper and Zwiener 1982, Tewes 1982, Deutsche Bundesbank 1982).

One common result of the studies is that an increase in government spending leads to a higher level of nominal demand both in the short run and in the longer run. Another common result is that an increase in government spending positively affects real output in the first two years after it has been initiated. Those of the simulations which cover a period of more than two years have arrived at mixed results about the long-run real effects of an increase in government spending. While Conrad and Kohnert (1980) find that the long-run real effect is relatively low but still positive, the study by the Deutsche Bundes-bank (1982) arrives at the result that after approximately two and a half years the initial positive effects on output are followed by an induced decline in real GNP which completely offsets the initial gains in output and employment. This result is attributed largely to the price–wage feedbacks operating in the model and is consistent with the hypothesis of a vertical long-run Phillips curve.

If one considers the implications of these results for the crowding-out debate two points should be noted. First, the simulations are based on the implicit or explicit assumption that an increase in govern-ment spending causes an additional expansion of central bank money (and other monetary aggregates).[11] The reason is that the Bundesbank is assumed either to fix directly short-run market interest rates or to fix its own lending rates (discount rate, Lombard rate) and, thereby, to dampen the increase in market interest rates which results from additional government borrowing.[12] The result, however, that a fiscal-cum-monetary expansion leads to an increase in aggregate nominal demand has never been a controversial issue of the crowding-out debate. Moreover, it is doubtful whether the assumption of an accommodating monetary policy reflects the actual behaviour of the Bundesbank. Central bank money has been used since 1973 as an intermediate target for the Bundesbank's policy and the Bundesbank has never considered an increase in government spending as a reason to pursue a more expansionary monetary policy.[13] Thus, at least for an analysis that goes beyond the very short run it seems more appropriate to base simulations of a fiscal expansion on the assumption that the Bundesbank reacts to an additional increase in the demand for central bank money by raising its interest rates (or lowering them less quickly than otherwise would have been done) in order to keep the expansion of central bank money on its preannounced course. In this case the demand effect of a fiscal expansion would most likely be lower than in the simulations which are based on the assumption of an accommodating monetary policy.

A second point is that the structural macroeconometric models on which the simulations are based incorporate only a part of the potential channels for a crowding-out of private demand.

Domestic interest rates have a negative effect on domestic investment demand in all models and in some models also on the demand for consumer goods; the role of crowding-out via a rise in domestic interest rates is, however, strongly reduced by the assumption of an accommodating monetary policy which completely or largely neutralizes the effect of deficit spending on domestic interest rates.

Foreign interest rates do not enter into any of the models as an endogenous variable so that a crowding-out of foreign demand for domestic products via the effect of deficit spending on foreign interest rates is not considered.

Exchange rates are endogenous in some of the models; it is, however, doubtful whether the effect of a fiscal expansion on the exchange rate is correctly grasped by the equations; Dornbusch (1982, p. 10) in reviewing the empirical evidence on exchange-rate determination arrives at the conclusion that 'claims for empirically successful exchange-rate equations are disappearing rapidly. . . . This is the case whether a monetary approach is adopted, a Mundell–Fleming–Frankel model or models that include, in addition, current account or relative wealth variables.'

Wealth effects are considered explicitly only by Westphal (1981). He finds that the introduction of a wealth variable reduces the effect of a fiscal expansion on demand but only to a very small extent.

Expectations usually represent one of the major problems of econometric research (Lucas 1976); expectation-induced crowding-out via direct substitution effects, the discounting of future tax payments or risk effects are not accounted for in any of the simulations.

Long-run effects on the budget are neglected in most of the investigations. Conrad and Kohnert (1980, Tables A4 and A9) arrive at the result that an increase in government spending reduces the budget deficit already in the first year (and in all of the following years). In contrast to this result Tewes (1982) finds that in the first two years (which is the time horizon of his simulation) budget deficits increase by about 50 per cent of the rise in government spending.

Evidence from small econometric models and reduced form estimates

Dewald and Marchon (1979) have presented a reduced form estimate of aggregate nominal spending for Germany on the basis of the St Louis model. They find that the elasticity of aggregate nominal demand with respect to changes in government spending is about 0.05.[14] This value is substantially lower than the estimates from the structural macroeconometric models for Germany. A general critique that has been advanced against reduced form estimates is that the fiscal policy coefficient may underestimate the actual fiscal impact in cases where government spending systematically neutralizes the effect of exogenous shocks (Blinder and Goldfeld 1972). In the German case, however, it appears doubtful whether such a systematic fiscal policy has been pursued in the past.

Neumann (1981) uses a small macroeconomic model with rational expectations to test for the effects of unexpected changes in the money supply and government spending. He finds that an unexpected change in public expenditure on consumption and investment goods has no significant effect on private-sector output (being defined as real GNP minus salaries of public employees at constant prices). Neumann explicitly mentions the empirical difficulties in separating the unexpected changes from the expected changes. Since the simulations are not also run for the overall changes in government spending the results of this study are not directly comparable to those of the other investigations.

The OECD (1982) has constructed a small macro-model for the purpose of estimating the effects of an increase in government spending both under an 'accommodating' and under a 'non-accommodating' monetary policy. The real sector of the model essentially follows that

158 HARMEN LEHMENT

used for the OECD interlink model; the monetary sector covers the supply and demand for money using parameter estimates from Boughton (1979).

In the OECD Study which covers seven major OECD countries 'accommodating' monetary policy is taken to imply that the central bank fixes the interest rate. A 'non-accommodating' monetary policy is taken to imply that the central bank fixes the money supply. The study also considers a case of fixed exchange rates where the central bank is supposed to keep both interest rates and exchange rates constant.[15] The results of the OECD study are reproduced in Table 6.1.[16]

TABLE 6.1

Multiplier Effects of Government Spending on National Income under Alternative Monetary Policy Assumptions

	Accommodating monetary policy, fixed exchange rates	Accommodating monetary policy, flexible exchange rates	Non-accommodating monetary policy, flexible exchange rates
United States	1.99	3.35	0.35
Japan	2.41	4.51	0.91
Germany	1.17	3.11	0.67
France	1.23	3.14	1.15
United Kingdom	0.98	3.28	0.97
Italy	1.18	3.45	0.41
Canada	1.33	3.35	0.64

Source: OECD (1982), Table 8.

When exchange rates are flexible a combination of fiscal expansion and monetary policy that fixes the interest rate causes a currency depreciation which contributes to the expansion of income. Under fixed exchange rates the expansionary effect of a depreciation is absent. This explains why for all of the countries under consideration the multipliers in the second column of Table 6.1 are larger than in the first column.

When monetary policy is 'non-accommodating' the effect of a fiscal stimulus on income is substantially lower than under an 'accommodating' policy. The reason is that with the money supply held constant the increase in government spending leads to a rise in interest rates and a higher external value of the country's currency as compared with the 'accommodated' flexible exchange-rate case. As a result there is a crowding-out of private expenditure and a relatively less favourable position for the external sector of the economy. A comparison of the secnd and the third columns in Table 6.1 shows that the effect of a fiscal stimulus on income under a 'non-accommodating' monetary policy is between three (France) to nine times (United States) lower than in the case of monetary accommodation. The substantial differences between these two figures implies that changes in the money supplies have a powerful effect on aggregate demand.

When the multipliers of the non-accommodation case are compared across countries one finds that multipliers are highest for France and the United Kingdom, and lowest for the United States. It is interesting to note that in this respect there is a close correspondence with the results of the Dewald–Marchon estimate according to which the income effect of a fiscal stimulus is strongest in France and the United Kingdom whereas it is relatively weak for the United States.

For Germany the assumption made in the OECD study that the Bundesbank controls M_3 under a 'non-accommodating' strategy comes close to the actual policy since deviations in the movement of M_3 and the movement of central bank money are usually relatively small. In order to check to what extent the results are changed if it is assumed that a 'non-accommodating' monetary policy involves holding the supply of central bank money constant I have estimated a demand function for central bank money of a similar structure as the M_3 function used in the OECD stimulations. The regression which is based on annual data of the period 1961–79 has yielded the following result:[17]

$$\ln(CBM/P) - 0.79 + 0.45 \ln GNP^r - 0.08 \ln R^1 + 0.60 \ln(CBM_{-1}/P).$$
$$\quad (4.64) \quad (5.68) \qquad\qquad (4.39) \qquad\quad (8.23)$$

$$\bar{R}^2 = 0.998 \quad SE = 0.010 \quad DW = 2.03$$

with CBM central bank money
      P GNP deflator
      GNP^r real GNP
      R^1 long-term government bond yield
t-values are shown in the parentheses.

The estimate implies a long-run income elasticity of 1.1 and a long-term interest elasticity of 0.20. If the estimated function for central bank money is substituted for the M_3 equation in the OECD model, the income multiplier for the 'non-accommodation' case is reduced from 0.67 to about 0.40.[18] The multiplier which is thus derived from the OECD model, under the assumption of non-accommodation in respect to the expansion of central bank money, is about twice as high as the multiplier in the St Louis model.[19] But it is also about eight times lower than the multiplier for the 'accommodation' case in the OECD model, under the assumption of flexible exchange rates, and about three times lower than the multiplier of 1.2 which has been derived in the OECD model, under the assumption of an accommodating monetary policy which fixes not only interest rates but also the exchange rate.

III. International Economic Policy Issues

The locomotive approach

The issue of international co-ordination of economic policy including the course of national fiscal policies emerged soon after the breakdown of the Bretton Woods system in 1973. The discussions intensified in 1976–7 when it became evident that the recovery from the 1974–5 recession was faltering. Moreover, the different reactions to the oil-price hike of 1973 had led to a division of industrial countries into so-called 'strong' countries including the United States, Germany, and Japan which had managed to keep their inflation rates on a relatively low level and so-called 'weak' countries like the United Kingdom, Italy, and—to a lesser degree—France which had reacted to the removal of the exchange-rate constraint by pursuing strongly expansionary monetary and fiscal policies and in 1976 found themselves with high inflation rates, strong devaluations of their currencies *vis-à-vis* those of the 'strong' countries, and high current-account deficits.

Against the background of this international economic situation a 'locomotive' approach was suggested by various economists and international economic organizations.[20]

The core of the locomotive strategy was that 'strong' countries should stimulate their internal demand and thereby help to pull the 'weaker' countries out of the prevailing stagnation.[21] The main elements of this demand-oriented version of the locomotive approach, which was supported especially by the OECD, may be outlined as follows (Gebert and Scheide 1980, Whitman 1978).[22]

First, a main reason for the slow-down of the recovery was seen in an insufficient level of aggregate nominal demand.[23]

Second, it was argued that the 'weak' countries had no room to pursue an expansionary policy on their own since this would lead to a 'vicious circle' of a further (real) depreciation of their currencies, additional increases in import prices, and higher wage claims. For the 'strong' countries, it was argued, a vicious circle was less likely to occur so they should go ahead with expansionary measures.[24]

Third, in the proposals for an expansion of demand large weight was given to fiscal deficit-spending. The OECD (1977, p. 10) explicitly encouraged governments in 'strong' countries to increase their budget deficits and to remove political, legal, and administrative barriers against a further increase in budget deficits. There may be several reasons why fiscal rather than monetary measures were regarded as the main instrument of the locomotive strategy.

One consideration is the result of a theoretical analysis of economic policy effects in the context of a Fleming–Mundell model with flexible exchange rates and international capital mobility. In this model a monetary expansion in one country has a negative effect on income in other countries whereas a non-accommodated fiscal expansion has a positive effect both on domestic and foreign income and, hence, a comparative advantage as an instrument of a locomotive strategy (Dornbusch and Krugman 1976). A non-accommodated fiscal expansion was, however, considered to be insufficient under quantitative aspects since much of the impact would be offset by the induced increase in interest rates (Solomon 1978).[25] However, an accommodated fiscal policy will be less efficient as a locomotive for other countries since the additional monetary expansion will strengthen the demand effect for the domestic country but weaken the demand effect that falls on other countries. If the monetary policy completely offsets all interest-rate effects of the fiscal expansion there will be no leakage of demand effects to other countries.

A monetary–fiscal expansion in one country—while having no or only small direct effects on the demand for foreign goods—may, however, indirectly contribute to an expansion in foreign demand since it tends to have a positive effect on the external value of foreign currencies and, hence, removes the exchange-rate constraint on expansionary demand policies in other countries. In fact this second aspect soon became a major point in the international policy discussions of 1977–8 where the original locomotive strategy was replaced by the suggestion of a concerted expansion in the OECD era (the so-called convoy strategy) according to which 'impetus would come from expansion not only by the stronger-currency countries but also from the intermediate countries taking advantage of their increased "elbow-room" ' (OECD 1978, p. xiii).

If the role of 'strong' countries, however, is reduced to a removal of the exchange-rate constraint for 'weaker' countries a fiscal expansion has no comparative advantage over a purely monetary expansion which—in contrast to a fiscal stimulus—has a clear-cut effect on the exchange rate in standard open-economy macro-models.

A second and very important reason for the weight which was put on fiscal measures must be seen in the use of macroeconometric models which did not allow for a separate analysis of money-supply effects. In the simulations with the OECD interlink model which provided the empirical basis for a large part of the discussion on the locomotive and convoy strategies the only instrument of demand management considered was an accommodated fiscal expansion (OECD 1979).[26]

A third reason for the dominating position of fiscal measures in the locomotive/convoy discussions (and a reason that became specially important for the transformation of the suggestions into actual policy decisions) has to be seen in the institution of economic summit meetings of heads of state and government. Since in several of the leading industrial countries monetary policy is not in the hands of the government, resolutions or decisions at summit meetings which aim at stimulating demand (as at the Bonn Summit of 1978) tend to show an inherent bias towards fiscal measures.

A critical reassessment of the locomotive and convoy strategies will have to focus especially on two points.

First, the underlying view that an expansion of demand would not create bottleneck problems[27] and would have only a rather small effect on prices[28] is not supported by the experience of the years 1978-80. Bottle-necks appeared already in 1979, for example in the construction sector in Germany. Consumer-price inflation in Western European OECD countries which had run at 9.9 per cent in 1978 increased to 15.6 in 1980. The increase in hourly wage rates rose from 12.2 in 1978 to 14.7 per cent in 1980 in Western European OECD countries exhibiting a substantial domestic element in the reacceleration of inflation.

The second point concerns the weight that was put on government deficit-spending as an instrument of demand expansion and the neglect of monetary policy, which—if considered at all—was given only the auxiliary function of accommodating the fiscal stimulus.[29] If we look at evidence that has been presented up to now on the relative efficiency of monetary and fiscal policy we do not find support for the view that fiscal expansion deserves priority when considering measures that affect aggregate demand. As is shown, for example, by the OECD (1982) study the effect of an 'accommodated' fiscal expansion for the countries listed is between three and nine times larger than in the case of 'non-accommodation' (p. 45), indicating the dominating role of money-supply changes in the context of a monetary–fiscal expansion.

At this point one may speculate about the way in which a stronger consideration of monetary factors in the international policy discussions of the years 1976-8 might have affected economic events. First, it is likely that with less weight being put on fiscal expansion, budget deficits would not have increased as strongly as they did. Second, the strong monetary expansion in several 'locomotive' countries including Germany, which could be observed from the autumn of 1977, would have implied a more cautious view on the need for a further monetary–fiscal expansion and might have contributed to avoiding the economic overheating of 1979-80 (which in turn can be regarded as a major factor for the sharpness of the subsequent recession).

The 1982 transatlantic controversy on US budget deficits

The plans of the US government to cut taxes substantially without proportionate reductions in government spending led to controversy among policy-makers in the US and Europe. On the European side there was concern that the increase in US budget deficits would raise interest rates not only in the United States but also in Western Europe and, thereby, contribute to a lengthening of the world-wide recession.[30]

The underlying view that a country should pursue a less expansionary fiscal policy in order to stimulate the economy of other countries stands in obvious contrast to the locomotive approach and hence invites a more detailed discussion.

An analysis in the context of a Fleming–Mundell model shows that a bond-financed increase in US government spending has a negative effect on aggregate demand for European products via the induced increase in world interest rates; at the same time, however, there are positive demand effects for Europe which result from the increase in US income and—possibly—from a real appreciation of the US currency. On balance the positive demand effects are stronger (although their quantitative impact may be rather small under a non-accommodating policy). These considerations suggest that a fiscal restriction in the US will not contribute directly to an economic recovery in Europe.[31]

It has also been suggested that US fiscal policy exerts a negative impact on world demand by causing US monetary policy to be more restrictive than it would otherwise be (Bergsten 1982). If we consider a combination of an expansionary fiscal policy and a restrictive monetary policy which fully neutralizes the effect of deficit spending on US income in the Fleming–Mundell model[32] we find that such a policy mix does not have a negative but rather a positive effect on aggregate demand for European goods, as long as flexible exchange rates are assumed; the reason is that the negative demand effect of the US monetary policy via the induced increase in interest rates is more than offset by the positive demand effect that results from the induced real depreciation of European currencies.

In order to arrive at a negative effect on aggregate demand for European goods one has to make the assumption that the fiscal expansion in the US (possibly combined with a US monetary restriction) leads to a tighter monetary policy (and/or a fiscal policy) in European countries.

A tightening of European monetary policies may occur if (1) the US fiscal expansion raises the external value of the US dollar and (2) the European monetary authorities wish to prevent or at least dampen the depreciation of their currencies in order to counteract imported inflation. There is, however, a substantial degree of uncertainty both about the effect of deficit spending on the exchange rate and about the reaction of central banks to exchange-market pressure. The uncertainty about the exchange-rate effect of an increase in public-sector deficits is illustrated by the observation that the depreciation of European currencies in 1980–2 has to some part been attributed to the negative confidence effect of the increase in European public-sector deficits, while the increase in US budget deficits has at least for some of the time been taken as a reason for the strength of the US dollar in the exchange market.[33] There are question marks also in respect to the reaction of central banks to exchange-rate changes. If we look at monetary policy in Germany (which because of the important role of the German currency in the EMS is of interest also to the other EMS members) we find that in 1982 despite the substantial increase in US budget deficits and despite a further appreciation of the dollar *vis-à-vis* the D-mark since the beginning of that year the increase in central bank money in 1982 was close to the upper limit of the target range of 4–7 per cent, and it may be doubtful whether the monetary expansion would have been significantly larger had the dollar been less strong in the exchange market.

One may therefore conclude that the positive effect of reduced US fiscal deficits for Western Europe should be seen in the longer-run allocative effects of lower interest rates rather than in a short-run stimulating effect on aggregate demand.

The domestic and international implications of strategies to reduce public-sector deficits

Several arguments have been advanced in favour of a reduction of the present structural budget deficits.

First, as a result of the growth of public-sector deficits in the last decade government interest payments as a ratio of GNP have increased substantially in Western Europe and have contributed to the overall government-sector expansion (Cassel 1982, Table 5). A reduction in public borrowing would contribute to slowing down or even reversing the public-sector expansion which frequently is regarded as a main impediment to economic growth. Second, a reduction in public-sector deficits tends to reduce real interest rates and, thus, has a positive effect on investment and long-term growth prospects; moreover, lower interest rates contribute to a reduction of public-sector interest payments and to a solution of the debt service problems which presently are regarded as a major threat to the stability of the international financial system. Third, a reduction of structural budget deficits has a positive effect on long-term economic planning in the private sector by removing the uncertainty which may otherwise exist in respect to the long-term financing of government expenditures. Fourth, large current-account deficits which often serve as an excuse for the introduction of trade restrictions usually reflect large government deficits (Emerson 1982, Graph 5). A reduction of budget deficits would reduce the scope for concern about the current account and, thus, help to prevent and remove protectionist policies.[34]

The major argument against a reduction in budget deficits concerns the negative aggregate demand effect that is expected to result from a fiscal restriction.[35] The weight of this argument depends on several factors including the size of the deficit cut, the quantitative impact of a deficit cut on aggregate spending, and the ability of the central bank to neutralize a negative fiscal impact on aggregate spending through a compensatory adjustment of the money supply. As an example for the effects of a deficit cut on nominal demand and its implication for monetary policy we may consider the case of Germany. The German Council of Economic Experts (1981) has suggested reducing the structural component of the budget deficit (which according to its estimates amounts to about 2 per cent of GNP) over a period of four years. With a fiscal multiplier of 0.4 derived from the OECD (1982) study under the assumption of a given expansion of central bank money an annual cut of public-sector deficits by 0.5 per cent of GNP reduces aggregate nominal spending by 0.2 per cent.[36] Since the elasticity of nominal GNP to changes in central bank money is close to one, a neutralization of the negative fiscal demand effect would require an additional increase in central bank money by 0.2 per cent. Time-lags of monetary policy have to be considered but they should not provide too large a problem since the effect of a fiscal restriction on aggregate demand also tends to operate with some time-lag (especially if the deficit cuts are brought about by a cut in transfer payments or an increase in taxes), and since the fiscal measures can be announced in advance so that corrective monetary measures can be taken at an early stage.[37]

A fiscal restriction combined with a monetary expansion that offsets the negative fiscal impact on domestic aggregate demand tends to have a negative demand effect for other countries to the extent that it leads to a reduction of foreign interest rates and, hence, a lower velocity of money. In the case under consideration this reduction in velocity should, however, be relatively small and could be offset by a somewhat more expansionary monetary policy in the other countries. With respect to the other EMS countries such a monetary response may at least to some extent be induced automatically since a German policy package of fiscal restriction and monetary expansion which is neutral in respect to domestic nominal GNP should reduce the upward pressure on the external value of the D-mark in the EMS.[38]

Conclusion

A main reason for the sharp increase in public-sector deficits in the seventies has been the attempt of governments to stimulate aggregate demand through expansionary fiscal policies. These attempts were supported by the results of macroeconometric policy simulations which suggested that a fiscal expansion has a substantial positive effect not only on nominal demand but also on real output and employment. These simulations are criticized on the ground that they tend to overestimate the demand effect of changes in government spending or taxation by (1) incorporating only a part of the crowding-out mechanisms which are discussed in the literature and (2) implicitly or explicitly assuming an accommodating monetary policy. The criticism is supported by the results of empirical studies. A study by the Deutsche Bundesbank (1982) for Germany arrives at the conclusion that an accommodated fiscal expansion leads to price–wage repercussions which after some time fully offset the initial gain in output and employment—a result that is compatible with the hypothesis of a long-run vertical Phillips curve. A study by the OECD (1982) for seven major OECD countries finds that the income effect of an increase in government spending is between three to nine times smaller if monetary policy is not accommodating.

The latter result indicates the dominant role of money supply changes in the context of a monetary–fiscal expansion and questions the large weight that has been given to fiscal demand expansion in the context of the so-called locomotive approach.

It is suggested that the targets of a reduction of public-sector deficits and of an adequate expansion of aggregate nominal demand can be achieved simultaneously by a policy mix where fiscal policy is assigned the role of reducing the structural component of the budget deficit and where monetary policy takes responsibility for keeping the expansion of nominal GNP on a level which is compatible with the maintenance or achievement of both price stability and a high level of capacity utilization.

Notes and sources

[1] See, for example, German Council of Economic Experts (1978–9, pp. 145–7).

[2] Matthöfer (1980, p. 125).

[3] There are two extreme cases in the IS–LM model in which deficit spending leads to a full crowding-out of private investment demand. The first is the case of a perfectly interest-elastic investment demand (represented by a horizontal IS curve); the second is the case of a perfectly inelastic demand for money (represented by a vertical LM curve).

[4] At this point it may be worth noting that financial innovations such as the payment of variable interest on demand deposits (which has become a widespread

practice in the United States during recent years) reduce the interest elasticity of the demand for M_1 and thereby lower the efficiency of fiscal demand management under an M_1-oriented strategy of the central bank.

[5] In the absence of capital mobility, deficit spending has the same effect on aggregate demand and interest rates as in the closed economy. The depreciation of the domestic exchange rate which results from the fiscal expansion in the absence of capital mobility fully offsets the income-induced increase in import demand so that there is no leakage of demand effects to other countries.

[6] In the original Fleming–Mundell model, which is based on the assumption of perfect capital mobility, there is no distinction between domestic and foreign interest rates. The negative impact of the world interest rate on the demand for domestic goods implicitly includes the negative response of the foreign demand for domestic investment goods in case of a rising world interest rate. Once imperfect capital mobility is allowed for, a distinction between domestic and foreign interest rates is required. The above consideration also suggests that export functions should include the level of foreign interest rates as an explanatory variable (Lehment 1982).

[7] Friedman (1978) has stressed the importance of the relative degree of substitution between bonds and capital for the analysis of wealth effects. In the standard IS–LM model, bonds and capital are treated as perfect substitutes. If the degree of substitution between capital and bonds is less than perfect and lower than the degree of substitution between bonds and money the LM curve may react to an increase in bond-financed government spending by shifting to the right rather than to the left.

[8] Most of the traditional IS–LM analysis also assumed that an increase in aggregate demand has no effect on prices. The extension of the analysis to the case of a less than perfectly elastic supply of goods showed that some part of the increase in aggregate demand is soaked up by an increase in prices so that the output effect is reduced; however, as long as the assumption of unchanged nominal wages is maintained, the output effect remains positive (Blinder and Solow 1973, p. 324).

[9] For a graphical and an algebraic analysis of expectation effects in the IS–LM model see Carlson and Spencer (1974) and Dieckheuer (1980).

[10] It should be noted, however, that expectation effects of public deficit-spending may in some cases also have a positive impact on aggregate demand as, for example, in the case of a public infrastructure project which improves the expected return on related private investment projects.

[11] An exception is the investigation by Krelle et al. (1979) on the basis of the Bonn model (Version 8.2) where additional government spending even causes a slight reduction in the monetary base and M_1. It should be noted, however, that monetary aggregates do not play an important role in the underlying model. This is shown by the fact that a simulated 20 per cent reduction of minimum reserves and the resulting increase in the money supply have practically no effect on interest rates, exchange rates, and GNP. The velocity of money is, thus, regarded as highly unstable and largely independent from changes in interest rates—a view which is not compatible with the results of empirical studies on the velocity of money (Langfeldt and Lehment 1980). This objection applies in a similar way also to the simulations by Conrad and Kohnert (1980) on the basis of Version 10 of the Bonn model.

[12] In the second case the increase in market interest rates will lead to an additional demand for central bank money which is assumed to be accommodated at least to the extent of existing lines of credit opened up by the Bundesbank.

[13] Central bank money is defined as the sum of currency held by non-banks

and banks' minimum reserve held against residents' deposits calculated at constant reserve ratios. Central bank money targets do not constitute 'base control'. The Bundesbank controls central bank money through changes in interest rates which affect credit expansion, the growth of bank deposits, and—via the induced effects on minimum reserves and currency holdings—central bank money (Bockelmann 1979).

[14] In their article Dewald and Marchon have also calculated respective long-run elasticities for other major OECD countries; the estimates are 0.195 for Canada, 0.284 for France, 0.214 for Italy, 0.285 for the United Kingdom, and 0.127 for the United States.

[15] The experience of the Bretton Woods system casts substantial doubts on the ability of a central bank simultaneously to control both interest rates and exchange rates. Economic theory suggests that in order to keep both variables constant in case of a domestic fiscal expansion the home central bank must pursue (1) an expansionary open-market policy to stabilize the interest rate and (2) sell foreign currency against domestic currency in order to prevent the depreciation which would otherwise result (Lehment 1980, Ch. III). In order to be successful such a policy requires that the domestic central bank has a sufficient stock of foreign currency and that the increase in the foreign money supply which results from the intervention in the exchange market is accepted by the monetary authorities of the other countries concerned. If a central bank does not sell foreign money but foreign securities (which is the general rule since central banks usually do not hold foreign currency), the effect on the exchange rate will be smaller and require an even larger amount of foreign assets. Moreover, the sale of foreign securities will tend to raise the domestic interest rate and, hence, have an adverse effect on the interest-rate target. If domestic and foreign securities are imperfect substitutes the effect will, however, not be fully offset—provided again that the foreign monetary authorities do not react despite the fact that the sale of foreign securities tends to raise foreign interest rates and the velocity of money abroad. With imperfect substitutability it can, however, no longer be assumed that an 'accommodating' monetary policy implies constant interest rates, since the operations by the central bank that are required to keep the exchange rate constant cause a divergence between foreign and domestic interest rates so that at least one of the two rates has to change.

[16] In addition to the effects on national income the OECD study also gives estimates for the effects on private expenditure and the current account.

[17] The underlying nominal adjustment hypothesis performs better in the estimations than the real adjustment hypothesis which implies a lag term of the form $\ln(CBM_{-1}/P_{-1})$; as has been shown by Goldfeld (1976) the nominal adjustment hypothesis assumes that nominal money balances are adjusted only gradually to price changes whereas the real adjustment hypothesis assumes an immediate proportional reaction of nominal balances to price changes. The introduction of real public debt into the equation did not lead to a significant improvement of the estimate; this means that we have found no support for the hypothesis that changes in the stock of government bonds cause a shift of the LM curve.

[18] This result is derived by substituting the parameter values of the CBM equation for the parameters of the M_3 equation in the formula for the income multiplier which is given in Table H of the OECD study. The lower value of the multiplier is largely due to the fact that the interest elasticity in the M_3 equation which has been estimated by Boughton is 0.40 and, hence, above the estimate for the interest elasticity in the CBM equation. The relatively high interest

elasticity in the M_3 equation is largely due to the underlying real adjustment hypothesis in Boughton's study. I have run a regression on the demand for M_3 analogous to the CBM regression (i.e. incorporating the nominal adjustment hypothesis) and found that in this case the long-run interest elasticity is about 0.20 and, hence, similar to the result for the CBM estimate. Moreover, I found that the nominal adjustment hypothesis performs better than the real adjustment hypothesis in the case of the M_3 equation also. It should be noted that the small OECD model also covers only part of the crowding-out mechanisms which have been discussed in the literature so that the multiplier may actually still be lower than the estimates from this model.

[19] The share of public consumption and investment is about 25 per cent of GNP in Germany so that the elasticity of 0.05 which has been found by Dewald and Marchon implies a multiplier of about 0.20.

[20] Cooper (1976, p. 47), Tripartite Group (1977), McCracken *et al.* (1977, pp. 30–1, 236–7), OECD (1976), BIS (1976, p. 7), and EC (1977, p. 4).

[21] The locomotive approach was not formulated in a unified theoretical framework and has been subject to substantial differences in interpretation.

[22] Apart from the demand-oriented interpretation there was also a supply-oriented interpretation stressing the importance of structural adjustment and innovation in advanced countries as an instrument to improve economic conditions in 'weaker' countries including the less developed countries (Giersch 1978).

[23] The alternative view that the stagnation had its main source on the supply side and especially in wage increases which exceeded the (adequate) increase in aggregate nominal demand received comparatively little attention in the international economic policy discussion.

[24] For a critical assessment of the vicious circle hypothesis see Haberler (1977). Moreover, the suggestion to stimulate demand in weaker countries through an expansionary policy in the 'strong' countries stood in apparent contradiction to the recommendation that restrictive demand policies should be pursued by the 'weaker' countries in order to reduce inflation (OECD 1976).

[25] The results of the OECD study (1982) which show relatively low multipliers for non-accommodated fiscal expansion support this view.

[26] For a critical review of the OECD interlink model and the policy simulations based on this model see Gebert and Scheide (1980, Ch. 4). It may be of interest that for Germany a fiscal multiplier of 1.5 has been assumed in the interlink simulation; this value is about four times higher than the value which we have derived for a 'non-accommodated' fiscal expansion in the OECD (1982) model.

[27] 'Concern about possible supply constraints may be more relevant from the point of view of medium-term problems than from those of the next 12 to 18 months. The fear of bottlenecks, even for fairly narrowly-defined sectors, seems, at the moment, unjustified' (OECD 1978, p. x).

[28] 'Although there would probably be some resulting upward pressure on prices it could be kept small, particularly if the fiscal stimulus consists of measures calculated to reduce cost and price pressures in the first place' (OECD 1978, p. x).

[29] In its discussion of possible different ways of implementing the convoy strategy the OECD (1978, p. xiv) considered various different forms of fiscal stimuli; monetary policy is not even mentioned.

[30] It should be stressed that concern about large US budget deficits was also expressed by economists and political representatives within the United States. The tax increases which were adopted in the summer of 1982 in order

to reduce part of the revenue shortfalls of the cut in income taxes and the subsequent decline in US interest rates seem to have largely settled the transatlantic dispute about US budget deficits—at least for the moment.

[31] The reduction in interest rates, however, tends to affect the composition of spending and—by favouring investment relative to consumption—may have a positive effect on long-term growth.

[32] Bergsten (1982) assumes that the negative demand effect of the induced monetary restriction is even stronger than the positive demand effect of the fiscal expansion; a reason for this assumption is not given.

[33] The observation that the recent increase in US taxes and the resulting reduction in the interest differential between the United States and European countries has gone along with a further appreciation of the dollar makes the argument appear doubtful.

[34] 'The current-account deficit of a country is the sum of the private financial deficit (excess of investment over savings) and the public deficit. If the current-account deficit increases this may be because the private deficit has risen—which is not a matter for public-policy concern—or because the public deficit has risen—which may indeed be a matter for concern. But the balance-of-payments figures in themselves will not tell one whether there is a problem. One must go directly to the public-sector (including central-bank) figures, so making the balance-of-payments figures redundant' (Corden 1977, p. 51). Once current-account problems are identified to be, in fact, government budget problems there is little reason to resort to trade restriction, which is a most inappropriate instrument for the removal of excessive budget deficits.

[35] The argument that a reduction in present deficits would be sub-optimal from the perspective of intertemporal burden-sharing has played no role in the recent policy discussion. Negative incentive effects may be brought forward as an argument against a reduction of public-sector deficits through tax increases but can hardly serve as an argument against a reduction of deficits through a cut in government consumption and transfers. For a discussion of the pros and cons of various possible measures to reduce public-sector deficits see Lehment (1981).

[36] If the multiplier of 0.20 which has been found in the context of the St Louis model (Dewald and Marchon 1979) is used, the effect on nominal GNP amounts to only 0.1 per cent. Moreover, it should be noted that the multipliers are derived for a change in fiscal expenditure on investment and consumption. To the extent that the deficit cut takes the form of a reduction in transfer payments or an increase in taxes, standard analysis suggests that the fiscal multiplier and the effect on aggregate demand should even be lower.

[37] In the context of the present policy of the Bundesbank a reduction in public-sector deficits could be included among the factors which the Bundesbank regards as justifying a monetary expansion in the upper part of the announced target range.

[38] The argument is analogous to the consideration that a corresponding policy mix in the United States would reduce the upward pressure on the external value of the dollar.

References

Bailey, Martin J. (1971), *National Income and the Price Level: A Study in Macroeconomic Theory*, 2nd edn. New York.

Barro, Robert L. (1974), 'Are Government Bonds Net Wealth?', *Journal of Political Economy* 82, 1095–117.

Bergsten, C. Fred (1982), 'The International Implications of Reaganomics', Kieler Vorträge, No. 96, Institut für Weltwirtschaft.

BIS (Bank for International Settlements) (1976), Annual Report, Basle.

Blinder, Alan S. and Goldfeld, Stephen (1972), 'Some Implications of Endogenous Stabilisation Policy', Brookings Papers on Economic Activity, No. 3, 585–640.

Blinder, A. S. and Solow, Robert M (1973), 'Does Fiscal Policy Matter?', Journal of Political Economy 82, 319–37.

Bockelmann, Horst (1979), 'Experience of the Deutsche Bundesbank with Monetary Targets', in John E. Wadsworth and François Léonard de Juvigny (eds.), New Approaches in Monetary Policy, Alpen, Rijn, 103–9.

Boughton, John M. (1979), 'The Demand for Money in Major OECD-countries', OECD Economic Outlook, Occasional Studies, Paris.

Brunner, Karl and Meltzer, Allan H. (1976), 'An Aggregative Theory of a Closed Economy', in Jerome L. Stein (ed.), Monetarism, Amsterdam, 69–103.

Carlson, Keith M. and Spencer, Roger W. (1975), 'Crowding Out and Its Critics', Federal Reserve Bank of St Louis Review, 57, 12, 2–17.

Cassel, Dieter (1982), 'Staatsverschuldung International. Stand und Entwicklung der öffentlichen Kreditaufnahme ausgewählter OECD-Länder im Vergleich', in Gottfried Bombach, Bernhard Gahlen, and Alfred E. Ott (eds.), Möglichkeiten und Grenzen der Staatstätigkeit, Tübingen.

Cebula, Richard J. (1973), 'Deficit Spending, Expectations and Fiscal Policy Effectiveness', Public Finance 3/4, 362–70.

Christ, Carl F. (1968), 'A Simple Macroeconomic Model with a Government Budget Restraint', Journal of Political Economy 76, 53–67.

Conrad, Claus and Kohnert, Peter (1980), 'Economic Activity, Interest Rates and the Exchange Rate in the Bonn Forecasting System No. 10', Discussion Paper No. 107, Institut für Gesellschafts- und Wirtschaftswissenschaft, Wirtschaftstheoretische Abteilung Universität Bonn, Feb.

Cooper, Richard N. (1976), 'Worldwide versus Regional Integration: Is there an Optimum Size of the Integrated Area?' in Fritz Machlup (ed.), Economic Integration — Worldwide, Regional, Sectoral, London and Basingstoke.

Corden, W. Max (1977), Inflation, Exchange Rates, and the World Economy: Lectures in International Monetary Economics, Chicago.

David, Paul A. and Scadding, John L. (1974), 'Private Saving, Ultrarationality, Aggregation and "Densions Law" ', Journal of Political Economy 82.1, 225–50.

Deutsche Bundesbank (1982), Monatsbericht, Aug., 32–41.

Dewald, William G. and Marchon, Maurice N. (1979), 'A Common Specification of Price, Output and Unemployment Rate Responses to Demand Pressure and Import Prices in Six Industrial Countries', Weltwirtschaftliches Archiv, 115, 1–19.

Dieckheuer, Gustav (1980), 'Der crowding-out Effekt. Zum gegenwärtigen Stand von Theorie und Empirie', Vierteljahreshefte zur Wirtschaftsforschung, Berlin, Heft 3/4, 126–47.

DIW (Deutsches Institut für Wirtschaftsforschung) (1981), 'Finanzpolitische Überreaktionen gefährden Wachstum und Beschäftigung', DIW-Wochenbericht No. 30, 16 July, 341–8.

Dornbusch, Rüdiger (1976), 'Comments on Brunner and Meltzer', in Jerome L. Stein (ed.), Monetarism, Amsterdam.

Dornbusch, R. (1982). 'Equilibrium and Disequilibrium Exchange Rates', unpublished manuscript.

Dornbusch, R. and Fischer, Stanley (1981), Macroeconomics, 2nd edn. New York.

Dornbusch, R. and Krugman, Paul (1976), 'Flexible Exchange Rates in the Short Run', *Brookings Papers on Economic Activity*, No. 3, 537–75.

EC (European Community) (1977), Commission, Die Wirtschaftslage der Gemeinschaft, Heft 4, Luxemburg.

Emerson, Michael (1982), 'The European Stagflation Disease in International Perspective and Some Possible Therapy', paper prepared for the Conference of the Centre for European Policy Studies on European Policy Priorities, Brussels, 15–17 Dec., published in this volume.

Fleming, J. Marcus (1962), 'Domestic Financial Policies under Fixed and Floating Rates', *IMF-Staff Papers*, 9, 369–79.

Friedman, Benjamin (1978), 'Crowding Out or Crowding In? Economic Consequences of Financing Government Deficits', *Brookings Papers on Economic Acitivty*, No. 3, 593–641.

Friedman, Milton (1968), 'The Role of Monetary Policy', *American Economic Review* 58, 1–17.

Gebert, Dietmar and Scheide, Joachim (1980), 'Die Lokomotiven-Strategie als wirtschaftspolitischer Konzept', Institut für Weltwirtschaft, Kiel.

German Council of Economic Experts (1978–9), Annual Report.

German Council of Economic Experts (1981), Special Report.

Giersch, Herbert (1977), 'IMF-Surveillance over Exchange Rates', in Robert A. Mundell and Jacques J. Polak (eds.), *The New International Monetary System*, New York, 53–68.

Giersch, H. (1978), 'Reflections on the "Locomotive Theory" ', paper prepared for the Seminar on 'The Locomotive Theory' at the American Enterprise Institute, Apr.

Goldfeld, Stephen M. (1976), 'The Case of the Missing Money', *Brookings Papers on Economic Activity*, No. 3, 683–739.

Haberler, Gottfried (1977), 'The International Monetary System after Jamaica and Manila', Weltwirtschaftliches Archiv, 113, 1–30.

Keynes, John M. (1936), *The General Theory of Employment, Interest and Money*, London, New York.

Krelle, Wilhelm, Conrad, Klaus, Grisse, Gerald, and Martiensen, Jörg (1979), 'The Effects of Foreign Monetary Impulses and of Fiscal and Monetary Policy Changes on the German Economy: Simulations with the Bonn Forecasting System', in John A. Sawyer (ed.), *Modelling the International Transmission Mechanism*, Amsterdam, New York, Oxford, 347–86.

Langfeldt, Enno and Lehment, Harmen (1980), 'Welche Bedeutung haben "Sonderfaktoren" für die Erklärung der Geldnachfrage in der Bundesrepublik Deutschland?', Weltwirtschaftliches Archiv, 116, 669–84.

Lehment, Harmen (1980), 'Devisenmarktinterventionen bei flexiblen Wechselkursen. Die Politik des Managed Floating', Kieler Studien 162, Tübingen.

Lehment, H. (1981), 'Zur Neuorientierung der staatlichen Schuldenpolitik'. Kieler Diskussionsbeiträge 79, Kiel, Sept.

Lehment, H. (1982), 'Wechselkurs- und zinsbedingte Crowding-out Effekte kreditfinanzierter Staatausgaben in der offenen Wirtschaft', Vorgetragen auf der Tagung des Vereins für Socialpolitik zum Thema 'Staatsfinanzierung im Wandel', Köln, 13–15 Sept.

Lucas, Robert E. (1976), 'Econometric Policy Evaluation: A Critique', in Karl Brunner and Allan H. Meltzer, *The Phillips Curve and Labour Markets*, Amsterdam, 19–46.

McCracken, Paul *et al.* (1977), *Towards Full Employment and Price Stability*, Paris.

Malinvaud, Edmond (1978), *The Theory of Unemployment Reconsidered*, Oxford.

Matthöfer, Hans (1980), 'Staatsverschuldung—Mittel oder Hemmschuh der zukünftigen Wachstums- und Beschäftigungspolitik?' in *Probleme der Staatsverschuldung. Beihefte der Konjunkturpolitik*, Heft 27, 123–30.

Mundell, Robert A. (1968), *International Economics*, New York.

Neumann, Manfred J. M. (1981), 'Der Beitrag der Geldpolitik zur konjunkturellen Entwicklung in der Bundesrepublik Deutschland 1973–80', *Kyklos* 34, 405–31.

OECD (1976), *Economic Outlook*, Paris.

OECD (1977), *Economic Outlook*, Paris.

OECD (1978), *Economic Outlook*, Paris.

OECD (1979), 'The OECD International Linkage Model', OECD *Economic Outlook*, Occasional Studies, Paris.

OECD (1982), 'Budget Financing and Monetary Control', OECD Monetary Studies Series, Paris.

Ott, David J. and Ott, Attiat F. (1965), 'Budget Balance and Equilibrium Income', *Journal of Finance* 20, 71–7.

Pohl, Reinhard (1981), 'Staatsdefizite, Kreditmärkte und Investitionen', Vierteljahresheft zur Wirtschaftsforschung, Berlin, Heft 3/4.

Siebke, Jürgen, Knoll, Dieter, and Schmidtberger, Wolf-Dieter (1981), 'Theoretische Grundlagen des crowding out Effekts', in Werner Ehrlicher (ed.), *Geldpolitik Zins und Staatsverschuldung*, Berlin, 227–62.

Silber, William L. (1970), 'Fiscal Policy in IS-LM Analysis: A Correction', *Journal of Money, Credit and Banking*, 2, 461–72.

Solomon, Robert (1978), 'The Locomotive Approach', paper prepared for the Seminar on 'The Locomotive Theory' at the American Enterprise Institute, Apr.

Tewes, Torsten (1982), 'Kreditfinanzierte Staatsausgaben und private wirtschaftliche Aktivität in der Bundesrepublik Deutschland. Eine Analyse mit Hilfe des ökonometrischen Modells des IFW', Die Weltwirtschaft, Heft 1, 38–47.

Tobin, James and Buiter, William (1976), 'Long-run Effects of Fiscal and Monetary Policy on Aggregate Demand', in Jerome L. Stein (ed.), *Monetarism*, Amsterdam, 237–309.

Tripartite Group (1977), *Economic Prospects and Policies in the Industrial Countries*, The Brookings Institution, Washington.

Vesper, Dieter and Zwiener, Rudolf (1982), 'Konjunkturelle Effekte der Finanzpolitik 1974–1981', DIW-Wochenbericht 19, 13 May, Berlin.

Westphal, Uwe (1981), 'Empirische Aspekte des Crowding-out', in Werner Ehrlicher (ed.), *Geldpolitik, Zins und Staatsverschuldung*, Berlin, 209–26.

Whitman, Marina v. Neumann (1978), 'The Locomotive Approach to Sustaining World Recovery: Has it run out of Steam', *Contemporary Economic Problems*, American Enterprise Institute, 245–84.

7

The Adaptation of Working Time as a Response to the Unemployment Problem

JEAN-MICHEL CHARPIN

There can be no denying the existence and importance of an unemployment problem. Unemployment has risen dramatically in Europe and America since 1980. Young people are specially affected. They are now getting used to the idea that the 'normal' way of entering the labour market is through unemployment. Long-duration unemployment is now more and more frequent, and leads to the existence of a new social category whose financial and moral situation is very difficult in most countries. Labour mobility diminishes, except for the cases of forced mobility. Structural adaptation is thus slowed down.

Existing forecasts and projections indicate that prospects are also quite gloomy. Possible economic strategies in both the demand and supply side can have only limited positive consequences on unemployment in the medium term, either because there is not much scope for these policies or because the lags involved are very long.

In this sense it can be said that when looking at ways of improving this situation we are not sure whether the adaptation of working time is a good solution, but we know it is the only one. In other words, everybody knows that if there is no adaptation of working time then unemployment will not decrease over the medium term.

However, adapting working time raises a lot of economic and social problems. This chapter tries to clarify the main issues at stake in this debate.

I. Experiences

The objective of this section is not to give a full account of all past experiences concerning the reduction of working time; for example, nothing will be said about the fairly important reduction of the working week which took place in Belgium. Its aim is only to exhibit the different problems which were raised in some very different cases of working-time reductions.

France 1936: The forty-hour legal working week under Léon Blum

In France, the decision to reduce the legal working week from forty-eight to forty hours was taken by the Assemblée Nationale in June 1936. This decision followed the Matignon agreements which were reached in the beginning of June between employers and unions and which led to substantial wage increases and to two weeks of paid holidays. In September 1936 the franc was devalued, and again in 1937. As a result the value of the franc dropped by about 57 per cent. At the beginning of November 1936 the legal working time of forty hours was introduced in the coal-mines, and in December in the metal industries. From the beginning of 1937 the forty-hour working week became general in industry.

The results for the French economy of the reduction of working time are given in Table 7.1. In 1937, the reduction of the legal working

TABLE 7.1
Economic Indicators of the French Economy 1936–1939

	Percentage change per year (Dec.–Dec.)			
	1936	1937	1938	1939[a]
Effective working time per worker in industry [b]	3.0	−11.6	−2.6	3.2
Employment in industry[b]	0.8	6.1	3.3	2.5
Industrial Production	7.5	4.7	−6.7	14.5
World Industrial Production	14.1	7.5	−6.2	n.a.
Exports (volume)	−5.5	9.6	7.0	n.a.
Imports (volume)	10.1	6.1	−10.6	n.a.
Consumer prices[c]	17.1	20.7	9.4	3.3
World commodity prices in gold	14.2	18.6	−21.4	n.a.
Import prices in French francs	12.0	55.0	12.9	8.7
Nominal wages per hour	10.9	37.7	14.2	5.1
Real wages per hour	6.7	8.6	−2.1	1.1
Real wages per week	8.5	−7.5	−1.5	7.3
Productivity per hour in industry[d]	3.5	11.8	−7.3	8.2
Changes in levels				
Trade balance (billion francs)	−10.0	−19.5	−15.1	−8.7
Unemployment rate (percentage points of active population)	−0.7	0.4	−0.1	n.a.

[a] Figures for the first seven months of 1939.
[b] Figures for firms with more than 100 employees.
[c] Index of the cost of living for a four-person family (Nov.–Nov.).
[d] Industrial production divided by the number of employed and by the effective working time.
Source: A. Sauvy, *Histoire Economique de la France entre les deux guerres*, Fayard, Paris, 1967, Part 2.

time led to a reduction of effective working time in large firms in industry of more than 10 per cent. This drop was almost completely offset by an increase in productivity per hour, partly due to an increase in the intensity of work and partly due to a higher level of output, so that employment nevertheless increased by 6 per cent. As a result of the devaluations, import prices rose strongly and led to a strong inflation, which was moderated by the imposition of price controls in October 1936, and to a deterioration of the balance of trade. The reduction of working hours per worker was compensated in part. Together with the higher employment, the wage sum in real terms remained unchanged. Although investment may have dropped a little, the volume of exports increased so that final demand increased and output followed the world-wide increase at a slightly lower pace. The trade balance deteriorated further due to the fall in the terms of trade, although the volume of exports increased more than that of imports. The rate of unemployment showed only a slight drop.

In 1938 both world output and commodity prices dropped. In France, the drop in industrial production was accompanied by an increase in prices and by a greater volume of exports.[1] These effects may be explained as follows. First of all, the devaluations in 1936 and 1937 totalled more than 50 per cent so that it may be expected that competitiveness in 1938 was high and the volume of exports increased. Consumption by households will have remained more or less the same, since the loss in real weekly wages was compensated by more employment. On the other hand, investment[2] dropped considerably and the lower level of investment depressed final demand. In 1939 the economy experienced the effects of the increased military buildup. This led to more output with a low inflation rate. The increase in the wage sum reflects the increase in productivity. The effective working time was allowed to fluctuate above the legal forty-hour working week. Due to the outbreak of war in September, the 1939 figures concern only the first seven months, excluding August, the normal holiday month.

As the statistical system before the war was relatively undeveloped, conclusions based on these figures include a large margin of uncertainty. The figure for effective working time includes paid holidays as working days. So the legal two weeks of paid holidays, which amounted to a 3.8 per cent reduction in working time per year, do not appear in effective working time, but do show up in the figure for output. Taking this into account, the actual drop in working time between 1936 and 1937 would then amount to approximately 15 per cent. Due to the fact that the total wage-bill and government spending, both in real terms, remained unchanged, final demand remained more or less unchanged. Whereas the picture looked quite bright for 1937, the lapse of world output in 1938 as well as the political and social unrest in France led to the abandonment of the forty-hour week after the fall of the second Blum government in 1938.

One could conclude that the supply side[3] did not suffer too much initially due to a big increase in the intensity of work, and to an ample supply of labour mainly in the form of hidden unemployment. Thus the aim of increasing employment by reducing working hours was achieved to a certain degree, even though the number of unemployed was not reduced much.

Federal Republic of Germany: the gradual reduction of contract working hours over the period 1955–1958

In the Federal Republic of Germany, contract working hours were reduced between 1956 and 1958 from forty-eight to forty-five hours per week, not with the specific aim of increasing employment. An extensive study by Kregel, mainly concerning manufacturing, concludes[4] that:

The employment effect was relatively minor (especially due to the economic downswing at that time);

The reductions of working time led to a rationalizing of production and thus stimulated the acceleration of productivity, so that strong economic growth could be obtained in the years after;

The reduction in working time stimulated structural changes, i.e. labour mobility.

From Table 7.2 it can be seen that contract working hours per week were reduced over a period of three years by 6.7 per cent and per

TABLE 7.2
Growth rates in the German economy 1955–1959

	Percentage change per year				
	1955	1956	1957	1958	1959
Contract working hours per week	0.2	−2.0	−2.9	−1.9	0.2
Contract workings hours per year	0.2	−2.6	−3.8	−2.5	0.4
Production	10.6	6.6	5.6	3.8	7.3
Investment	20.0	8.9	−0.1	4.7	11.2
Production price	2.0	3.3	3.0	3.6	1.2
Employment	3.8	2.6	2.1	0.4	0.9
Unemployment rate	2.4	2.0	1.7	2.0	1.6
Productivity per head	6.8	4.0	3.5	3.4	6.4
Real-wage rate per head	7.0	5.3	3.8	4.8	3.4

Source: COMET–ESA data bank and Commission of the European Communities.

year by an estimated 8.6 per cent. The figures for 1955 represent those of post-war industry working at nearly full capacity. As the capital stock increases, the unemployment rate steadily decreases. In this scenario a reduction of working hours does not seem an ideal policy to increase employment because production would be expected to decline as capacity is lost. The high level of capacity utilization, together with the large compensation of real wages (and so a rise in unit labour costs) gives an explanation for the acceleration of inflation from 1955 to 1958. Due to the loss of capacity, and the subsequent loss of production in an economy working at nearly full capacity, employment hardly increases. Thus productivity per head slows down but, if corrected for the drop in contract hours since 1955, productivity per hour shows an acceleration of the rate of increase due to a higher intensity of work. This is in line with Kregel's conclusion, quoted above.

The Netherlands 1961: The five-day working week

In the Netherlands, working time was reduced abruptly in 1961, due to increased pressure from organized labour for more leisure time, in particular for the five-day working week (see Table 7.3). Whereas the reduction of working hours was 2 per cent in January 1961, it had increased to 4.3 per cent by July and at the end of the year the reduction totalled 4.7 per cent (5.5 per cent in industry). In March 1961,

TABLE 7.3
Annual Growth Rates for the Netherlands 1960–1964

| | Percentage change per year | | | | |
	1960	1961	1962	1963	1964
Effective working hours per week	0.0	−4.7	0.0	0.2	−1.0
Exchange rate of the guilder	0.0	3.0	0.0	0.0	0.0
Production	9.6	2.9	4.3	3.3	8.6
Investment	11.5	6.5	4.4	1.9	18.9
Exports	14.0	2.1	6.5	5.6	12.1
Imports	16.6	6.3	6.7	9.5	14.8
Production price	3.4	2.6	3.2	5.0	8.4
Export price	−0.4	−1.8	−0.9	2.4	2.2
Import price	−3.0	−2.0	−1.4	1.4	2.5
Real-wage rate per head	5.7	5.2	4.1	5.3	9.0
Employment	1.9	1.5	2.0	1.4	1.8
Unemployment rate	0.7	0.5	0.5	0.6	0.5
Productivity per head	7.8	1.5	2.3	2.0	6.8
Trade balance	0.4	−0.3	−0.3	−0.9	−1.8

Sources: COMET–ESA data bank and Commission of the European Communities, *European Economy*, No. 7, Nov. 1980.

the Dutch guilder had been revalued in relation to the dollar by 5 per cent. According to the Centraal Planbureau, this revaluation had the following consequences:

An increase in the terms of trade, so that exports decreased and imports increased, which resulted in a deterioration of the trade balance;
Lower profits, giving less investment;
Fewer exports, meaning less production and thus less employment;
A reduction of inflation due to the increase in the terms of trade.

Three factors determine the background against which the reduction of working hours must be set. First of all, the revaluation of the guilder by 5 per cent, which reduced the level of utilization of capacity and therefore increased over-capacity. Secondly an extremely tight labour market in which the unemployment rate reached a historic low of 0.5 per cent, which enabled employees to demand and obtain the reduction of working time. Thirdly, there was the peak of an economic upswing in 1960, so that capacity at the time was utilized to a high degree.

The shock to working hours and the revaluation were restricted solely to the year 1961. The drop in production has been attributed partly to the turn in the business cycle and to the revaluation, but mainly to the reduction in working hours. After 1961 investment grew at a considerably lower rate. Factors which presumably played an important role are:

The increase in unit labour costs due to the more or less full compensation for the reduction of working hours by a higher wage rate per hour. This is reflected in the steady increase in real wages.
A decrease in productivity, reflecting the drop in production.
The lower profitability of firms, due to the rise of labour costs above productivity and the decrease of margins in foreign markets, so that industrial investment slowed down.

The increase in the volume of exports dropped due both to the revaluation and to the reduction in working hours. Employment growth remained unchanged, absorbing the supply of labour and keeping the unemployment rate very low. The nearly constant growth of productivity per hour indicates that there is no extra increase in the intensity of work. This is contrary to the German experience, described above, where intensity did increase. For subsequent years not much can be said due to the incidence of second-order effects, but in general a high level of utilization of capacity has persisted. The price controls limited the additional effect on inflation.

Summarizing, work sharing in the Netherlands in 1961 was introduced at a time when there was hardly any over-capacity, neither in

men nor in machines. As a result production slowed down, compared
to the previous year, with a percentage equal to the reduction of working time. As there was no deceleration in wages, unit labour costs increased. No additional employment above the trend was created under
these circumstances. Furthermore there was no apparent increase in
the intensity of work, compared to before the reduction of working
time. Although the reduction of working time was not meant specifically to create more employment, it can be concluded that the circumstances have prohibited any increase in employment.

The three-day working week in the United Kingdom in the beginning of 1974

In the United Kingdom working hours were reduced in January and
February 1974 when industry worked a three-day week as a result
of a widespread labour dispute. This means that working time was
reduced across the board by almost 40 per cent.

The figures in Table 7.4 show no large impact of the working-time
reduction. If the reduction had been the only determining factor of
economic performance, the reduction of working time by 40 per
cent would have led to a drop in production of 5 per cent. There
would have hardly been any effects on consumption and exports.
The drop in production is possibly reflected in the reported degree
of utilization of capacity (DUC) in the EC Business Survey. In the
fourth quarter of 1973, the DUC amounted to 90 per cent and fell
to 80 per cent in the first quarter of 1974, and regained 85 per cent
in the second quarter. However, in Germany, where there was no
major reduction of working time, the same pattern was observed
(88, 78, 86). We may conclude that the experience with the three-
day working week shows that in the short term large increases in
intensity of work can be achieved. In this case actual loss of capacity

TABLE 7.4

United Kingdom: Economic Indicators for the First Quarter on Annual Basis

	1971	1972	1973	1974	1975	1976	1977
Gross domestic product[a]	−3.8	−1.1	29.4	−5.7	−1.7	11.6	−5.7
Volume of exports	−13.9	−4.3	8.2	1.7	1.5	8.7	3.1
Final domestic demand[a]	−2.0	5.8	19.5	−3.4	1.9	5.1	−9.0
Degree of utilization of capacity[b]	82.1	77.2	85.1	79.6	83.3	76.0	81.8

[a] Percentage change on preceding quarter, annual rates, seasonally adjusted.
[b] From the EC Business Surveys, full utilization equals 100 per cent.
Sources: European Commission estimates and *European Economy*, No. 7, Nov. 1980.

may well have been only approximately one-eighth of the reduction of working time, as was reflected by a 5 per cent loss of production compared to a 40 per cent reduction of working time.

France 1981–1982

In the post-war period, the working week remained very high in France, in fact increasing until 1963. In 1963 the average working week in non-agricultural firms reached 46.2 hours. Then it began to diminish, fairly slowly at the beginning then increasingly rapidly. Between 1969 and 1979, the average annual rate of decrease was around 1 per cent leading to an average working week of 41.0 hours in 1979. But the movement was already slowing down impressively at the end of the period; in fact, the decrease was very moderate in 1979 (−0.4 per cent), 1980 (−0.3 per cent), and 1981 (−0.5 per cent), in spite of the recession experienced during these last two years. The reason for this decrease in the rate of reduction was fairly clear: almost no agreements between employers and employees contemplated a reduction of the working week going further than the forty-hour week level. It was evident that this level was going to stabilize quickly: in April 1981, 54 per cent of the workers and 75 per cent of the employees were working exactly forty hours a week. This relates not only to the fact that the level of forty hours was the legal level of the working week, beyond which hours were considered as overtime and consequently paid at a higher rate and under which the allowances for partial unemployment could be paid, but also the extraordinary impact of the forty-hour legal week of 1936 on the collective French sensitivity. In fact the forty-hour week was not only considered as legal, but really as 'normal'.

Negotiations between the social partners began in 1978 in order to try to modify and reduce working time. They were interrupted in 1980, no possibility of agreement being in sight. Prime Minister Barre then asked M. Giraudet, Chairman of Air France, to consult with the social partners and propose a way out. The Giraudet report[5] did not favour any reduction of the legal working week or a fifth holiday week: but it proposed a reduction of the annual working time and measures aimed at improving the use of equipment. It was very discreet on the question of wage compensation. Nothing much happened afterwards; but the issue of the reduction of working time was a central one during the presidential campaign.

After the elections, a national, but imprecise, agreement was reached between the social partners in July 1981 about the fifth holiday week and the reduction of the working week. The modalities of these measures were supposed to be defined by decentralized negotiations at the industry level. This proved very difficult and the government had to intervene, deciding in January 1982 on the thirty-nine hour legal week and other measures leading to working-time reductions (the *ordonnances*).

After this intervention from the government, agreements were quickly reached in the different industries about the modalities. From a level of 40.3 hours during the last quarter of 1981, the average working week went down to 39.5 hours during the first quarter of 1982. In January 1982, 92 per cent of the workers were working forty hours a week or more; there were only 36 per cent in this situation in April. The corresponding figures for employees are 87 per cent and 23 per cent.

There were some examples of large reductions (BSN, SAB, Europ-Assistance, etc.), but most of the time the reductions were moderate.

Looking at the precise content of the agreements between social partners, one can see that almost nothing was said about the reorganization of production processes and that wage-earners were generally fully compensated.

It is still too early to know whether the reduction of the working week has had, through lack of capacity, accelerated inflation, or reduced profits, any negative consequences on output. The first available studies[6] suggest that by mid-1982, the modification of the usual link between output and employment due to the reduction of the working week had resulted in manufacturing industries in the following split: 20 per cent for additional employment, 80 per cent for additional productivity.

For the first time since 1976, there was an increase in employment in manufacturing industries (very small indeed: 0.1 per cent) during the second quarter of 1982. It seems that this was partly a consequence of the reduction of working hours.

II. Macroeconomic Analysis

The first, and very simple, conclusion to be drawn from the wide range of experiences described in the first part is that a reduction of working hours cannot reduce unemployment if there is no involuntary unemployment. In this section, it will be assumed that present unemployment is to a large extent involuntary. This means that most registered unemployed would, if offered a job, accept to work at the existing level of wages. Such an assumption sounds sensible considering the present very high level of unemployment. In any case, it is obvious that if unemployment were to be of a voluntary nature, a reorganization of working time would be of no avail.

Basic considerations

The first question to look at, as is done in several studies,[7] is the following: Is the reduction of working hours likely to have a direct negative effect on production, or are the risks limited to indirect effects?

In general, the reduction of working time will lead to a reduction of capital hours, the amount of which depends on the possibility of implementing shift systems. Consequently, the production capacity is going to be reduced also. If there is no spare profitable capacity available in the economy, a reduction of capacity is equivalent to a drop in production. This case has been studied by Van den Goorbergh and Schouten;[8] they show that, depending on the wage compensation, such conditions for working-time reductions may have no effect or even negative effects on employment.

In the opposite case, that is when enough spare profitable capacity is available in the economy, it can be assumed that the reduction of working time has no direct effect on production, even without any extension of shift systems.

Let us take the following textbook example (Fig. 7.1): production capacity is represented by three machines, each working eight hours a day in effective working time. The demand is met by letting two machines run at full capacity, so that sixteen machine hours of the total capacity of twenty-four hours are used. The degree of utilization of capacity is 67 per cent and over-capacity 33 per cent.

Let us suppose that the daily working time is reduced to seven hours a day. The capacity is then reduced to twenty-one machine hours and the third machine can be utilized by employing more labour. The

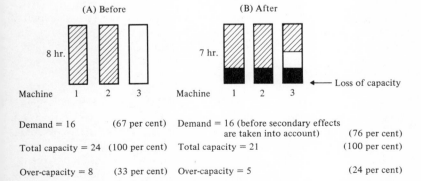

Fig. 7.1: The *ex ante* effect of the reorganization of working time on production (shaded area) and on capacity (white area) in a firm (A) before and (B) after the reorganization.

production can be maintained at sixteen machine hours; the capacity has been reduced as well as over-capacity.

In this set-up, the crucial assumption is that there exists enough spare profitable capacity before working hours are reduced. Of course, as over-capacity is reduced, there could be second-round effects on inflation, foreign trade, and so on; but these effects differ in nature from a direct effect on production.

It thus appears that the answer to the initial question depends on the answer to another question: does spare capacity exist today in our economies?

An indicator of the amount of over-capacity is given by the business surveys. A major drawback is, however, that these figures do not necessarily relate to the utilization of profitable capacity. Generally the business survey questions are formulated in a very general way; therefore the answers probably take into account some equipment which has become unprofitable, but has not yet been scrapped. However, the figures given by these surveys are the 'least wrong' answers one can get on this difficult topic.

Spare capacity, as measured by the business surveys, though generally far from the very high levels of 1975, is still fairly important. At least it can be said that there seems to be some room today in our economies for a reduction of working hours without directly having a drop in production.

In the future, two factors may cause a decrease of profitable over-capacity: an economic upswing or an increase in labour costs. In both cases, the room for manœuvre for the reduction of working time would be reduced.

Under present circumstances, one can consider that the direct effect on production of the reduction of working hours is negligible and that the debate is more on other issues raised by the past experiences discussed in the first section. These issues have been more or less dealt with by some recent quantified research; consequently a rapid survey of some of these exercises will now be given.

Recent quantified research

In the studies on the reorganization of working time in France,[9] three main effects have been analysed through the two macroeconometric INSEE models, DMS and METRIC. First of all, a shock to employment is applied equal to the reduction of working hours, while wages are assumed to drop by the same percentage. The additional employment takes some time to materialize, the so-called productivity cycle. A short-term increase in intensity of work is assumed, so that initially the level of production is maintained. Furthermore, effects of the Phillips type, due to strains in the labour market, induce wage increases, so that part of the additional employment may be lost. Secondly, work sharing could lead to a loss of capacity. It is assumed that this does not lead to an *ex ante* loss of production. Due to an increase of imports and a decrease in exports the trade balance deteriorates. Furthermore, the resulting drop in production leads to a rise in unit labour costs. Together with the increased strain on productive capacity, this produces higher inflation. Thirdly, the wages compensating for hours lost amount to an increase in hourly wages. This leads to different effects per model. In METRIC higher wages lead to an increase in final demand, so that output goes up. In its turn this results in higher investment and more employment. In DMS the profits are eroded by the increase in the costs of labour. In this model investment decreases as the return on investment diminishes and in the medium term employment is lost.

A reduction of working hours can lead to an increase in the intensity of work. This means that productivity per hour increases and so reduces the effects of the working-time reduction. If we denote the increased *ex ante* intensity of work by i per cent, then the *ex ante* shock on employment will amount to $(100 - i)$ per cent of the nominal reduction. The effects of the shock on employment must accordingly be reduced. In this manner changes in the assumptions on intensity can be accounted for.

An important element in the French exercises is that the three shocks (on employment, capacity, and wages) are independent and linear. This implies that it is possible to add the variants and to multiply them by a factor, in order to obtain a grid of results, relating to different a priori assumptions. If we denote the results of the variant of a shock on employment of 2.5 per cent with an equivalent loss of wages per head by A, on capacity of 2.5 per cent by B, and on wages of 2.5 per cent by C, the variants discussed in the French exercises can be given as follows. In Variant 1 a reduction of effective working time by 1 hour (= 2.5 per cent) with no wage compensation, no increase in the intensity of work, and measures which completely offset the loss of capacity, results in an *ex ante* increase in employment of 2.5 per cent (Variant 1 = A). In Variant 2 it is additionally assumed that an equivalent loss of capacity occurs in industry and services, with the exception of those working twenty-four hours a day (12 per cent), so that Variant 2 equals A + 0.88B. In Variant 3 and 4, the same assumptions as in Variant 1 are made but in these cases wages are taken to be fully made up for employees earning up to one and a half times the minimum wage. This compensation is equal to about 70 per cent of the loss of wages and comes on top of the wage rises due to the Phillips-type effects as a result of the shock on employment. The total wage compensation is thus considerably higher than

TABLE 7.5
The Reorganization of Working Time in France

	Average percentage deviation after three years			
	Variant 1	Variant 2	Variant 3 (METRIC)	Variant 4 (DMS)
GDP	−0.1	−0.8	+0.8	−0.7
Consumption	−0.1	−0.5	+1.5	+0.2
Investment of enterprises	+0.3	−0.5	+2.2	−3.1
Exports	−0.2	−1.6	−1.9	−2.1
Consumer prices	−0.2	+0.2	+0.8	+1.7
Labour productivity per hour	+0.6	+0.2	+0.8	+0.2
Wage rate per hour	+1.1	+1.4	+4.0	+4.6
Changes in levels after three years				
Employment (thousand)	+248	+179	+326	+216
Unemployment (thousand)	−108	−74	−143	−84
Trade balance (billion francs)	−0.8	−4.6	−10.2	−2.8

Source: Oudiz, Raoul, and Sterdyniak op cit.

the initial loss, as has been pointed out by Görres.[10] Variants 3 and 4 are equal to A + 0.7C. The results are given in Table 7.5.

This presentation, where the 'user' of the exercises can choose his own weighting of variants A, B, and C, has some advantages; it shows very clearly that the economist cannot be expected to anticipate what the conditions of the reorganization of working time are going to be, especially as far as wages and work organization are concerned. This kind of expertise, as has been stressed by J. Drèze, is not really to be expected from economists. What economists can try to do is to associate each set of conditions with their economic consequences.

In the *Netherlands*, the reorganization of working time has been studied using the Vintaf II model.[11] The results are presented in Table 7.6. In the first variant (variant A), working time is reduced by 2.5 per cent per year, while wages follow the drop in productivity per head. Intensity of work increases by 0.3 per cent per year. The additional employment amounts to 1.5 per cent per year, which equals 60 per cent of the reduction in working time. Thus the reduction in working time does not materialize completely as additional employment. As no Phillips curve effects have been taken into account, this is due to the loss of demand caused by the lower level of social benefits to households, which are linked to wages.

In the second variant (variant B) the additional assumption is made of a 2.5 per cent loss of capacity.

The third variant (variant C) gives the effects of an autonomous wage

TABLE 7.6
The Reorganization of Working Time in the Netherlands

| | Average percentage deviation per year (over five years) | | |
	A	B	C
Production in manufacturing	−0.4	—	−0.3
Consumption	−0.9	—	0.7
Exports	0.1	—	−0.8
Consumer prices	0.0	—	0.7
Real-wage rate per head	−1.7	−1.7	1.0
Employment[a]	1.5	0.3	−0.4
Labour productivity per head	−1.9	—	0.2
Changes in levels after five years			
Employment (thousand)	295	60	−85
Unemployment (thousand)	−195	—	55
Net lending by government[b]	1.9	0.1	−1.2
Trade balance[b]	1.9	—	−1.4

[a] Change in level after five years as a percentage of total employment in manufacturing and services (3.9 m.).
[b] Percentage of net national income.
Source: Centraal Planbureau, The Hague.

increase of 1 per cent per year. Employment will be reduced by 0.4 per cent per year due to the increase in unit labour costs which leads to an increase in scrapping and to lower profits and so to a lower level of investment. An increase in wages to compensate for the loss in variant A of 1.7 per cent per year would halve the additional employment effect of the reorganization of working time while leading to a deterioration of the trade balance.

These two studies give a sound idea of the econometric work which has been undertaken on the topic. We will not discuss all other similar studies.[12] But two special notes will be made.

In a British study,[13] the implementation of worksharing was examined against the background of a tight monetary policy. In the case of full wage compensation, a tighter monetary policy leads to lower inflation, a higher exchange rate, less output and also less employment.

In the European Commission study,[14] besides discussion of the issues raised by other studies, it was stressed that the favourable consequences of a reduction of working hours on the public deficit could be fairly important and that, in the case of no or partial wage compensation, the total effect on the disposable income of households could be negative, especially when unemployment allowances are of a magnitude comparable to wages.

Main issues

Now that the question of the direct effect of reducing working hours on production has been put aside and the historical and econometric material analysed, it is possible to list the main macroeconomic issues at stake.

Wage compensation. This is of course the main issue both for firms and for employees. It is also an important issue at the macroeconomic level. Most studies indicate a negative elasticity of employment with respect to the real-wage rate, at constant foreign balance and exchange rates.[15] Thus the point of view of the economist on this issue is clear: if work sharing is to be implemented, it must at the same time be income sharing. As will be seen in the third section of the paper, this is contrary to the position of the trade unions and consequently it raises a difficult implementation problem which we will discuss later.

Work organization. This issue is very important both for firms and at the macroeconomic level. On the one hand, historical experiences and quantified studies show that if capacity is lost because of reduced working time, then inflation is accelerated and the foreign balance deteriorates, leading to a decrease of potential beneficial effects on employment. On the other hand, a reduction in working hours can be an opportunity for firms to modify work organization, extend shift systems, and increase the utilization of existing equipment; a growing number of firms are proposing this sort of trade-off to their employees: fewer labour hours against more capital hours, especially in industries with a high capital/output ratio. But such a work re-organization creates some problems, both for firms and for employees. In particular, the trade unions very often resist the generalization of shift systems.

These two issues are by far the most important ones. More precisely, it can be said that a reduction of working hours without too large a wage compensation for the employees and without a decrease of capital hours is very likely to create employment and thus to lower unemployment. The third section of the paper will examine whether such conditions are possible, and if so which negotiation modalities can favour such conditions.

Nevertheless there are a number of other important issues, though less crucial than the two previous ones.

Productivity gains. Most studies consider and historical experiences confirm that very large productivity gains are feasible in the short run. The question is to know whether these gains are just transitory or if they can be consolidated in the long run. Or, to put it another way, how much does productivity increase in the long term when working hours are reduced?

The literature is not very helpful on this matter. Denison,[16] following the 1947 study of the Bureau of Labor Statistics,[17] argued in favour of fairly large productivity increases, around 100 per cent of the reduction of working hours at a level of 48.6 hours a week and still around 40 per cent at a level of 40 hours a week. But other authors consider this second percentage as irrelevant and favour a 0 per cent assumption.

If the long-term increases in productivity are important, then the question of wage compensation is not so crucial, but the increase of employment cannot be expected to be very large.

Unemployment allowances. It is often said that a large part of the financing problems of the social security systems comes from the unemployment situation. Huge figures can be computed, adding unemployment allowances, early retirement schemes expenditures, and contributions not received because people are not employed. But only the first category is to be taken into account when measuring the beneficial effects of the reduction of working time on the public-sector deficit. Nevertheless these effects are far from negligible, especially in those countries where the cost of the marginal unemployed is very high.

One conclusion following from this remark is that governments can envisage partially subsidizing the reduction of the working week because, in spite of these subsidies, their financial situation may eventually improve.

Concerted action. If the reduction of working time could be implemented without any cost, that is at constant unit labour cost and constant production capacity, it would not be necessary to consider the idea of internationally concerted action. Therefore, the idea behind concerted action is that there are some costs which cannot be fully avoided and that these costs will be more easily tolerated if they also appear in other countries.

This argument is correct but should not be carried too far, as Charpin and Hanekuyk have shown.[18] The reduction of working hours is basically a stagflationary measure, in the sense that, except when a very important reorganization takes place, it can only accelerate inflation and reduce output (its main advantage being the improved employment situation). The stagflation, when countries are taking concerted action, is passed through the trade flows between countries, which multiplies the undesirable effects on inflation and output.

That is the reason why, in any case, whether the reduction in working time be an individual action or a concerted action, the conclusion of this macroeconomic analysis stresses the importance of lowering the costs (both labour costs and capital costs) in order to get a positive effect on employment.

III. Implementation Problems

The conclusions reached in the second section are for the moment abstract ones. They only give the conditions the macroeconomist can exhibit for an improvement of the employment situation following a reduction of working hours. Now we must have a look at the concrete situation, especially by taking into account new trends of work organization in enterprises and the positions of the trade unions.

New trends of work organization in enterprises

It has been said that an important condition for the success of a reduction of working time is a reorganization of work in enterprises, in order to maintain or, if possible, increase capital hours.

At the same time, and for reasons largely independent from the reduction of working time, new types of work organization are being experimented with and implemented in numerous enterprises. These new types all present the same basic characteristic: they have more flexibility than the classical eight hours a day, five days a week, forty-seven weeks a year system.

The new organization either adopts one or several techniques (variable hours, condensed week, shift systems, holidays in rotation, sabbatical years, part-time employment, etc.),[19] or consists of a unified system which includes all techniques. A famous example in France of such an integrated system is the PIEC system[20] introduced by Citröen and Peugeot in 1977. It is a very sophisticated system of individual management of working time through a system of points, which workers can freely earn, save, and spend, subject to some fairly simple rules. Citröen and Peugeot are not regarded as philanthropic or even social employers. But such systems are very profitable for the firm: through a number of rules they incite employees to work according to the production needs;[21] absenteeism is generally considerably reduced; capital hours can be increased and so capital costs per unit are reduced.

On the other hand, there is no doubt that, at least for some categories of employees, such flexible systems correspond to an improvement of their situation, especially when combined with a reduction of working time, be it a reduction of hours per day, days per week, or weeks per year. This combination justifies the title of this paper. Working time is then not only simply reduced, but really adapted in response to the unemployment problem.

There are of course, as always, some difficulties:

In some cases, the trade unions fear a dilution of the work community, which may reduce their implantation and role;

Medium- and high-level staff can be penalized by such systems, first because they may be forced to work longer hours, second because their authority may be more difficult to impose;

Finally, there is often a temptation for the firm's management to use the implementation of these systems as an opportunity to strengthen controls and discipline, which may cause employees and their representatives to resist the introduction of these systems.

But, on the whole, there is no doubt that, if a reduction of working time is to occur without increasing capital costs, it must be accompanied by important changes in work organization.

Position of the trade unions

The reduction of working time is at present an important objective for most European trade unions. The reasons may differ. Some trade unions stress the importance of more leisure time in order to improve the quality of family, social, and cultural life; other trade unions put more emphasis on the reduction of working time as a means of improving employment and reducing unemployment. Rather than giving an extensive list of the positions of all the different trade unions,[22] the position of the CES[23] will be given, as stated at the Munich Congress 1979.

The objective of the CES was to reach a 10 per cent reduction of working time in the near future, by using various means: thirty-five hour week, six-week holidays, retirement age brought down to sixty, compulsory school attendance until the age of sixteen, vocational training, etc.

On the two main issues which were raised in the second section of the paper, the position was clear: this reduction of working time was to take place without any reduction of wages, the limitation of shift systems was considered as an important objective.

These statements were made in 1979. Since then, the economic situation has deteriorated rapidly, unemployment has almost doubled in Europe and some trade unions have taken more flexible positions, especially concerning wage compensation. But there is still a considerable distance between what the economist would consider as reasonable conditions for an efficient reduction of working time and what trade unions seem prepared to accept, at least considering their public statements.

However, some room for manœuvre seems to exist. At the firm level, trade unions may accept a wage reduction when the reduction of working time is important[24] or when the only alternative solution is massive lay-offs or bankruptcy. At the national level, trade unions may accept only partial wage compensation, if only because they are more and more concerned by the unemployment problem and aware of the poor financial situation of most firms.

The negotiations

To begin with, it must be recalled that a reduction of working time which is accompanied by full wage compensation and no change in work organization is more likely to have negative than positive effects on employment in the long run. When such a situation is considered as the most likely, and unless there are really strong aspirations for more leisure time, doing nothing to reduce working time may be a better policy than doing something. But in this case and whatever the demand or supply policies applied, our societies would have to reconcile themselves to growing unemployment, with all its potential dramatic consequences.

Forced with such a choice, the only courageous policy is at least to try to formulate and implement an economically sound adaptation of working time.

An important issue concerns the right 'place' for negotiations between social partners. The recent experience in France suggests that:

(i) The negotiations about the precise modalities of working-time reductions and changes in work organization are possible only at the firm level;

(ii) However, at this level and with the exception of only a few examples, the pressures for full wage compensation are very difficult to resist. If only for an obvious reason: unemployed people, who are by far the most interested in an efficient reduction of working time, have no say in the matter. Consequently my feeling is that it is only at the national level, where trade unions actually take into account the interests of the unemployed, that an agreement between social partners on the wage compensation issue must be sought. Even at intermediate levels, for example the industry level, the pressures for full wage compensation would be very strong.

If this last intuition is right, then matters become difficult, though not impossible, to organize, because two levels of negotiations would have to be involved.

Governments can help the process through various subsidies, if only because the potential decrease of unemployment can reduce their expenditures. However, given the present financial situation of government accounts in most European countries, this help cannot go further than these potential savings.

All these elements show first that the manner of organizing the negotiations is an important issue, and secondly that there is no available solution to the problem which will guarantee a favourable conclusion.

But, in response to the unemployment problem, our countries and our governments have, as usual, no other dilemma than the one of will: to give up or to try.

Notes and Sources

[1] The increase in exports was mainly due to the strong increase in exports of agricultural products (+25 per cent) but also to an increase in exports of manufactured goods (14 per cent).

[2] Sauvy (op. cit., p. 281) reports that whereas output of the main branches of industry dropped by 5 per cent between May 1936 and May 1938, output of investment goods decreased by 11 per cent during the same period.

[3] In 1936 with only a slight reduction of working time, the increase in French output was only 50 per cent of the world increase of output, and in 1937 with a large reduction of working time, it was above 60 per cent of the increase in world output.

[4] See *European Economy*, No. 5, Mar. 1980, 101.

[5] Pierre Giraudet, *Rapport sur la durée du travail,* La Documentation Française, Paris, Apr. 1980.

[6] *Tendances de la conjoncture,* INSEE, Sept. 1982.

[7] See, for example, G. Oudiz, E. Raoul, and H. Sterdyniak, 'Réduire la durée du travail, quelles conséquences?' *Economie et Statistique*, No. 111, May 1979; and J. Drèze, 'Réduction progressive des heures et emploi', Congrès des économistes belges de langue française, Mons, Nov. 1980.

[8] W. M. Van den Goorbergh and D. B. J. Schouten, 'The Case of Labour Time Reduction without Wage Compensation: More or Less Unemployment?', *De Economist* 128, 4, 1980.

[9] G. Oudiz, E. Raoul, and H. Sterdyniak, op. cit.

[10] P. A. Görres, 'Will a Shorter Workweek help to reduce Unemployment?', University of Munich, Mar. 1981, mimeo.

[11] See Social Economische Raad, *Advies sociaal economisch beleid op middellange termijn,* No. 7, The Hague, 1980; and A. B. T. M. Von Schaik, *Naar een nieuwe macro-economic,* Leiden, 1981.

[12] For a review of these studies, see *European Economy,* No. 5, Mar. 1980.

[13] R. Allen, 'The Economic Effects of a Shorter Working Week', Government Economic Service Working Paper, No. 3, London, June 1980.

[14] Basic Economic Considerations in quantifying the Effects of a Reduction in Working Hours, Commission of the European Communities, Feb. 1981, mimeo.

[15] See also J. Drèze and F. Modigliani, 'The Trade-off between Real Wages and Employment in an Open Economy', *European Economic Review,* 15, 1981.

[16] E. Denison, *Why Growth Rates differ,* Brookings Institution, Washington DC, 1967.

[17] US Bureau of Labor Statistics, *Hours of work and output,* Washington DC, 1947.

[18] J. M. Charpin and D. Hanekuyk, 'Reducing Working Time in the European Community', *Cambridge Journal of Economics* Conference, July 1982, mimeo.

[19] For an extensive description of these techniques, see, for example, J. L. Michau, *L'horaire modulaire,* Masson, Paris, 1981.

[20] Dossier PIEC, Cahiers techniques de l'UIMM, No. 24, Paris, May 1977.

[21] For example, in the PIEC system, the capital of points is doubled at age thirty-five; so the worker is encouraged to work very hard until this age, which corresponds to the firm's interest. In other firms, the rules could reward work during seasonal peak periods.

[22] For such a list, see: Institut Syndical Européen, *La réduction du travail en Europe occidentale*, Brussels, 1979.

[23] Conféderation Européenne des Syndicats, a grouping of thirty-one trade unions from eighteen European countries.

[24] For example, in France, the working week was reduced to thirty-five hours without full wage compensation at Europ-Assistance (May 1982) and at SAB (April 1982), in this last case even with the agreement of the CGT (Confédération Générale du Travail).

8

The European Stagflation Disease in International Perspective and Some Possible Therapy

MICHAEL EMERSON

I. The Relative Condition of the European Economy

With the 1980-2 recession Western Europe suffered a renewed, bad attack of stagflation disease. But the idea of economic diseases seems to have developed in deeper ways in many countries of the region.

One hears even West Germans talking about having caught the Swedish disease (over-indulgent welfare state?) although many other Europeans still look to the German economy as their model. Then there is the Dutch disease (something like the Swedish, compounded with gastro-enteritis of the exchange rate). There is the Belgian disease (same family, but with complications: swollen budget deficit and galloping indexation). A relation of the Belgian virus is found in Italy (with more inflation). And there is our old friend the British disease (multiple sclerosis of the economic arteries; daring surgery has recently been tried, but the patient remains in the intensive-care unit). Nor should we forget *le mal français,* an ailment thought to relate to over-centralization. The diagnosis is given a more sociological bent in Denmark, where the governor of the central bank has used the analogue of the rake's progress.[1]

The economic miracles seem to have gone. There may still be a Swiss model, despite some unlikely demonstrations by young people in Zurich in recent times. Finland seems to have done well in the seventies. But the European models have surely reduced to minority corners of the continent. The miracles have gone east, not just to the land of the rising sun, but to the Pacific basin at large, to Silicon Valley, Seoul, and Singapore.

If one tends to the view that the European disease is not incurable, we should get on with the job of diagnosis and therapy.[2]

Deficiencies in employment creation and related ills

Europe's number-one problem is its failure to increase employment at a time of exceptional demographic expansion of the working-age population, which for some years will remain at the present rate of 1 per cent per year. This failure is particular to Europe in two senses. It is a problem common to almost all European countries; and one that runs much deeper than in either of the region's two main industrial competitors, the US and Japan. For the US we must look at the employment record for at least a decade before the current recession. The latter has caused a renewed rise of unemployment, but this is distinct from the longer-run employment performance that will be commented on below.

Within Europe, half of the region has inflation more or less under control, but virtually the whole of the region is afflicted by high unemployment levels. No family with children heading for the labour market would doubt it even if economists argue fine points about the statistics, and about concepts of voluntary unemployment. Only in a few smaller countries are the apparent unemployment rates very low: Sweden, Norway, Switzerland. Even in these cases qualifications are important (unemployment transposed into vast training schemes in Sweden, or exported with the repatriation of immigrant workers in Switzerland).

Among Europe's main competitors (as Figs. 8.1 and 8.2 show) the rate of employment creation over the last two decades has been incomparably higher: 30 per cent up in Japan, 40 per cent up in the United States, 2 per cent up in the EC. Nor have the seventies been different to the sixties. After a pause around 1974 following the first oil shock, employment resumed its strong upward path in the US and Japan, whereas in Europe it remained flat. Particularly striking as between the US and Europe is the 15 per cent growth of employment in 1975–80 in the United States, alongside practically none in Europe (+0.5 per cent), whereas GDP grew by comparable amounts (18 per cent, 16 per cent respectively). Thus the US found itself puzzling over a productivity problem (up 4 per cent, compared to the EC's 13 per cent, and Japan's 16 per cent), whereas Europe found itself puzzling over an employment problem.

Looking more closely into the US–Europe comparison, we note that the 15 per cent employment growth in the US permitted a very large increase in the labour-force participation rate as well as a drop in unemployment, even at a time of very fast demographic growth of the working-age population. The female labour force's participation rate increased in the United States from 53 per cent in 1975 to 60 per cent in 1980, whereas in Europe it grew much more slowly

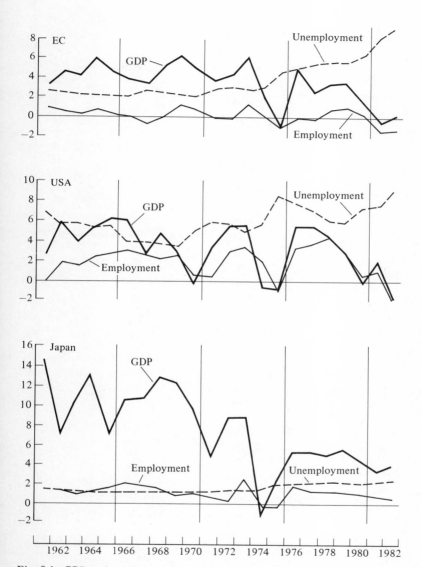

Fig. 8.1: GDP and employment growth and unemployment rate, EC, USA, and
Japan 1961–82

Source: EC Commission, 'Annual Economic Review 1982-3', *European Economy*, No. 14, Nov. 1983.

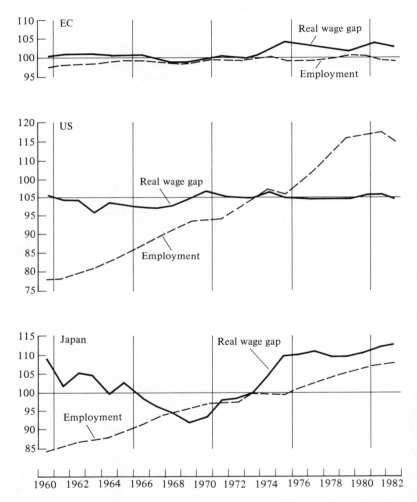

Fig. 8.2: Real-wage gap and employment, EC, US, and Japan 1960–82
(1973 = 100)

Souce: EC Commission, 'Annual Economic Review 1982–83', *European Economy*, No. 14, Nov. 1983.

from 46 to 49 per cent. Not unrelated was the exceptionally large contribution to this growth of jobs in the US of the service sector, often in small enterprises with flexible conditions of part-time employment.

There may be more than a suspicion that Europe's less bad labour productivity performance compared to the US has not represented an attractive trade-off against the employment shortfall. Suppose, for example, that labour productivity has held up in Europe because relative labour-market costs and rigidities have encouraged capital deepening in labour-saving technology, and discouraged small-scale employment creation in service sectors. In the US, on the other hand, the extension of service-sector employment to increasing numbers of women, who earlier were housewives, may have partly caused aggregate productivity performance to drop, but this is hardly an economic problem. Total factor productivity is thought to have slowed much in the US, but more study of this in Europe—where there are data problems—might show similar results.

The fact that the US unemployment rate has in the present recession shot up to European levels is also hardly comforting. There is a shared cyclical problem. But Europe has a longer-term and deeper structural employment problem.

On the whole, financial policies in Europe have been quite supportive of nominal demand. The budget balance of EC countries, which hardly moved from a surplus of 0.4 per cent of GDP in the EC's inaugural year 1958 to a deficit of 0.3 per cent in 1970, rose to 3.5 per cent in 1980 (a cyclical peak year), reaching high points of 5.5 per cent in 1975 and 5.0 per cent in 1982 at the troughs of the oil-shock recessions. Nominal GDP growth in the sixties was 8.7 per cent on average, and in the seventies 11.8 per cent, with money supply respectively 10.4 per cent and 13.9 per cent, and real long-term interest rates respectively 3.6 per cent and 1.1 per cent.

While one may discuss the influence of US interest rates in the prolonged 1981–2 recession, clearly it would be misplaced to suppose that this was at the heart of the structural unemployment crisis that has grown during the seventies.

Rather one should enquire why the demand stimulation of the seventies was diverted into increased inflation rather than real demand and employment growth. This turns the spotlight on to the other conditions for employment and investment: income distribution between profits and real wages, and flexibility versus rigidity in the conditions of employment more generally. There are admittedly measurement problems here. Interpretation of incomplete data on profitability is befogged by uncertainties over the income of the self-employed, intersectoral differences in profitability between internationally exposed versus sheltered activities, and the influence of

TABLE 8.1
GDP and Unemployment 1960–82

	EC	Europe–OECD	US	Japan
GDP, growth %				
1960–73	4.6	4.8	4.0	10.3
1973–82	1.7	1.8	1.8	3.6
GDP per capita, growth, %				
1960–73	3.8	3.8	2.8	9.1
1973–82	1.4	1.3	0.7	2.6
GDP per employed, growth, %				
1960–73	4.4	4.4	2.0	9.1
1973–82	1.9	1.9	0.3	2.7
Unemployment rate, %				
1960	2.5	2.9	5.3	1.7
1973	2.5	3.6	4.7	1.3
1982	9.4	10.0	9.5	2.3
GDP per capita, ECU[a]				
1960	1,062		1,752	572
1973	3,272		4,786	3,201
1982	9,339		12,805	9,538

[a] At current purchasing power parities.
Source: OECD and estimates of EC Commission.

inflation on real versus apparent profitability. The stickiness of real wages in Europe, contrasting with sticky nominal wages in the United States, has been tracked econometrically by Sachs.[3]

Available data from the national accounts suggest that the net rates of return on fixed capital in Europe have been low compared to the United States and to Japan over the whole of the last two decades (see Table 8.3). In the second half of the seventies, the rate of return fell in all regions; only slightly from a very high level in Japan, substantially from a high level in the United States, and substantially from a lower level in Europe (four large EC countries). More critically, it seems that in Europe the net rate of return has now perhaps fallen even lower than the cost of capital. By 1979, the last year for which the rate-of-return data exist, the EC rate of return had fallen to 14 per cent compared to 24 per cent in the United States and 35 per cent in Japan. With the recession these rates of return have presumably now dropped further, whereas in mid-1982 long-term interest rates stood at $14\frac{1}{2}$ per cent in the EC, $12\frac{1}{2}$ per cent in the US, and $7\frac{1}{2}$ per cent in Japan. As between the four largest European countries it is clear

TABLE 8.2A

Indicators of Macroeconomic Disequilibria and Constraints in 1982 (EC countries)

	Unemployment rate	GDP deflator, percentage change	Balance-of-payments current account, percentage of GDP	Real rate of interest[a]	Public finance Budget balance, percentage of GDP	Corrected balance, percentage of GDP[b]	Public debt, percentage of GDP (1981)[c]
Belgium	13.9	7.3	−4.0	3.7	−12.8	−5.8	88.6
Denmark	9.1	10.6	−4.1	12.0	−9.5	(−9.0)	(46.4)
Germany	6.9	4.8	0.1	4.6	−3.9	−3.1	5.1
Greece	(3.8)	21.7	−2.4	(−7.0)	−9.2	−1.4	40.4
France	8.3	12.4	−2.6	5.4	−3.0	−1.9	(17.3)
Ireland	12.1	18.6	−9.0	1.1	−15.2	−3.7	98.4
Italy	9.9	17.5	−1.3	6.0	−11.6	−1.1	64.9
Luxembourg	1.2	8.7	19.7	0.6	−0.9	1.2	(21.0)
Netherlands	10.4	6.2	4.0	5.7	−5.7	−2.5	(34.0)
United Kingdom	12.2	8.4	0.8	6.9	−0.9	2.4	56.0
EC	9.4	10.6	−0.7	4.8	−5.0	−1.6	(42.3)

[a] Long-term interest rate in July 1982 less the increase of consumer prices over six months (Jan.–July) in annual rate.
[b] Budget balance corrected for the impact of inflation on the real value of domestic public debt (see Ch. 6).
[c] Central government debt for DK, GR, F, IRL, L, NL; general government debt for D, '*settore statale*' for I, public sector for B and UK.

Source: EC Commission, 'Annual Economic Report, 1982–3', *European Economy*, No. 14, Nov. 1982.

TABLE 8.2B

Indicators of Macroeconomic Disequilibria and Constraints in 1982 (other OECD countries)

	Unemployment rate	GDP deflator, percentage change	Balance-of-payments current account, percentage of GDP	Real rate of interest[a]	Public finance: Budget balance, percentage of GDP
Austria	3.4	5.50	−1.9		−1.8
Switzerland	5.9	5.75	3.6	−2.1	
Finland	2.0	9.50	0.4	−1.8	
Norway	3.0	8.25	−0.1	−0.7	
Sweden		7.00	−2.3	1.7	−5.9
Portugal		24.50	−9.3		−
Spain	15.0	12.50	−2.1		−4.0[b]
OECD Europe[a]	10.5	10.25	−0.8		
Japan	2.2	3.50	0.6	5.4	−3.4
United States	9.3	6.00	0.4	5.8	−3.6
OECD[a]	9.0	10.25	−0.2		−4.0

[a] Including OECD forecasts for EC countries.
[b] 1981 figure.
Source: OECD, *Economic Outlook*, July 1982.

TABLE 8.3
Rates of Return on Fixed Capital[a]
(Percentages)

	1960–73	1974–9
High		
Japan	35.6	21.0
Average		
United States	29.1	20.6
Below average		
France	20.3[b]	14.4[c]
Italy	16.6	15.4
Germany	21.9	16.0[c]
Very low		
UK	12.7	5.0
EC (above countries)	18.7	13.4
OECD (above countries)	26.0	17.8

Note: The figures represent net rates of return on the net capital stock at replacement cost for all countries except Japan, for which they are gross. For France, Germany, the United Kingdom, and the United States, for which both net and gross data are available, the differences between the net and gross figures over long periods are not very great.

[a] Manufacturing industry.
[b] 1963–7.
[c] 1974–8.

Source: OECD and estimates of EC Commission.

that the UK's private sector is in a class of unprofitability of its own, with net rates of return down to 5 per cent, compared to around 15 per cent in the other three large European countries. Belgium could be close to the UK, to judge by some indications.

Striking figures also emerge in comparisons of hourly labour-cost levels (Table 8.4). In 1970, European wage costs were broadly half the US level, the exchange-rate changes of the early seventies corrected an undoubted element of over-valuation of the US currency, and by 1974 the high end of the European wage scale (Germany and Benelux) was on a par with the US. By 1980, at the trough of the dollar's devaluation, German wages had risen almost 30 per cent above the US level. Belgian workers treated themselves to even higher wages, 34 per cent above the US level, while Italian and French wages were brought almost to a par with the US. No wonder that multinational enterprises were concluding that Europe was too expensive, when one also takes into account the inefficiencies of Europe's imperfect internal market. The exchange-rate changes of the last two years have redressed this situation,

TABLE 8.4
Hourly Labour Costs in Manufacturing ($US)

	1970	1974	1980	1981
United States	4.3	5.4	10.0	11.1
Germany	2.6	5.6	12.9	11.1
Netherlands	2.2	5.4	11.7	10.4
Belgium	2.2	5.2	13.4	11.6
Italy	1.9	3.6	9.6	8.5
France	1.8	3.6	9.6	8.8
UK	1.6	2.9	7.3	7.1
Japan	1.1	2.4	6.8	7.2
EC (above countries)	2.1	4.3	10.5	9.3
OECD (above countries)	3.2	4.5	9.7	9.8

Source: **Institut der Deutschen Wirtschaft.**

maybe excessively, but that is not yet clear. The full adjustment process is not yet complete. By 1981 the high-wage groups in Europe— Germany and Belgium (coupled to Sweden and Switzerland outside the EC)—were still about on par again with the US on hourly labour costs (Table 8.4). Taking into account social security costs, which are substantially higher in Europe (see Table 8.5), it is not obvious that the US worker has become overpriced.

Meanwhile the Japanese worker has caught up the middle-income European countries, such as the UK, without eliminating the massive relative profitability of Japanese industry. Moreover the much greater flexibility of employee compensation in Japan remains an additional advantage from the employer's point of view. Bonus payments there, amounting to a quarter of total cash earnings, are related to the company's performance.[4] While these are becoming more integrated into the annual wage round negotiations, it seems that the latter are becoming increasingly influenced by company performance. Surveys conducted by the Ministry of Labour in Japan on the most relevant factors in wage determination suggest that the number of companies for which its own performance was the number-one factor rose from 40 per cent in 1972 to 65 per cent in 1979, whereas for the 'going rate' of wage increase the proportions fell from 29 to 18 per cent, and the cost of living fell from 11 to 7 per cent. It would be interesting to obtain comparable figures for European countries and the US, but one may suppose that the results for European countries would show the 'going rate' and cost-of-living increases to be easily predominating factors.

One attempt to clarify the wage cost factor is seen in calculations

TABLE 8.5

Ratio of Non-wage Labour Costs[a] to Total Labour Costs 1981
(Percentages)

Italy	51.9
Austria	47.4
France	45.1
Netherlands	43.8
Germany	43.5
Belgium	43.0
Sweden	40.1
EC average	40.1
Spain	37.3
Greece	35.5
Switzerland	32.0
Norway	32.0
United States	27.8
Canada	25.9
United Kingdom	24.3
Ireland	24.0
Japan	21.0
Denmark	18.2

[a] Principally social security contributions of the employer.
Source: Institut der Deutschen Wirtschaft, *Informationsdienst,* No. 18, Köln, 1982.

of 'real-wage gaps'. This gap aims at measuring the difference between the actual real-wage evolution and that which would have resulted in unchanged factor shares of the enterprise sector in GNP; or, put another way, it measures the wage increase 'warranted' by the evolution of productivity and the terms of trade. The long-term profile of the real-wage gaps of the EC, US, and Japan are set out alongside employment in Fig. 8.2. During most of the sixties, the real-wage gap opened up to the advantage of profits in the US and Japan, alongside very rapid employment growth. For Europe the story becomes dramatic in the wake of the first oil shock. The real-wage gap then increased sharply, in favour of wages and against profits, and has since remained significantly above the 1973 baseline (which was close to the previous long-term average). This increase in real-wage gap coincided broadly with the accelerating demographic labour-supply increase. Combined with a continuing stagnation of employment, unemployment in Europe began its catastrophic rise. Meanwhile, the US quickly reversed in 1975 the incipient emergence of a real-wage gap, and then saw the strong employment growth expansion of the seventies that stands in such stark comparison with Europe's stagnation during this same period. In Japan the rise in employment halted in 1974–5 alongside a very sharp rise in the real-wage gap in favour of wages. The real-wage gap then stabilized over the remainder of the decade, and employment resumed its growth. The Japanese experience must no doubt be interpreted in the context of the high levels of profitability and flexibility of wage costs that have been seen before and since their passing inflationary aberration of 1974–5.

Finally, Europe can see worrying symptoms of a relative weakening of economic performance in the technological quality of its industrial output, which, for a region not well endowed with natural resources, will mean a gradual decline in its relative income. The evidence on this point has been summarized in three indicators: export market share performance in equipment goods, export–import ratios for these goods, relative specialization of exports in high technology goods (defined in terms of the high-grade human skill component in value added).[5] All these indicators show the same overall picture of rapid progress in Japan, approximate stability on the part of the US at a high level of technological performance, and a declining position on the part of the EC. Data for Korea, Taiwan, Singapore, and Hong Kong would no doubt also show a build-up in high technology exports, reflecting their growing economic maturity, and conversely their lesser reliance on such products as textiles and footwear. In these latter products the EC has increased its relative specialization.

Further indications emerge from data on overall investment performance. Europe's investment ratio has declined from 24 per cent of GDP around 1970 to $21\frac{1}{2}$ per cent around 1980. That of the US has remained rather constant at the low level, of about 18 per cent, which fits with the combination of low productivity and high employment growth already noted. Japan's investment ratio has declined somewhat, but from an exceptionally high level of 35 per cent of GDP around 1970 to 32 per cent around 1980. Within the composition of investment, the share of non-residential construction may be taken as a rough indicator of capacity extension, as opposed to capital deepening. On this account Europe's performance has declined from a 33 per cent share around 1970 to 31 per cent around 1980, similar to the decline seen in the United States but contrary to an increasing share in Japan. According to fragmentary survey evidence in Europe (IFO for Germany, INSEE for France) an increasing share of equipment investment has been going into capital deepening rather than capacity extension.

Excesses of the public sector and related ills

Europe has another clear structural difference with its industrialized competitors, the growth and extent of its public sector.

Institutional non-comparabilities are perhaps minimized in looking at current government spending, which cuts out capital expenditure and transfers. The latter involve non-comparable arrangements for financing public investment and sectors in which state enterprises are sometimes important.

Countries of the OECD area can be arranged, as in Table 8.6, in groups labelled 'below OECD average' (current spending under 35 per cent of GDP), 'above OECD average' (above 35 under 45 per cent), and 'very big government' (above 45 per cent). The US and Japan both lie well within the 'below OECD average' group, despite which the Reagan Administration is undoubtedly cutting public expenditure

TABLE 8.6
Levels and Growth of Current Public Expenditure in Europe, US, and Japan
(Percentages of GDP)

Levels in 1980		Growth from 1960 to 1980	
Sub-OECD average, < 35		*Sub-OECD average, < 10*	
Japan	25.4	*United States*	6.2
Spain	29.1		
Switzerland	29.1		
United States	31.7		
Above-OECD average, < 45		*Above-OECD average, < 15*	
Italy	41.1	*Japan*	11.8
Germany	41.2	United Kingdom	11.8
United Kingdom	41.7	France	12.2
Austria	42.4	Finland	12.5
France	43.1	Switzerland	12.5
		Germany	13.5
		Italy	14.9
Very big government, > 45		*Very big growth, < 20*	
Norway	45.4	Spain	15.4
Belgium	48.1	Austria	16.9
Ireland	48.5	Norway	19.0
Denmark	55.7	Belgium	19.7
Netherlands	56.7		
Sweden	57.7	*Runaway growth, > 20*	
		Ireland	25.7
		Sweden	26.6
		Netherlands	27.9
		Denmark	33.0
EC average	42.8	EC average	14.2
OECD Europe average	42.0	OECD Europe average	14.6
OECD average	35.6	OECD average	10.1

Source: OECD, 'Historical Statistics, 1960–80', *Economic Outlook*, 1982.

growth now to a lower level than the European average. In the same camp we find among European countries only Switzerland, Finland (which made a strong adjustment policy in the mid-seventies, setting a 37 per cent of GDP ceiling on public expenditure in 1977), and some underdeveloped Mediterranean countries.

The second 'above average' group interestingly covers all four of the major European economies, France, Germany, Italy, and the UK, and only one small country, Austria. This sets the centre of gravity in Europe for current public expenditure at around 42 per cent of GDP, about 10 percentage points above the US and 15 points above Japan.

With the third group we move into the upper stratosphere of the welfare state with seven small European countries (the Benelux trio, the Scandinavian trio, and Ireland) whose current public spending averages about 50 per cent of GDP. In the Netherlands, Sweden, and Denmark it exceeds the 55 per cent level. If in these countries one adds capital spending and transfers, total public expenditure reaches 60–65 per cent of GDP.

One may wonder how far these differences reflect long-standing institutional arrangements, deeply embedded into the political and social system.

For example, Europe and the US both spend on average about $8\frac{1}{2}$ per cent of GDP on health care, and the 85 per cent public financing in Europe, compared to 43 per cent in the US, accounts for about 3 out of 10 of the percentage points of GDP excess of Europe's public expenditure ratio.[6] However this kind of explanation is hardly an end to the matter. The higher levels of European public expenditure compared to the US are in fact a comparatively recent phenomenon. In 1960 current government spending in the EC was 28.6 per cent of GDP, compared to 25.5 per cent in the US. Denmark's figure (21.4 per cent) was then lower than that for the US, Sweden's was barely higher (26.9 per cent).

Only in the two past decades have the major differences emerged. Over this period current public expenditure rose a relatively moderate 6.2 per cent of GDP in the United States; it rose about twice as much in the four major European countries, about three times as much in Austria, Belgium, and Norway, and an astonishing four to five times as much in Ireland, Denmark, the Netherlands, and Sweden. In these extreme cases, called the 'runaway growth' group in Table 8.6, current public expenditure in two decades has in total grown by between 26 and 33 per cent of GDP. Japan increased its current public spending in the two decades twice as fast as the US in GDP (four times as fast in volume terms), but from a low base, thus only reaching in 1980 the level of the EC average in 1960 ($25\frac{1}{2}$ per cent of GDP).

Why did the extremely fast European growth of public expenditure happen, and what are its consequences for the growth of production and employment?

In part it was the political choice of broadly speaking social democratic regimes in Europe, compared to relative conservatism in the US. But one could also hazard the guess that a negative answer would be obtained from polls of politicians in the small European countries concerned to the question whether they had intended the 20 to 30 or more precentage point increase from 1960 to 1980 in the share of GDP taken by current public expenditure; and to the question whether they would have wished to have done it all with the benefit of hindsight in 1982. One interpretation is that as the golden sixties rolled by, with year upon year of 5 per cent GDP growth, the public sector's advance began with increases in the degree of income parity accorded to pensioners, unemployed, handicapped, and other welfare recipients, and also with increases in the degree of indexation of these benefits on prices or nominal wages. This seemed no more than a normally equitable distribution of the fruits of growth. But then as part and parcel of the oil-shock and stagflation crises, real wages overshot their economically warranted level. Thus, automatically, transfer payments were also lifted above their economically warranted level. And then the problems interacted and compounded. Recession raised the number of welfare recipients and further drove up the public expenditure share of GDP. Nor was economic thinking adapted to trying seriously to arrest this process. The then-conventional, Keynesian theoretical framework emphasized above all the deflationary, low-growth-trap risks of cutting real wages, or real welfare benefits, or budget deficits. The econometric models functioning in official institutions largely ignored classical employment relations and the monetary consequences of deficit financing, and thus continued to buttress the status quo.

The effects of enormous public-sector growth on real economic performance are still only dimly perceived. Economic analysis of incentive effects of taxation and social security regimes remains in its infancy, as it is also regarding more classical views of the real wage/ employment relation. An heroic attempt to draw out a relationship between the relative growth of public expenditure and the relative decline in GDP growth performance was made in the recent BIS annual report, reproduced here as Fig. 8.3. Some shaky relationship seems visible, with a rough trend relating public expenditure growth negatively to output performance. But, of course, simple presentational techniques cannot be expected to do too much, when growth has multiple determinants, with institutional and efficiency variables behind the public expenditure figures, and, perhaps most important

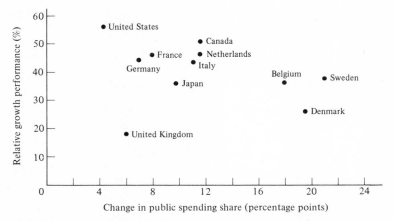

Fig. 8.3: Growth performance and the share of public spending in GNP. (Annual average rate of growth 1973–81 relative to 1960–73 plotted against change in public expenditure share between 1973 and 1981)

Source: Bank for International Settlements, 'Annual Report 1981/82', Basle, 14 June 1982.

of all, uncertain, although surely rather long time-lags in the process of cause and effect.

Other less heroic approaches to the question, linking public expenditure growth to public deficits and to the balance of payments are still instructive.

A first point about public deficits supports the proposition that the growth of current public expenditure was far from wholly intended. The strong relation with the growth of the public deficit (see Fig. 8.4) shows that the present generation has not been prepared to pay for its own current public expenditure over the last decade where the growth of this expenditure got out of line with economic capacity. The cross-section of data in Fig. 8.4 suggests that EC countries were prepared to finance only about half of the public expenditure growth of the last twelve years with taxation, but after that the rise of current public expenditure was entirely borne by increased deficits. Thus, to take extreme cases, the UK increased its deficit some 3 per cent of GDP compared to public expenditure growth of some 6 per cent; Belgium increased its deficit 12 per cent of GDP compared to public expenditure growth of 23 per cent. Overall this cross-country evidence undermines the force of the argument that cyclical influences explain at all adequately the increased recourse to deficit financing.

A second point is that the economy as a whole has hardly been more prepared to pay for the public expenditure. Fig. 8.5 shows the relationship between the public-sector deficit and the balance-of-payments

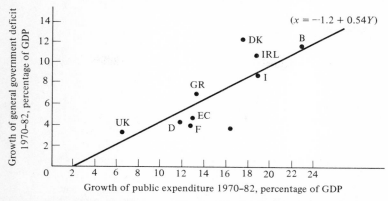

Fig. 8.4: Growth of public expenditure and budget deficits in EC countries
Source: EC Commission.

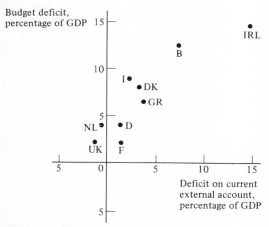

Fig. 8.5A: Budget and current external account deficits in EC countries 1981
(Percentage of GDP)

Source: EC Commission.

deficit. Domestic private savers were not prepared to buy the debt instruments of the government, and so foreign savers were invited to subscribe. The risk of course for the borrowing countries lies in the exchange rate. In the event of subsequent devaluation the borrowing would prove very expensive in real terms as well as being inflationary. An alternative, also malignant, course is to finance public expenditure by a purely domestic inflation tax; i.e. let a monetary financing of the budget deficit fuel domestic inflation, and then see

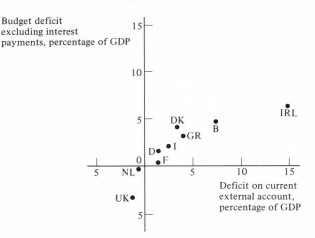

Fig. 8.5B: Budget deficits excluding interest payments and current external
account deficits 1981 (Percentage of GDP)

Source: EC Commission.

domestic inflation erode the value of bonds held by savers. The savers
then are willing to absorb more bonds in order to maintain the real
value of their savings, demanding however compensation in high
nominal interest rates to offset the inflation tax on their assets. The
budget then finds interest payments to be absorbing a fast increasing
share of its expenditures. At this point the double ills of high inflation
and large public deficits become very painful to cut back. Real public
services or transfers have to be compressed already to pay for rising
interest payments, in order to prevent a further increase in the budget
deficit and public expenditure. To reverse the process requires deeper
cuts in public services or transfers, especially taking into account the
transitional demand deflation which may add a further automatic
cyclical rise in the deficit.

To summarize, a very fast public expenditure growth may be associated with either of three financing models, with different economic
dangers:

Increased domestic borrowing with monetary financing, leading to
increased inflation and inflation taxing of bond holders;
Increased foreign borrowing, with hard exchange-rate policies
initially, but leading after some time to devaluation and higher inflation;
Correspondingly high taxation growth, and no monetary financing,
with dangers here for the supply side of the economy.

Reviewing again in this framework the experience of countries with fast-rising public expenditure, the stories fall into place.

Italy is the outstanding case of a country almost wholly financing its public expenditure growth by an increase in the budget deficit alongside an accommodating monetary policy and accelerating inflation. The domestic inflation tax increased, and so did the nominal interest rate, but the balance-of-payments deficit was kept quite low on average over the years. Indeed interest payments on the public debt account for almost all of the present public-sector deficit, and almost all this goes to compensate the inflation tax on bond holders. But the institutionalization of inflation also advanced to the point that almost all debt instruments are now quite short term, and three-month Treasury Bills came to be included in the official definition of M_2.

Belgium, Ireland, and Denmark have to an important degree financed their excess public expenditure by foreign borrowing, thus allowing the domestic absorption of imports to run up very large balance-of-payments deficits. Since the breakup of the Bretton Woods system all have constrained monetary policy by an exchange-rate link to the Snake or EMS (or the pound sterling, in the case of Ireland until the EMS started). External debt has built up at an ultimately unsustainable pace, and the process of painful adjustment is now recognized as inevitable. Belgium acted in early 1982 with a package of budget measures, wage de-indexation and devaluation. Denmark's new government announced important budget and wage de-indexation measures in October 1982, and in the same month Ireland announced new plans to eliminate its current budget deficit by 1985.

Sweden, the Netherlands, and Norway have to a greater degree financed their enormous public expenditure growth with taxation. In the Dutch case, in particular, gas revenues explain the relatively limited budget deficit and balance-of-payment surplus; with a very hard monetary policy and exchange rate the loss of manufacturing employment has been the severest in Europe. The Norwegian case differs from the Dutch mainly in the choice of a softer monetary policy since leaving the Snake exchange-rate system in 1978. It also seems that the Norwegians were for a while rather carried away with their seemingly unlimited spending possibilities. When the oil price weakened in late 1981 they found themselves exposed to rising public finance and balance-of-payments deficits as well as accelerating inflation. A retrenchment of policy has since begun.

It falls therefore to Sweden to be the real European champion of taxation growth in the sense of the burden placed upon the normal domestic economy with no exceptional rent to redistribute. Its tax burden now amounts to 57 per cent of GDP compared to a European average of 42 per cent and an OECD average of 37 per cent; its recent experiment with centre-right government did not really change this situation, and the renewed social democratic administration set off in October 1982 with new tax increases.

The UK case has several features comparable with the Netherlands hydrocarbon revenues and an ever harder exchange-rate policy. Combined with much more restrained public expenditure, the UK emerges as the only country in Europe to have reduced its budget deficit in GDP share terms in the ten years from 1973, and almost the only one to be experiencing in the early eighties an inflation rate significantly below its average record of the seventies: its unemployment rate, though, is also now one of the highest.

Over the next five years sharper differences in the growth of output and consumption levels may emerge between the European countries which need to make severe public-finance adjustments, and those which have followed more cautious financial policies. It is to be feared, for the countries with most exposed financial situations, that the negative relationship suggested in Fig. 8.3 between changes in growth performance and public expenditure growth will become clearer with time, as they struggle to master and cut back on their various excesses: regular taxation, inflation tax, or foreign debt.

II. Some Actions for Internal Adjustment

The menu of adjustment policies

Solution of Europe's 10 per cent unemployment crisis needs more than an escape from the prolonged world cyclical recession. Return to a 3 per cent growth trajectory in Europe is not likely, on recent experience, to do much more than stabilize the unemployment situation. There also may be legitimate fears that this modest figure exceeds the potential growth rate in Europe of the early eighties. In the 1978–9 recovery, which saw a 3 per cent growth rate for two years, there was a mere flattening of the unemployment rate, but also a rapid emergence of capacity tensions in key industrial regions and skill categories of the labour force.

A therapy for Europe as a whole, following the foregoing diagnosis, would involve a redistribution of income in favour of enterprise profitability, a reduction in total labour costs (wage and non-wage) relative to competitors, a reduction in capital costs, an increase in flexibility in the conditions of employment, with real cost increases only in the energy domain to further aid factor substitution in favour of employment. If these structural conditions for employment growth were respected, there would be less difficulty in being able to sustain demand through financial policy—a subject to which we must return later. But, first, let us examine schematically what the menu of policy action might consist of:

(i) Wage costs:
    (a) devaluation
    (b) real-wage adjustment (irrespective of the exchange rate)
    (c) greater real-wage flexibility
    (d) employment subsidies

(ii) Non-wage labour costs:
    (a) reduced social contributions, with corresponding expenditure cuts
    (b) reduced social contributions, with increased other taxes
    (c) reduced social contributions, with increased budget deficits

(iii) Cost of capital:
    (a) increased investment subsidies
    (b) reduced interest rates

(iv) Cost of energy:
    (a) increased excises on hydrocarbons
    (b) import levy.

Since the menu is à la carte, a more selective guide is called for.

From the starting-point of autumn 1982, we note that the exchange-rate changes of the past two years, led by the dollar's rise, have already delivered an improvement of over 20 per cent in the relative unit-labour-cost position of the EC (1982's average level over 1980). The relative levels of hourly labour costs have by 1982 probably moved back, as between Europe and the United States, to a situation not seen since the early seventies, with, for example, US wage costs now again distinctly higher than those of Germany.

If this *fait accompli* were to be exploited as a way into a structural adjustment strategy, Europe should be working on the next moves in the process. For left on its own, the adjustment process may well lead to a partial reversal of these cost positions as US real interest rates decline from their unsustainably high levels, and the exchange rates move back to a weaker dollar; except that the extra inflation incurred in Europe during its devaluation phase in 1981–2 may notch down the medium-run exchange rates of Europe *vis-à-vis* the US.

A strong European adjustment strategy, on the other hand, could consist of matching US interest rate declines rapidly to prevent erosion of the competitiveness gains of the past two years through an unwinding of the exchange-rate movement; and suspending, partially at least, wage indexation in Europe to permit deceleration of inflation and a gain to enterprise profitability. After the resumption of growth, continued profitability gains and investment growth would be assured by approximately unchanged real wages for a period of years, or at least until the employment situation was clearly on a new substantially rising trend.

Vis-à-vis Japan, Europe's competitiveness could also be expected to gain through an exchange-rate appreciation of the yen resulting from the unwinding of recent interest-rate differentials. Japan's low and administratively protected domestic interest rates failed to match the rise of dollar and European rates in the recent past, and should correspondingly fail to decline in the period ahead.

The techniques for securing the real-wage adjustment in Europe —through sustained devaluation and less than total price compensation—have to be adapted to very varied national situations. However, for the first time in a long period, the prospects seem not unpropitious for achieving a broadly concerted adjustment across Europe. For many years Europe was polarized, at the level of official opinion as well as that of the social partners, between advocates of indexation and greater real-wage flexibility. Practice varied across a complete spectrum, from Germany where wage indexation has been illegal in the post-war period, to Belgium and Italy, where extremely rapid and complete indexation (two-point threshold, or two-month time-lag) was defended as the inner citadel of the work-force's rights and interests. In between there have been many variants in which qualified indexation operated (exclusions of indirect taxes or energy products from the index, a flat sum compensation worth less than each point of the index, the presumption that negotiations are reopened after a threshold is passed, etc.). In the course of 1982 both Belgium and Italy have seen movements from their traditionally extreme positions. Special powers were obtained and used by the Belgian government to secure a real-wage reduction. In Italy, after unfruitful tripartite discussions, the employers unilaterally announced their intention to discontinue the prevailing indexation system as of the end of this year. In France and Denmark too, in the autumn of 1982, the governments hardened their positions against wage indexation for the foreseeable future. These changes, while still controversial, may signal a certain coming to terms in Europe with the necessity and modalities of achieving real-wage adjustments. The campaign against complete and unconditional wage/price indexation—for example that sustained by the EC Commission since its 1981 recommendation[7]—has not denied the case for a large measure of cost-of-living insurance for wage earners when the economy is in a reasonable equilibrium condition. It has rather been aimed at preventing economic rigidities reaching the point that vital real adjustments are blocked, be it in relation to energy price changes, devaluation, or public finance reforms.[8]

Wage flexibility is important at the micro- as well as macro-level. The indexation question tends to be the focus at a national macro-level for the real-wage discussion. But there is the separate question whether wages are adapted to the performance of the enterprise. Europe as a whole does this relatively little. There have been recent crisis cases, in which the threat of bankruptcy such as in SABENA, some steel firms, British Leyland, etc., has led to agreement on substantial real-wage cuts, in some cases nominal cuts. But there is all the difference in the world, for the prospects of investment and employment growth, between a certain labour-cost flexibility assured at a time when the enterprise plans its future, rather than just when it is hovering on the brink of disaster. For the latter, there has been quite an interesting recent proliferation of workers' co-operatives in several European countries taking over insolvent enterprises facing the prospect of shut-down.[9]

Away from the shadow of the liquidator there have flourished some regional examples of flexible and participatory enterprise of which the most important case is the small-business sector of central and eastern Italy, in which improvised organization and family participation seem to be the keynotes. High levels of export specialization, productivity, and incomes appear to have been achieved there, alongside continuing controversy about tax evasion or 'backward' economic dualism.[10] Formalized systems of industrial co-operatives have emerged and prospered in the Mondragon community in the Spanish Basque province.[11] A controversial centrally legislated approach has been advocated by the social democrats in Sweden, whereby large-scale transfers of equity capital in the enterprise sector would be made in favour of the trade unions. It remains to be seen how the new Palme administration implements this. At the authoritarian end of the spectrum, and as regards real-wage flexibility, Professor Meade has advocated for the UK a legally institutionalized arbitration system which would decide between claim and offer on the basis of that which would enhance employment prospects best.[12]

The key distinction between wage flexibility versus a straight wage cut or profit boost, is that employment and investment can be more strongly boosted at a lower level of profit in the former case. How to organize this is of course the difficult question. No doubt it has to be a deep socio-political process, more than mere legislation, and certainly extremely diverse in its forms in the European countries —as the few examples quoted would already suggest.

Prescription of employment subsidies stands in principle as the theoretical opposite to the greater real-wage flexibility. The former accepts real-wage rigidities, and tries to improve the employment situation in cohabitation with the rigidities. The latter seeks to improve the adaptation of wages to market economics. In practice it is not impossible to work with both at the same time, at the cost of criticism for philosophical inconsistency perhaps to the point of losing some of the value of each approach. If subsidies are seen to be 'available', the strength of the drive for labour-cost flexibility may be fatally eroded. Conversely, the Achilles' heel of wage subsidies is the adjustment of wage differentials to the point that the intended employment incentive effect is eroded. Worth noting in this connection has been the creation recently of youth employment subsidy schemes in the UK with conditions requiring that certain wage ceilings are not passed (these ceilings widen traditional differentials for young employees versus experienced workers). There may be also opportunities to include selected employment subsidies in social contracts of wider scope. For example, greater flexibility in certain conditions of employment (limitation of indexation, a modest real-wage norm, etc.) may be accepted by trade unions where the government is prepared to concede subsidies for recognized minority groups that are disadvantaged (youths, handicapped persons, etc.).

But if the overall diagnosis of the European economy's ills stresses problems of market rigidities and excesses in public expenditures and deficits, it would be difficult to justify more than an exceptional and temporary use of employment subsidies.

In contemplating reductions of non-wage labour costs (social contributions and payroll taxes) there are three approaches to choose from: (a) a parallel reduction of public expenditures; (b) a shift to forms of taxation that may discourage employment less; and (c) increased deficit financing.

Of countries with extremely high levels of social contributions, France may be cited as an outstanding case whose general level of taxation is not so high. In this case a shift in tax burden, especially on to a higher personal income tax, would be a move closer into line with the average European tax structure. In fact the Mitterrand government seems to be converging in this respect more closely on the European average, although it is also increasing social contributions further.

In the Netherlands, among EC countries, social contributions are of the same importance (19–20 per cent of GDP), but in this case total public expenditure and taxation are also exceptionally high. The warranted prescription in this case would seem to be a parallel reduction of both social expenditures and taxes. Similar action could be considered appropriate also in Belgium, Denmark, Ireland, Sweden, and Norway where public expenditure levels are similar; however the latter countries also feature high budget deficits, which puts even stronger question marks against the level of social expenditures.

Reduction of social contributions or payroll taxes with more or less explicit increases in the budget deficit might be considered where the macroeconomic conditions for an easing of budgetary policy are present: no severe balance-of-payments constraint, an unemployment problem, an acceptably low starting budget deficit level, a low or satisfactorily declining inflation rate, and the prospect of low or normal real-interest-rate levels. Unfortunately few countries find themselves in this situation in the early eighties. The UK and Germany are closest, but qualifications are still called for in these cases.

The UK is convalescent rather than cured with respect to inflation. The prospects of re-exciting inflation expectations and adversely affecting interest rates are not remote. As regards Germany it should be remembered that its current budget deficit is considerably higher than the EC average in real terms (i.e. after deducting the inflation tax—which is small in the German case—on the existing stock of public debt). This, as well as international monetary influences, could be responsible for Germany's high real interest rates, and constitute a warning of crowding-out effects.

Among actions to cut the cost of capital and boost investment a primary choice may be made between measures reducing the rate of interest and those subsidizing investment. Several attempts are being made in the present recession to advance the timing of the investment cycle by providing temporary investment incentives (Germany, France, Belgium) to compensate investors for the high interest-rate levels, but without conspicuous success. Given evidence of capital deepening and labour economizing investment in Europe, and the narrowness of investment subsidy instruments for the purpose of general economic stimulation, increased investment subsidies seem a doubtful priority. The case for pushing European interest rates down in the foreseeable future with less regard to those of the US if necessary, but with more attention to de-indexing imported inflation should the dollar further appreciate, may be the more attractive next step.

Finally one might add a plea for a strong energy taxation policy now at a time of energy price weakness, as the only cost-increasing element in the package. Europe, unlike the US, has hardly yet felt the world oil-market-price weakening of the last year because the exchange rate of the dollar has hardened. But already at the OECD-wide level there is the sad spectacle of major energy projects being abandoned as their profitability prospects (over what time horizon?) are eroded. The US administration has contemplated an energy import levy or excise duty, but not pursued the idea, particularly unfortunately in view of the budget deficit crisis there. The EC Commission has advanced similar proposals in recent years, without Council action as yet. The process of the oil importing world failing to insure against a third OPEC shock, with Europe in particular leaving the labour factor of production underused and overpriced, would be the most appalling of economic blunders—even if the precise substitution elasticities between the factors of production remain uncertain. Some individual European countries have, it should be noted, taken more resolute energy tax measures since the second oil shock: one can mention Belgium, Denmark, and France as positive examples, Germany as a case in which energy tax levels are now becoming conspicuously low by average European standards.

Managing the transitional problem of demand

The important question not yet treated is if or when a recovery of output and employment should be expected to follow spontaneously from strong policies of real-wage and public-finance adjustment— the latter covering the unwinding of excessive deficits in some countries and of public expenditure and taxation growth trends in many. Or should a substantial problem of transitional demand deflation be feared?

Except where devaluation is added to give a kick-start to the adjustment process, there is not much evidence to support optimistic hopes for rapid business recovery. As regards the devaluation option in practice, for Europe as a whole, this has been somewhat accidentally employed in the last two years *vis-à-vis* the dollar, and could be added to *vis-à-vis* the yen in the near future. This said, devaluation is a difficult instrument for Europe to manage internationally as a bloc, and could quickly run into problems of competitive reactions within Europe if used too much in an unco-ordinated way by individual countries (viz. Sweden's 16 per cent devaluation in October 1982).

For Europe as a whole the apparent elasticity of employment to real wages seems to be weak or uncertain enough to discourage trade unions from acquiescing in an employment strategy based on a large real-wage adjustment, except when the external constraint menaces disaster. Most econometric models in prominent use in Europe will not easily simulate an encouraging real-wage strategy, for example one that could transform the employment situation within the lifetime of a parliament. The transitional depression of demand dominates the two-to-five year time horizon. Maybe the models will change in this respect with new research, as is suggested by Layard, who finds typically elasticities in the range of -0.7 to -1.5 for the elasticity of employment to real wages in the major OECD economies.[13] Small open economy examples are of course unreliable for the region as a whole. Casual empiricism seems not to be more encouraging than the conventional models, if one were to judge, for example, by the substantial German unemployment problem bequeathed by a period of model real-wage behaviour on the part of the social partners; not model enough some would say,[14] but still an impressive example for the rest of Europe. However, if the German real-wage adjustment managed after the second oil shock had not been overlaid with the depressive effects of US monetary policy, the results would certainly have been more favourable. With respect to the public finance reforms, there is little encouragement for believing in miracles either, by way of triggering spontaneous dynamism in the short run. Cutting public-sector deficits from very high levels (10 per cent of GDP or more) may well generate benefits from monetary and expectational quarters to offset negative Keynesian demand effects in some degree quite quickly, and will avert greater disasters. But such policies are typically unlikely to have a stimulative impact within two years. A parallel cutting of current public expenditure and taxation may well have far-reaching supply-side effects in due course, but here too in the short run it would be prudent in Europe to echo the supply-side caution of Professor Feldstein in his recent congressional testimony. 'I think it is most unfortunate that this idea of stimulating supply rather than demand got a bad name when the label "supply-side economics" was attached to some extreme rhetoric about self-financing tax cuts and to euphoric forecasts of a painless transition to rapid but inflation-free growth.'[15]

For these reasons it is not surprising that demand-side worries are manifest in the writings of Malinvaud and Meade, the two leading theoretical proponents in Europe at present of an important real-wage adjustment in the employment strategy. Professor Malinvaud's demand-side worries have brought him to advocate a strategy based on 'wage restraint supported, during the first years, by an expansionary fiscal and monetary policy. Later on, when the requirement would increase, demand management would have to become more restrictive so as to avoid a labour shortage.'[16] However his most recent contribution (just quoted) ends on a somewhat pessimistic note. He notes that many Western European economists are reluctant to advise expansionary policies, and that the difficulty of organizing incomes policy may require a transitional period of restrictive demand policy so as to achieve the real-wage decrease appropriate in the long run for full employment.

Meade, in his recent 'Stagflation' book goes on in effect where Malinvaud breaks off, with a strong double proposition to increase real-wage flexibility through institutional means but to safeguard against demand deflation, as against excessive inflation, through setting targets for evolution of nominal gross domestic product over a medium-term period.[17]

In Europe as a whole one could envisage this proposal being implemented in a co-ordinated way as follows. Countries would prepare together preliminary multi-year trajectories for nominal GDP growth and submit them for discussion both domestically to the social partners, and internationally, within the EC and a broader forum if other countries wished to participate. They would obtain feedback from both the social partners and the international discussion before deciding on their objectives. Countries participating in the European Monetary System, or informally associated with it, would choose their nominal GDP targets with a special eye on objectives for monetary and price convergence.

Countries with the severest structural unemployment problems would then endeavour to settle for real-wage adjustments that would enhance competitiveness, investment, and profitability. If this resulted in an outcome for nominal GDP evolution falling below the normative trajectory, financial policy would presumably be eased. Where interest rates were constrained to maintaining an exchange-rate objective, budgetary policy would be the instrument to change. Where nominal GDP overshot the trajectory, financial policies would presumably be tightened, i.e. they would be non-accommodating.[18]

The combination of nominal GDP targeting with incomes policy could be arranged as a safety net against the demand deflation risks of an ambitious real-wage adjustment strategy. It could help formation of social contracts, or social insurance policies. If the real-wage adjustment led into a deflationary spiral of unexpectedly low activity and price rises, the social partners could count on a financial policy stimulus. This in turn could help business confidence with a lesser degree of uncertainty. The final outcome in terms of the real versus inflation split of nominal GDP could not be known in advance, but some of the risks of the adjustment policy would be dampened.

For the medium run it can be argued that the setting of nominal GDP targets is in principle similar to the setting of money-supply targets, since over a period of two or three years or more the money supply/nominal GDP relationship is a close and faithful one. But in the shorter run there would be important differences. Short-run money-supply management is bedevilled by technical problems— changing institutional arrangements, instability of the demand for money, unexpected external shocks. The recent experience of its most devoted exponents has continued to show this (viz. the FED's temporary suspension of M1 targeting in autumn 1982, and the UK's recourse to the same target range for three M definitions after two years of wayward behaviour from the £M_3 aggregate). In addition there are many, especially smaller, countries that do not target M at all in deference to the exchange rate. This in itself is understandable, but in a continent of adjustable parities within the EMS and sometimes abrupt changes by other countries, it is often difficult to know what the nominal constraints on the economy are meant to be. For these reasons there are advantages in attempting to organize internal and external policy co-ordination around normative nominal GDP trajectories, rather than around money-supply objectives.

Admittedly in the short run there are for nominal GDP special problems of information and control. There are long time-lags in availability of the national accounts and in the impact of financial policy adjustments on the economy. This means that the monitoring of economic performance in relation to targets would have to rely in practice on rough estimates of the current year and uncertain forecasts of the next, rather than sure data. But these problems should not be overrated. There is considerable competition and transparency in the production of short-term forecasts in most countries and policy in any case will in practice take into account a view of the near future.

On balance the Meade proposal would seem worth examining further as a supplementary aid to economic policy review and co-ordination in Europe. Nominal GDP targeting will hardly by itself banish stagflation from Europe as if with the wave of a magic wand. But it may be a helpful technical ingredient in the policy co-ordination discussion. It may help articulate incomes policy discussions with macro-financial policy and avert some of the perils of over-rigid reliance on intermediate financial targets, without lurching back into dangerously accommodating financial policies. Thus it would seek a safe escape from the 'expectations trap', wherein policy defined very strongly in terms of intermediate financial objectives is immobilized because of the credibility losses that its more flexible management might risk incurring. It could contribute to the continuing debate about the appropriate assignment of instruments to objectives in an economic setting in which the real-wage variable needs to be addressed more seriously to the employment objective. It may have some unexploited uses in international co-ordination, for example within the European Monetary System, but not only there, for providing more clear and balanced responsibilities for all countries in a group seeking greater convergence in macroeconomic performance. Samuel Brittan has argued for an international co-ordination strategy along these lines.[19]

The proposition of a more generalized and explicit nominal GDP targeting system would be an evolutionary rather than revolutionary step, especially for three of the largest European countries: Germany, France, and the UK. The Bundesbank has for several years indicated three components behind its central bank money targets, an 'inevitable' inflation rate, a potential growth rate and a velocity of monetary circulation factor; the first two sum to a nominal GDP norm. At the same time, the Bundesbank has never made an extreme or exclusive religion of its money target. France writes normative GDP forecasts (real, prices, and nominal) explicitly into its budget documents, and uses these data in incomes policy discussions, but not as yet as a criterion for subsequent demand management adjustments. The UK, in the third budget statement of the Thatcher administration, introduced a nominal GDP norm alongside three monetary targets, marking the end of the solitary reign of £M$_3$. The EC Commission in its 1982–3 Annual Economic Report advocated 'a closer monitoring of aggregate nominal GDP trends. . . . Financial, i.e. budgetary and monetary, policy would have to assure a certain trajectory for nominal GDP and external equilibrium, while income developments, free collective bargaining or incomes policies and supply side policies would be responsible for determining the rate of employment and productivity growth.'

Outside Europe one might suggest that the FED in the United States takes nominal GDP targeting on board as part of the technical equipment for a more flexible management of its monetary aggregates. When the targeting of M1 was suspended in October 1982, with recognition that its evolution in the near future would be meaningless as a macroeconomic indicator, the world was left with a new uncertainty as to the future evolution of policy; beyond qualitative pledges to stability. The nominal GDP evolution of the US economy could be used as a safer monetary indicator for the guidance of US financial policies. James Tobin has been arguing this for some time, and was joined in December 1982 in this by Herbert Stein and colleagues from the American Enterprise Institute.[20]

Postscript. In early February 1983 the Council of Economic Advisers presided by Martin Feldstein endorsed, in its *Annual Report*, the nominal GDP principle for guiding the FED's operations in 1983.[21] However, later that month Mr Volker did not retain this so clearly in his statement of policy objectives to the Congress, although he moved somewhat in the right direction.[22]

III. Summary and Concluding Remarks

A worrying indication of Europe's economic and political condition has been the tendency in recent years to blame its economic misfortunes on the anti-social behaviour of the rest of the world. If only the US were less insular in its internal versus external demand management, if only OPEC adopted more rational pricing policies, if only the NICs introduced trade union and social policies 'appropriate' for the industrial trading community, then our problems would be eased, maybe to the point of removing the need for disagreeable adjustments at home.

Taken on their own, each of these international issues seem entirely reasonable pressure points for European diplomacy. However if together they take over the centre stage of explanations of Europe's economic ills, one must surely stop and think again. To paraphrase Oscar Wilde, to lose out in one international economic accident may be unfortunate, to lose out in two is looking distinctly careless . . .

Looking inside the Western European economy as a whole, taking both the EC and EFTA countries, and comparing them with the US and Japan over a period stretching well before the present generalized recession, one cannot fail to be struck by some major structural differences: first, the much greater rise in Europe of public expenditure, taxation, and, often, public indebtedness too; secondly, the weakness in industrial profitability and the high level and real rigidity of labour costs; thirdly, a weakening in industrial technological performance, linked in part to the political fragmentation of the region; fourthly and gravest socially, and resulting from the foregoing, failure to create employment growth sufficient to reduce unemployment to anywhere near socially desired levels. Western Europe of course contains country differences which include still some examples of outstanding economic success among both medium- and small-sized countries. But these examples are now so few and the interdependence factor among European countries is so great that the region needs surely to consider on a continental scale how to steer the European economy out of its alarmingly faulted performance.

One can think of remedies in two categories: (a) improving the organization and external policies of Europe so as to protect it more successfully against external economic shocks, and to enable it to negotiate internationally with more effect; (b) making deep internal improvements to the economies of most European countries, sufficiently parallel in time and compatible in the sense of not beggaring neighbours to get the whole European macroeconomy on to a better track.

In the first category there are interesting possibilities, for example in the domains of monetary and industrial policy in Europe, which fall to others to discuss.

In the second category, it is suggested that the agenda for internal European economic policy should feature widespread measures to reduce the real-wage and non-wage labour costs of enterprises, to reduce the nominal or real rate of interest, and to increase enterprise profitability, *inter alia* through introducing much greater flexibility into employment conditions. The recent history of the United States and Japan interestingly offer two very different examples—in both high and low productivity growth settings—of sustained, rapid rates of employment growth in excess of what is now needed in Europe to solve the unemployment problem. In these examples it can be argued that the critical differences *vis-à-vis* Europe have basically been in public finance, and wage/profit relations.

The use of demand policies, taking a long view that carries over the seventies, does not appear to offer systematic explanation of the relative macroeconomic performance of Europe *vis-à-vis* the US or Japan, especially as regards employment. Moreover many countries in Europe have now got themselves into positions of multiple disequilibria that rule out the possibility of taking a demand policy escape route from their structural problems. There are cases, such as Germany and the UK, where one may discuss the prospective real versus inflation effects of demand policy adjustments from present starting-points, but most other European countries are now far from meeting the basic preconditions of stability for successful recourse to domestic demand stimulation.

On the other hand, if one advocates a policy of adjustment based on improving profitability, holding back real wages, and unwinding excesses in public expenditure and indebtedness, there is a serious risk of creating a transitional demand deflation of unacceptable length and depth. A framework is therefore needed to manage demand alongside the process of income redistribution and resource reallocation. Professor Meade suggests that targets should be set for nominal GDP, and that the maintenance of demand along this trajectory—in most European countries a declerating one would be suitable—should be the degree of protection afforded against transitional deflation. The split of the nominal GDP growth between real production and inflation cannot be determined by demand policy, and to achieve a favourable production and employment result would be the task of income and resource allocation policies.

Targeting quantified objectives in macroeconomic policy is at any event extremely hazardous given uncertainties surrounding many key economic relationships. But other systems of targeting are seriously defective, or, in many countries, non-existent. Merely targeting money supply (and maybe budget variables) with a view to attaining an inflation objective leaves too many open gambles as regards what will happen to activity and employment. The separate targeting of nominal and real GDP components with only demand policy in support tends to amount only to normative projections, equipped with insufficient policy instruments to be an operational plan aimed at the two objectives.

The targeting of nominal GDP, with demand policy in support, provides at least a safety net against depression, which financial targets do not on their own assure. If managed in conjunction with a wage/ employment policy its potential can be much increased. The advantage of such a framework in an international setting is that it can well accommodate a wide range of country situations as regards the strength of the wage/employment policy instrument. In the minimal case, it amounts to the government setting some parameters for wage bargaining and saying how it feels responsibilities for employment results are distributed between the social partners; in the maximalist case it would be the framework for co-ordinated income and financial policies entailing a social contract with real (output, employment) as well as inflation objectives.

The system could also provide a framework for international co-operation in the sense of a set of indicators set in parallel by a number of countries (typically the EC, and countries that could be associated to the European Monetary System), and serving several purposes: a guide to policy reactions of partner countries in the light of economic developments, a defence against both inflation and depression, and a more explicit framework for the convergence of policies in Europe. Analogous to the 'divergence indicator' of the European Monetary System, deviations from the targeted course of nominal GDP would imply, in the system of international policy co-ordination, only the presumption to act. It would remain for each country to decide if, or to what degree, it would seek to establish a social contract linking demand and incomes policies.

Notes and Sources

[1] W. Hogarth, satirist and painter of the eighteenth century, depicted eight stages in a young man's progression from a promising early life to an unfortunate end. Governor Hoffmeyer thought Denmark had reached stage four.

[2] Unless otherwise indicated, data are taken from: 'OECD Historical Statistics, 1960–1980', OECD, *Economic Outlook,* 1982; and Commission of the EC, 'Annual Economic Report and Review 1982–83', *European Economy*, No. 14, Brussels, Nov. 1982.

[3] Jeffrey D. Sachs, 'Wages, Profits, and Macroeconomic Activity: A Comparative Study', *Brookings Papers on Economic Activity*, No. 2, Washington DC, 1979. Sachs's analysis of the big seven OECD economies shows econometric evidence of real-wage stickiness in Europe, contrasting with nominal-wage stickiness in the United States.

[4] Data extracted from OECD, *Economic Survey of Japan,* Paris, July 1981. See an interesting chapter on 'Selected factors of the Successful Adjustment Process'.

[5] Commission of the EC, 'Communication on the Problem of Investment', *European Economy,* No. 10, Brussels, Nov. 1982.

[6] *Financial Times,* 4 Oct. 1982.

[7] Commission of the EC, 'Communication to the Council on the principles of indexation in the Community', 23 July 1981, reproduced in *European Economy*, No. 10, Brussels, Nov. 1981.

[8] The legal form and considerable growth of worker co-operatives in Europe has been documented by the Mutual Aid Centre, 'Prospects for Workers' Co-operatives in Europe' (Volume I: Overview), memo., Dec. 1981, available from Commission of the EC (DG V), Brussels.

[9] G. Fuà, 'Experiences of diffuse industrialisation in Italy', Mimeo, paper

submitted to OECD symposium on rural change and public management, Oct. 1981. Fuà's short paper contains several other references on Italian experiences.

[10] J. Meade, *Stagflation. Volume I: Wage-fixing*, George Allen & Unwin, London, 1982.

[11] R. Layard, D. Grubb, and J. Symons, 'Wages, Unemployment, and Incomes Policies', Chapter 3 of this book.

[12] Jürgen Roth, 'Mehr Beschäftigung durch Reallohnzurückhaltung' (More Employment through Real Wage Adjustment), *Kiel Discussion Papers*, No. 85, Mar. 1982.

[13] Layard *et al.*, op. cit.

[14] Roth, op. cit.

[15] M. Feldstein, in his congressional testimony upon appointment as President of the US Council of Economic Advisers, Oct. 1982.

[16] E. Malinvaud, 'Wages and Unemployment', *Economic Journal*, London, Mar. 1982.

[17] Meade, op. cit.

[18] J. Meade, 'Domestic Stabilisation and the Balance of Payments', *Lloyds Bank Review*, London, Feb. 1982. This paper proposes a detailed set of rules for the consistent international application of these ideas.

[19] Samuel Brittan, 'How to End the "Monetarist" Controversy', *Hobart Paper No. 90*, Institute of Economic Affairs, London, 1982 (2nd edn.).

[20] Philip Cagan, William Fenner, Rudolph Penner, and Herbert Stein, *Economic Policy for Recovery and Growth*, American Enterprise Institute, Washington DC, 8 Dec. 1982.

[21] Council of Economic Advisers, *Annual Report*, Washington DC, Feb. 1982.

[22] Chairman Volker's testimony to Congress on 16 February 1982. In this statement considerable attention was paid to recent velocity problems that bedevilled money-supply targeting in 1982, and to nominal GDP projections for 1983 underlying the FED's revised objectives for monetary policy. Principal innovations were as follows: 'the (Open Market) committee set forth for the first time its expectations with respect to growth of total domestic non-financial debt, and felt that a range of $8\frac{1}{2}$ to $11\frac{1}{2}$ per cent would be appropriate . . . While the credit range during this experimental period does not have the status of a 'target', the Committee does intend to monitor developments with respect to credit closely for what assistance it can provide in judging appropriate responses to developments in other aggregates. The range would encompass growth of credit roughly in line with nominal GNP in accordance with past trends; the upper part of the range would allow for growth a bit faster than nominal GNP in recognition of some analysis suggesting a moderate increase in ration of debt to GNP may develop.'